Micheal Twaddle

The Population Factor in African Studies

The Population Factor in African Studies

The proceedings of a conference organised by
The African Studies Association of the United Kingdom, September 1972

Edited by R.P.Moss & R.J.A.R.Rathbone

 UNIVERSITY OF LONDON PRESS LTD

Maps and diagrams drawn by Judy Crumpton
Cover design by David Brown

ISBN 0 340 18353 5

First Printed 1975

University of London Press Ltd.
St Paul's House, Warwick Lane, London EC4P 4AH

Represented in West Africa by
C M Kershaw, P O Box 62, Ibadan, Nigeria
Represented in East Africa by
K W Martin, P O Box 30583, Nairobi, Kenya

Printed in Great Britain
Computer Typesetting by Print Origination, Bootle, Merseyside, L20 6NS

Introduction

Every two years the Council of the African Studies Association of the United Kingdom faces an awkward decision; it has to devise a theme for its conference. In some senses this is a delightful problem, for an association of specialists in a wide variety of academic fields, linked by their interests in many facets of the continent of Africa, can naturally generate any number of ideas. But delight becomes quandary when high-flying is substantially grounded by the fact that few themes can satisfy the demanding criteria of intellectual imperatives and viability, and at the same time concern and attract all members of an Association whose disciplines range from soil science to literature. In retrospect, the decision of Council for the 1972 Conference was a particularly happy one. The theme of the population factor in African studies, as will be seen, generated genuinely inter-disciplinary discussion of a constructive sort, suggested new avenues of research and, above all, if the tenor of discussion and interest at the crowded sessions were anything to go by, was felt to be relevant by a gathering representative of diffuse disciplines.

Beyond the simple, and rather voguish, interest in population lay the fundamental importance of the demographic factor in all our areas of study, a factor that is always a nagging presence, for outside the work of the professional demographers it remains unsystematically dealt with to say the least. Guesses abound, and assumptions drawn from European or other extra-African paradigms substitute for conclusions based upon the analysis of data. The reasons for this are not those of either indolence or unawareness. As will be plain in paper after paper, many areas of African studies as a whole remain hobbled by the poverty of our data. Population is by no means the only factor subject to this powerful constraint. Our relative ignorance of the population factor rests then, not only upon the data gap. Perhaps more significantly, population, more than any other theme, is demandingly interdisciplinary. As the non-experts became increasingly aware during the Conference, the proper consideration of population demands a fairly sophisticated grasp of human biology, ecology, sociology, history and statistics as well as a mastery of a discrete, specialised and weighty literature. Awareness of this last point might act as a further inhibitor but happily it is more likely to act as restraint upon the wilder, unfounded generalisation on population that is too frequently found outside the specialist literature. There are no excuses now; non-demographers with problems of demography emerging in their research now know who or what to consult and this is a healthy development. It is to be hoped that this constructive and hopeful mood, typical of an exciting and thoroughly enjoyable conference, comes across in this collection.

Contents

Historical Aspects

Introduction

R. J. A. R. Rathbone

Common sense informs the historian of Africa that population ranks amongst the most significant of the variables he juggles; it clearly matters enormously how many people we are dealing with; their rates of increase or decrease, their age and sex ratios, their density, their epidemics and so on are crucial items of evidence for all historians. But experience equally informs the African historian that such material is, until the very recent past at least, largely irrecoverable. Unlike the near and middle East, Asia and Latin America, Africa combines in one continent all the worst features for such reconstructions: pre-literate societies do not keep accurate records; African settlements of the past do not as yet appear to give the archaeologist the chances of population estimation over time that the Central American cultures have done; in addition, the continent is spatially gigantic, its historical populations scattered, and in some cases disconcertingly mobile. If these critical shackles were not burdensome enough, we are also bound to admit that the paradigms of Europe, the middle East and Asia probably do not provide us with even a theoretical framework for constructing hypotheses about the population factor in the African past. African societies, their various family types, and their systems of land-use and tenure appear to be sufficiently unlike those of the well-documented and researched historical populations of other parts of the world to inhibit assumptions about Africa based upon work in other parts of the world.

There is perhaps comfort in two thoughts. The first is that the historians of pre-Columban America for example might have felt similarly restricted twenty or so years ago, and such pessimism, while not totally discredited, would look a trifle excessive in the light of subsequent technical breakthroughs. The boom in European and other work on historical reconstructions of populations, while never supplying us with templates of the development of African populations, does provide us with a whole range of questions. For this reason it was perhaps a pity that the session of the Conference devoted to historical aspects was largely inward-looking. Brave though the attempts of Messrs. Birmingham, Fage, Flight and Wrigley were, and they are important first shots in a dark that must be lightened, there is a negative quality to them [1] if they are to be considered as suggestions for further research, or at least as suggestions to be borne in mind in the course of future research. It would have been instructive to have heard from a non-Africanist, historical demographer, well-versed in the study of non-African, pre-industrial societies, about methodology and, more particularly, about the areas of inquiry that such scholars have found to be vital to the explanation of significant change in their own regions. This area of possible cross-fertilisation [2] would seem to be an absolutely essential starting-point for any consideration of historical populations in Africa. Handicapped as we must concede we are, we can at least learn from the achievements and errors of historians of other areas.

The second cause for comfort is more concrete. Mary Tiffen's piece is a more than adequate demonstration of just how detailed population reconstruction can become with rigorous methods, the right questions and exemplary thoroughness. Her work on Gombe Emirate seems to show, among much else, that there is a rich field for research in the history of populations at the sub-national level and in the more recent past. Her sources seem to show that the high-level of detail she achieves owes as much to a sensitive use of African oral information as it does to her thoroughness with the written data. Such information, as with all oral data, is perishable and it would be tragic if it were to be lost.

Notes

[1]   Negative in the best way of course. All try to de-mythologise in an energetic and helpful manner. As pointers to where we go from here, they are a little less happy.

[2]   Jack Goody, whose work and ideas have proved so generally exciting to many scholars, has clearly deepened his understanding of Africa, and hence that of his readers, through his contacts with his Cambridge colleagues in Ancient and European history and not least the members of the Cambridge Group for the History of Population and Social Structure. Although many historical demographers openly doubt the wide-open possibilities of such studies in Africa—e.g. Hollingsworth in his *Historical Demography*, London, 1969—the key seems to lie in the Africanists' ability to perceive where other studies of pre-industrial societies are relevant to our concerns.

Population in the Archaeological Past

How far have population density and movements of population been major causative factors in African history, and how much can we hope to know about any of these, at least in the period before reliable census data become available, a date which some would still place in the future for certain parts of Africa?

During the last ten years or so, archaeologists have become increasingly aware of the possibility of using changes in population density, or in population 'pressure', as explanations of cultural changes [Smith, 1972]. Why this idea should suddenly have caught on is an interesting question; but it is of course an old idea, and one which was, for example, very characteristic of Scottish historical philosophy in the late eighteenth century. Its reintroduction into archaeological thinking seems due largely to the influence of two writers: Wynne-Edwards [1962] on the regulation of animal populations, and Boserup [1965] on the relation between agricultural land use and population density. Thus it has been suggested that the origins of agriculture in the Near East may be explained in terms of increasing pressure of populations on food resources. The classic desiccation or 'oasis' theory as expounded by Gordon Childe and others admittedly will not do; but it can now be regarded simply as a special case of the general theory. Yet of this special case, perhaps an instance is provided by the 'Neolithic' sites investigated by Munson [1968, 1970] in Mauritania.

The weakness of such explanations has been that generally they bear little direct relation to the empirical data. It is often possible to argue quite convincingly that some cultural change *could have been* an effect of population pressure; it is seldom possible to find any evidence to suggest that it *was*—evidence, that is, other than the fact that the change which might have been so caused did in fact occur. The difficulties of estimating the population of a site or of a region from archaeological data, in absolute or even in relative terms, are enormous. Probably nowhere in Africa is it possible yet for an

5

archaeologist to make an estimate of population which is anything like reliable—except in the Nile valley [Trigger, 1965]; and circumstances there are exceptional. Sites are concentrated in one narrow zone, they are mostly dateable quite closely, and there is a long history of research. This favourable conjunction of circumstances does not exist elsewhere. On a more optimistic note, however, it seems likely that interest in the explanatory potential of demographic factors will encourage archaeologists to pay more attention to the problem of estimating population on the ground.

Notes

Boserup, E.I. (1965) *The Conditions of Agricultural Growth*, London.

Munson, P.J. (1968) 'Recent archaeological research in the Dhar Tichitt region of south-central Mauritania', *West African Archaeological Newsletter*, 10, pp. 6-13.

Munson, P.J. (1970) 'Corrections and additional comments concerning the Tichitt tradition, *West African Archaeological Newsletter*, 12, pp. 47-8.

Smith, P.E.L. (1972) 'Changes in population pressure in archaeological explanation', *World Archaeology*, 4, pp. 5-18.

Trigger, B.G. (1965) *History and settlement in Lower Nubia*, New Haven.

Wynne-Edwards, V.C. (1962) *Animal Dispersion in Relation to Social Behaviour*, Edinburgh.

This section is a summary by Marion Johnson of a paper written by Colin Flight which sadly did not arrive in time for discussion at the 1972 conference. The author was at the time busy with archaeological investigation 'on the ground' in West Africa.

Population and the State.

Absolute numbers of African populations in earlier periods, and the rate of increase even in the immediately pre-colonial period, are probably unknowable; but disease and uncertain rainfall almost certainly kept natural increase slow, and it is possible that even by the nineteenth century in eastern and southern Africa the settlement of land by organised farming communities was still in progress. Nearly everywhere in tropical Africa there was land to spare, even in the early colonial period.

For these reasons, Christopher Wrigley suggests, it is unlikely that population growth was often a dynamic factor in African history. Though elsewhere this has been the most powerful generator of change, African history, once the introduction of agriculture and metallurgy had been completed, was not particularly dynamic. Internal tensions could be relieved by lateral secession, and there was no need for a society to evolve highly specialised judicial and executive organs.

The theory that abundance of land made state-formation impossible or very difficult rests upon a belief that pre-capitalist states are based on control of land, and therefore of subsistence, which is surely an illusion; even in medieval Europe 'land' rights were, in the first instance, rights over people, an expression of power based upon military force. Forest clearance kept pace with the growing population until the late thirteenth century. Land was therefore not scarce, the scarcity being of military resources—horses and armour and the ability to use them—leading to Goody's minority control over the 'means of destruction'.

But in eastern, southern and central Africa at the critical period there were neither horses nor firearms; states ought therefore not to have existed at all. However, military force was not the only power. The religious position of the King—his unique ability to mediate between the people and the supernatural powers—was also a source of power. The true divine King was a mascot rather than a ruler, but there must always have been opportunities for converting reverence into obedience. Moreover, even where there was no minority control of scarce weapons, the organised company of young warriors was a powerful military force.

Robert Stevenson has argued for a positive correlation between population density and state formation, and his work was strongly criticised, by Goody among others, not only for classifying the Ibo as being organised in 'states', but also for failing to mention that more politically centralised peoples such as the Hausa do not have higher population densities. The causality might be the other way round: chieftainship might be a necessary pre-condition for a fully agricultural economy, acephaly being secondary among flourishing agricultural societies such as the Ibo, Tiv, Kikuyu and Luo.

A better case, both empirical and theoretical, could perhaps be made for the opposite hypothesis—that, ecology for ecology, population density tends to be higher in stateless areas. In West Africa this is supported by the case of the Ibo, but contradicted by parts of Hausaland. Over much of East Africa it fits well; only the dense populations of Rwanda and Burundi appear to controvert the argument. Most high density areas are mountainous, defensible and malaria-free, so the correlation may not be significant. 'Democratic' societies are likely to have been more prolific, since the extreme form of polygamy of the larger states would tend to lower the birth-rate. However, this adverse effect of polygamy on the birthrate was challenged by several speakers.

Notes

This section is a summary by Marion Johnson of a thought-provoking paper contributed by Christopher Wrigley on population density, political and economic change in pre-Colonial Africa, and of the consequent discussion. Mr. Wrigley made reference to the following:

Colson, Elizabeth in L.H. Gann and P. Duignan (eds), (1969) *Colonialism in Africa*, I: 33-35, Cambridge.
Goody, J. (1971) *Technology, tradition and the state in Africa*, London.
Horton, W.R.G. (19ʌ) 'The Ohu system of Slavery in a Northern Ibo village-group'
Stevenson, Robert F. (1967) *Population and Political Systems in Tropical Africa*, New York.

Population Movement

We now turn from problems of population density to questions of population movements. Most African people see their history in terms of migrations, and earlier historians of Africa have taken these traditions at their face value. David Birmingham quoted five historians of very diverse outlook—Seligman, Julien, Trevor-Roper, Oliver and Boahen—who were nevertheless agreed on placing great emphasis on the movement of ethnic groups. In a deliberately provocative contribution, Birmingham first dismissed the received traditions of the Ngoni, according to which they were uprooted from Natal and, in the course of a generation or so, migrated northward through the Transvaal, Rhodesia, Malawi, Zambia and Tanzania, leaving swarms of their ethnic brothers settled along the route. The alternative suggested was that, having lost land and stock in Natal, the Ngoni were driven to cattle-raiding for their subsistence. This raiding was so successful that a new economic way of life grew out of it; cattle-raiding caught on like an infection among neighbouring pastoralists, and the chain reaction swept from the Limpopo to Lake Victoria. The more successful the raids, the greater was the number of cattle-less people seeking a new livelihood. Some fled into exile, but others joined the raiders, and rapidly learned and modified Ngoni speech, acquired Ngoni pedigrees, and practised Ngoni initiation rites. During the Ngoni raids, some migration took place, mostly small in scale and short in distance. Far more important was the adoption of new fighting techniques and a new economic way of life in many areas of the cattle-keeping belt of eastern and south-eastern Africa.

Although pastoralists might have been expected to move more rapidly and more readily than people tied to the soil, migrations are almost as ubiquitous among the traditions of sedentary farmers. Occasionally such traditions may have a little historical validity. Successful agricultural societies grow and expand the scope of their activity and, as population increases, new lands are colonized. Such migrations are not necessarily preserved long in oral traditions; the

9

more important function of oral tradition was to justify the political relationships between various power groups, commonly symbolized by movement in space and time.

The 'mythical migrations' of Ghana, written up in the old Gold Coast histories were believed to have taken place around the fifteenth century, but the basic peopling of Ghana must have taken place several millenia earlier than the traditions allege. None of the later technical innovations necessarily or even probably, involved any large-scale diffusion of new populations.

The migration of Luba and Lunda titles in Zaïre might be compared with the use of the imperial title of *Caesar* by the Russian *Czar*, few of whose supporters were Romans, or even spoke Latin. In Zambia, too, the continuity of genes, if not of customs, may well have been more pronounced than is suggested by proponents [e.g. Fagan, 1969] of the Bantu hypothesis and of population replacement from the Congo in the first millenium AD. Probably no Zambian tribe was so directly, and frequently, afflicted by the loss of all its ancestors as is suggested by these theories.

The popularity of migration theories was partly due to their dramatic impact. A rising tide of new central African peoples fully equipped with cereals, bananas, hoes, pots and a Bantu lexicon is more intellectually pleasing than the thousand and one long-drawn-out experiments and compromises embarked on by late stone-age peoples faced with a huge variety of new and distinct cultural influences. Historians had been mesmerized for years by the expectation that research into the common vocabulary of Bantu would provide an historical outline. It is now clear that we know neither how, nor why, nor when, Bantu language diffusion occurred in late stone-age or early iron-age Africa. If correlation of the common features of Bantu have yielded disappointing historical rewards, we should perhaps concentrate on the uncommon features, on the relationships with non-Bantu languages, on the possible survivals of older languages, and on structural as opposed to lexical features. There are unlikely to be any instant, clear-cut solutions to the problem of 'ethnic movements', but a few more of the variables which make up the historical process may become visible. Birmingham's views did not pass without criticism, both from linguists and from historians. Professor Roland Oliver concluded that his rejection of major population movements was like suggesting that North America was peopled by Anglo-Saxonised Red Indians; no doubt some Amerindians were, but there had also been some migration.

Notes

This summary by Marion Johnson is based on a paper presented in absentia by Dr. David Birmingham, and on the resulting discussion, Dr. Birmingham's paper made reference to the following works:

Fagan, B. (1969) *The Iron Age Cultures of Zambia, II.* London.

Lucas, S. (1968) *Luba et Arund.* Unpublished Sorbonne doctoral thesis.

Miller, J. (1971) *Kings and Kinsmen: the Imbangala Impact on the Mbundu of Angola.* Unpublished Ph.D. thesis, University of Wisconsin.

Case studies of migration

In discussing the validity of migration theories of African history, it may be of use to consider the scale of various kinds of migration known to have taken place in recent times—migrant traders in tens and hundreds; victorious armies in hundreds or thousands; refugee populations in thousands or tens of thousands; migrating peasants, over the years, in tens or hundreds of thousands; and, largest of all, the continuing movement of slaves for export, going into millions over a matter of three or four centuries.

The two papers published here in full deal with the two cases of migrating peasants and the external slave trade. Mrs. Mary Tiffin documents a migration (not to say five distinct migrations) into Gombe Emirate in the present century, which enlarged the population by some half million people in a half century, and analyses some of the forces behind this movement.

Professor Fage's paper deals with the enforced migration of millions of slaves from West Africa in the centuries of the Atlantic slave trade. In this paper he is concerned with the probable effects on West African population of this movement. He is thus led to attempt, with Dr. Peter Mitchell, a population geographer, to reconstruct past sizes of the West African population and, perhaps even more hazardous, to estimate the population that might have been, had the Atlantic slave trade not taken place. This exercise came in for a good deal of criticism from Conference members, who were happy neither about the extrapolation backwards of population growth rates in a smooth curve, since population growth tended to proceed cyclically, nor about the assumption of a growth rate as low as 1.2 per 1000 before 1500 AD. Dr. W. Brass suggested that, while the calculations *proved* nothing, they served to illustrate that even a quite low rate of population growth would have been sufficient to offset the loss of population due to the slave trade.

At the latter end of his paper, Professor Fage turns to the

possible effects of the Indian Ocean slave trade, whose main impact was for a shorter period but on less densely populated areas. He concludes that the effects of slave-trading and the accompanying disturbances there might have been more serious demographically, and hence socially, economically and politically. He might, perhaps, have added that this may be reflected in the great areas of East Africa where tsetse fly has evidently been advancing into under-populated areas.

The concepts of 'overpopulation' and 'underpopulation' were subject to some criticism; one speaker suggested that they might be replaced by 'shortage of land' and 'shortage of labour'. There are limiting cases where the terms have real meaning: 'overpopulation' where, without major changes in the techniques of food production, the land cannot produce sufficient food without permanent deteri-oration through over-cropping or over-grazing; 'underpopulation' where failure to clear secondary bush leads to the development of impenetrable jungle or thornbush scrub filled with tsetse fly and dangerous wild animals. The two situations can occur side by side, where a small population concentrated on favourable or defensible sites is over-cropping its farmlands, while great areas of the surrounding countryside revert to tsetse-infested bush. Shifting cultivation, or bush-fallowing, represent an alternation in time between over-cropping and under-use which can, at least for a time, avert the disastrous consequences of either.

Major changes in the techniques of food production have occurred, as several of the contributors pointed out: the change from gathering to cultivation, and changes between pastoralism and cultivation. Such changes are often adaptations to population pressure or 'overpopulation'. What of adaptations to under-population? In colonial times the government of Tanganyika hit upon the method of establishing concentrated villages to form islands of cultivation in the fly-bush. Similar concentrations of population, whether for defence or to keep tsetse fly at bay, could have arisen in earlier times. A correlation between low population density and centralised states, as tentatively suggested by Wrigley, could have arisen in this way.

It is possible to see African history, whether concerned with state formation or with migrations, as a continuous attempt to keep on the knife-edge between overpopulation and soil exhaustion on the one hand, and underpopulation and tsetse fly encroachment on the other. There is indeed no necessary reason (other than a belief in the beneficence of Providence) for thinking that a permanently occupi-able area exists at all between the two slippery slopes of disaster. Is the recurring story of the decline and fall of African states a tale of shifting cultivation on a continental scale? Can development, based on the right kind of research, provide the new technology which will enable the African population to establish a stable relationship with its environment[1]?

Notes

[1]   Dr. R.W.J. Keay, in his Presidential Address to the Conference, reprinted in *African Research and Documentation* 1973, No 1, discussed a number of points of interest in this connection, including several cases where development without adequate research has led to disaster.

The effect of the export slave trade on African populations

J. D. Fage

Some academic eyebrows have been raised, though perhaps not as many as I had expected, at the estimates I have published as to the possible effect of the Atlantic slave trade on the population of West Africa[1]. Some explanation of my motivation and method may not be out of place so that there can be further discussion of this important question.

My motivation was extremely simple. There is no gainsaying that, for something like 200 years, from the first half of the seventeenth century to about the middle of the nineteenth century, the export slave trade was a major factor in the economic and social history of a very large part of West Africa. Indeed the enforced emigration of Africans to the New World was one of the major population movements of world history. The only real comparison is with the transatlantic emigration of Europeans that took place about the same time, though with a somewhat later peak.

Such a population movement must have been a powerful force, possibly at the time *the* most powerful force, for change in West African society. It has been commonly assumed that the export of manpower on such a scale, together with the accompanying warfare and slave-raiding, must have had disruptive and destructive effects. This was an assumption which I initially shared[2]. But in western Europe, large-scale emigration did not necessarily have this effect. Between 1815 and 1914, for example, something like 19 million people emigrated from the British Isles (probably three times the loss of population from West Africa during the whole period of the Atlantic slave trade). But during the same time, the population of the British Isles increased from some 16 million to over 45 million, and Britain as a whole reached the height of its prosperity and power.

Admittedly such a broad observation can be subjected to any number of qualification. Some of the British emigrants later returned, often after enriching themselves in the New World, others remitted money to their relatives at home, all provided enlarged

15

markets for British industry—and nothing comparable with these things applied to the West African case. It might also be observed that, in these 100 years, the population of Ireland was in fact halved. But to this it could be answered that, if all the Irish had stayed at home, they would probably have all starved. Nevertheless the fact remains that it is possible for a population to experience great growth in its numbers and in its aggregate wealth while experiencing extremely high rates of emigration—indeed, in the British case, the rates were as high as any known to history.

It thus occurred to me that the stock view of what happened to West African society, in particular to the size and wealth of its population, might well be coloured by the nineteenth and twentieth century revulsion against the slave trade and its methods. In particular, I began to wonder whether it was right to think of West Africa simply as a passive victim of an external demand, and whether in fact its great emigration might not also have been associated with internal changes and pressures comparable, at least in some measure, with those in western Europe. The first thing to be done, obviously, was to try and assemble some quantitative data for the Atlantic slave trade and for the demographic and economic history of West Africa during the slave trade period.

Professor Curtin's book [3] provided much better quantitative data for the size and distribution—in time and in space—of the slave trade than had been available before. He suggests, in fact, that his figures may be within ±20% of the truth, which is really as good as one might hope for. It should also be noted that his conclusions concerning the overall volume of the trade are appreciably lower than the guesses that had previously been in circulation.

The next stage was to try and match Curtin's figures for the export of slaves with data for the population of West Africa at the relevant times. In fact of course, there are virtually no figures available for the size of African populations before the twentieth century, and even the twentieth century data are not very reliable (and this applies to the more recent censuses as well as to the official estimates which were the most common form of population data in the colonial period). Nevertheless these figures are the only possible starting point for any calculation, and the picture they give, for what it may be worth, is as follows:

	c.1910	c.1940	c.1965
Estimated total population of West Africa [4]	36,000,000	48,000,000	88,000,000
Approximate growth rate per 1000 per year		10	24

In consultation with my colleague Dr. P.K. Mitchell, who knows much more about demography than I do, it was decided to take these figures as a section of an exponential curve, and to attempt to reconstruct its earlier sections. Dr. Mitchell suggested that, in view of the complexity of the problem, uncertainty as to the strength and—in some cases—the direction of various factors, it was desirable to use a very simple model involving few assumptions. These were that

1) Before c.1500, the West African population was growing at a low rate of 1.2 per 1000 per annum—a notional figure implicit in the estimates of Carr-Saunders and others for Africa as a whole and adopted by the U.N. demographers[5].

2) The subsequent opening up of sea trade with other parts of the world occasioned an increased rate of growth culminating in the high growth rates, often of 30 per 1000 per annum, that are implied by the most recent demographic data.

3) The rates of natural increase of the population were unaffected by the slave trade and concomitant disturbances.

4) The twentieth century growth rate might be related to that of the fifteenth century by a smooth curve of increase.

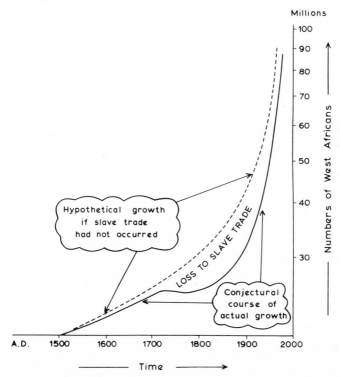

FIGURE 1   *The size of the West African population from c. 1500 AD to date (based on certain assumptions detailed in the text)*

On the basis of those assumptions, Dr. Mitchell was able to 'job-back', decade by decade, to 1850. At that point, to produce the 1965, 1940 and 1910 estimates, the total population would have been 28 millions, and its mean annual rate of increase 3.9 per thousand. Further back than this, a continuously falling rate of natural increase needed to be partly offset by the addition to the total population at the beginning of a decade of the slaves exported during its course, and the numbers of these were derived from Curtin's tables. The result of this calculation led to a hypothetical population for West Africa of 25 millions c.1700, when the export slave trade began to assume large dimensions; and of 20 millions for the beginning of the sixteenth century, which was also the effective beginning of the export of slaves from West Africa.

It is virtually impossible to gauge the accuracy of these estimates. The c.1700 figure of 25 millions, which is the key one (since some two-thirds of the slaves were removed in the next 110 years, and 85% in the next 170 years), could easily be out by 20%, i.e. by ±5 millions. However it is unlikely that the rates of natural increase have been overestimated. Given the size of the present population of West Africa, therefore, it seems more likely that the figures suggested for its population during the slave trade era may be smaller rather than larger than the actuality.

In fact, of course, there is no means of knowing what the population of West Africa was at any date before very modern times, and the argument about the degree of accuracy of our estimate is not very meaningful. What is important is to gain some idea of the probable order of the size of the population for the period when the export of manpower from West Africa became a significant part of its history, and this we think we have done. Given this, then we can gain some idea of the demographic effect (and, by extension, the social, economic and even political effects) of the loss of people due to the export of slaves.

On the basis of Curtin's figures, we can be tolerably sure that, for the period 1701-1810, when the West African trade was at its peak, West Africa lost people to the export slave trade at an average of the order of 40,000 a year. If the population were of the order of 25 millions, this would represent an average rate of loss of 1.6 per thousand per year. Two things are at once apparent: i) this is not an outstandingly high rate of loss; and ii) it is of much the same order of magnitude as the likely natural growth rate. In gross, therefore, the quantitative demographic effect of the slave trade on the population of West Africa is likely to have maintained it at an approximately static level over a period of up to one hundred years.

I am the first to admit that this is a very crude result. It is possible to refine it in a number of ways though, because of the crudity of the underlying assumptions, not all of these are very meaningful. However the following remarks may have some value.

Only about a third of the slaves exported were women, and those West African men who could afford it were polygynous. Therefore the birthrate may have been less affected than would have been the case had men and women been exported in direct proportion to their numbers in the population. Therefore the natural growth rate may well not have been depressed by the slave trade (as in fact was assumed).

The crude calculation assumes that the incidence of the slave trade was equally distributed throughout West Africa and throughout the eighteenth century. Of course this was not so.

Very roughly, Curtin's figures suggest that, during 1701-20, the mean annual loss was about 30,000 a year; for 1721-40, 33,000; for 1741-60, 43,000; for 1761-80, 48,000; and for the thirty years 1781-1810, 42,000. Thus the loss would seem to have been more serious in the second half of the period, and especially between about 1760 and 1790. For this time, the absolute peak of the trade from West Africa, we know that Upper Guinea was contributing a very small proportion of the slaves, only about 13%; from Ghana to the Cameroons. It therefore looks as though these coasts and their hinterlands should have been much more seriously affected, especially during this peak period, than the crude overall figures for all West Africa for 1700-1810 might suggest.

But it is difficult to substantiate this. There is little direct contemporary evidence bearing on population densities within West Africa in the eighteenth century. But such evidence as there is, e.g. from the accounts of travellers who did penetrate inland into Dahomey to about 70 miles from the coast, suggest that population densities were by and large relatively high in the lower Guinea coastlands in the eighteenth century. A glance at any modern population map shows that this area stands out as having one of the densest population clusters anywhere in West Africa—or in the whole of tropical Africa for that matter. Furthermore the hinterland of the Niger Delta, particularly of the eastern Delta, in Ibo and Tiv country especially, has some of the highest rural population densities anywhere in the world—densities, indeed, that are disproportionately high in relation to the available resources of soil and water and the existing agricultural technology[6].

This last point is of some interest. The New World demand for slaves from Africa increased consistently throughout the eighteenth century, and the prices offered for slaves on the West African coast moved in parallel with this demand. But all parts of Lower Guinea did not respond equally to this stimulus. Throughout the century, exports from what we now know as Ghana, Togo, Dahomey and western Nigeria did not vary significantly from the levels achieved at the beginning of the century, but there was a great surge in the

Delta-Cameroons trade. It looks, therefore, as though the volume of exports was in some way related to the capacity of the hinterland to export population without too adversely affecting the balance between its manpower and its resources.

I have attempted to elaborate on the economic and political implications of this in my article; here I will limit myself to the opinion that I cannot see any evidence that, by and large, the Atlantic slave trade had a crippling effect on the growth of population in West Africa. Within West Africa, there must in all probability have been some redistribution of population. But at worst population growth for the area as a whole is unlikely to have been more than checked for a period of at most about 100 years, more or less corresponding to the eighteenth century, and perhaps more probably for only part of this time. In the worst affected areas, the effect may have been no more than to cream-off surplus population, i.e. those whom it was more profitable to sell in return for imports than to employ in production at home.

More recently, I have been speculating on how relevant this conclusion from West Africa might be to East and Central Africa. Curtin provides figures for the slaves taken from these Bantu-speaking areas by the Atlantic slave trade. The trade was most significant there between about 1780 and 1830, when an average of perhaps 38,000 slaves a year where being taken, mainly from the territories we now know as Gabon, Congo (Brazzaville), western Zaïre, northern Angola, and Mozambique. This gives a total of just short of 2 millions for the period of about 50 years.

But Bantu Africa was also subjected to the Indian Ocean slave trade. Reliable estimates for the numbers involved here are almost impossible to obtain. It seems reasonable to accept the view that the numbers of slaves exported from the east coast south of Somalia were insignificant before the eighteenth century[7]. The best evidence I can find suggests, indeed, that slave-exporting from the eastern Bantu coast on any scale really only began about the beginning of the nineteenth century, that it reached its peak in the 1840s, and that, during the 1870s it was reduced to negligible proportions. Such figures as I have been able to find suggest that, by the 1810s, 10,000 slaves a year may have been exported; that by the 1840s and 50s, the figure may have risen to 40,000 a year, and that in the 1860s there was some decline, to perhaps 35,000 a year. These figures seem more likely to be maxima than minima[8].

The conclusion then would be that the Indian Ocean slave trade may have taken something of the order of 1.75 million people out of Africa, mainly from the territories now known as Tanzania, eastern Zaïre, Zambia, Malawi and northern Mozambique, between about 1800 and 1870. This period overlaps, of course, with the peak of the Atlantic trade from Bantu Africa, and leads to the very tentative conclusion that something like 3.75 million people may have been removed from Bantu Africa by the two trades in a crucial period extending from about 1780 to about 1870. With an average over the period of nearly 42,000 a year, we would seem here to have a volume of slave-exporting of the same order as that of the West African slave trade at its eighteenth century peak.

However, the area from which slaves were taken in Bantu Africa was considerably greater than the area from which we know that the bulk (about 87%) of the slaves were taken from West Africa. It would be virtually impossible to calculate with any exactitude what either area was. But in terms of modern political geography, the areas most affected in West Africa were Nigeria, Dahomey, Togo and Ghana, and in Bantu Africa: Congo (Brazzaville), Gabon, the northern half of Angola, Mozambique, Malawi, Tanzania, Zambia and Zaïre. These Bantu-speaking countries have a total area of nearly 2,400,000 square miles, compared with some 500,000 square miles for the four West African territories, i.e. their area is nearly five times greater.

It is also apparent that, in modern times, these Bantu-speaking territories are, by and large, less densely populated than the West African territories most affected by the export slave trade. On the basis of figures for the mid 1940s (chosen because they are late enough to have some pretensions to accuracy, but early enough to exclude major distortions due to modern changes such as industrial-isation), the four West African countries had an average population density of about 54 persons to the square mile, compared with only about 13 to the square mile in the Bantu-speaking area[9].

But it may be doubted whether slave-exporting could be a primary explanation of this marked difference. The main point as I see it is that there are a number of 'Bantu' territories which are not known to have contributed significantly to either the Indian Ocean or the Atlantic slave trades, the obvious examples being Rhodesia, Kenya and Uganda—though of course the latter did export a few slaves. In the 1940s these had an overall population density of some 26 persons to the square mile, i.e. a density closer to the 'Bantu' figure than to the West African figure. If Uganda is included with the 'slave-exporting Bantu territories', their overall average density goes up to 14 per square mile, but that of the 'non-slave-exporting Bantu territories' goes down to 19. In other words, population densities in the group of 'Bantu' territories are today significantly lower than population densities in those West African territories which are known to have contributed most to the export slave trade, and this is broadly true irrespective of whether or not these 'Bantu' territories were affected by the slave trade.

I think it is a reasonable presumption that this was also the case during the height of the slave trade. For one thing, though the modern population densities of the 'Bantu' territories are appreciably lower than those of the West African territories which once exported slaves, their modern growth rates (except for Gabon, for which the latest figure I have seen, of 11 per 1000 per annum, is unusually low for tropical Africa) are of the same order, ranging between 22 and 32 per 1000 per annum, compared with a range of 25-35 for the West African territories. (The range for West African territories which were not notable contributors to the slave trade, incidentally, is 19-27.) Secondly, and perhaps more to the point, there are historical grounds for thinking that the emergence of agriculture and the iron age, with all that these imply for population growth, may have been appreciably later in Bantu Africa than in West Africa.

But if population densities for Bantu-speaking areas were appreciably lower than those of West African areas when each became subjected to the demand for slaves for export, then it would be reasonable to expect that the effects of slave-trading (and of securing slaves by raiding or warfare), might have been more serious demographically and, by extension, socially, economically and politically also. Perhaps this is in any case the impression given by the nineteenth century European explorers of East and Central Africa.

Notes

[1] 'Slavery and the slave trade in the context of West African history', *J. Afr. Hist.*, X, 3 (1969); *A history of West Africa; an introductory survey* (Cambridge, 1969; reprinted with corrections, 1972), pp.81-95. The major comment that I have seen is by Christopher Wrigley in *African Affairs*, 70, 299 (1971), but see also A. Adu Boahen in *The Horizon History of Africa* (New York, 1971) at pp.326-7.

[2] *An introduction to the history of West Africa* (Cambridge, 1955; 3rd. ed., 1962), Ch.V.

[3] Philip D. Curtin, *The Atlantic Slave Trade : a census* (Madison, Wis., 1969).

[4] West Africa may be defined here as being equivalent to the modern territories of Senegal, Gambia, Guinea, Guinea (Bissau), Sierra Leone, Liberia, Mali, Ivory Coast, Upper Volta, Ghana, Togo, Dahomey, Nigeria and Niger.

[5] See, for example, Colin Clark, *Population Growth and Land Use* (London, 1967), pp.63-7, especially 66 and Table III.1.

[6] Akin L. Mabogunje 'A typology of population pressure on resources in West Africa' in *Geography and a Crowding World* (ed. W. Zelinsky et al), O.U.P., 1970, 114-128 *passim*.

[7] In the first volume of the *History of East Africa* edited by Roland Oliver and Gervase Mathew (Oxford, 1963) at p.152.

[8] These estimates derive mainly from figures in R. Coupland, *East Africa and its invaders* (Oxford, 1938) and *The Exploitation of East Africa, 1856-1890* (London, 1939), and Christopher Lloyd, *The Navy and the Slave Trade* (London, 1949). However Professor J.R. Gray has pointed out to me that A. Sheriff, in his London Ph.D. thesis 'The rise of a commercial

empire: an aspect of the economic history of Zanzibar, 1770-1873' gives ·
good reasons for supposing that the figure for the 1860s should be nearer
20,000 a year.

[9]   It will be seen that Cameroun has not been included in either the West
African or the 'Bantu' exporting areas. I thought it best to regard it in this
respect, as in so many others, as a transitional zone between the two. In
fact, its mid-1940s population density was of the order of 13 persons to
the square mile. Since this is the same as the overall average for the 'Bantu'
area, it could well be included with it.

Population movements in the twentieth century: a Nigerian case-study

Mary Tiffin

Summary

The migration of farmers from overcrowded or unproductive areas to areas where land is under-utilised is an important aspect of rural economic development. This paper describes five types of rural population movement which have taken place between 1900 and 1968 in Gombe Emirate, Nigeria, and which have resulted in the cultivation of new agricultural land, the adoption of new crops and new agricultural methods, and the growth of two new towns to serve the commercial needs of a prosperous agricultural community. The paper concludes by considering the economic, social and political influences on migration, and the changes in farming methods which migration has helped to cause [1].

Gombe Emirate occupies the eastern part of Bauchi Province, North-Eastern State. It is divided into six districts—Dukku and Nafada in the north, and Ako, Yamaltu, Kwami and Gombe town in the south (Map 1). Settled Fulani probably constitute the largest single tribal group. Other indigenous people include the Bolewa and the Tera; there are also substantial numbers of Hausa, Kanuri and other immigrants.

The economy of Gombe Emirate, c. 1903-1916

When the British arrived, the northern towns of the Emirate, inhabited by Fulani and Bolewa people, had been plagued for fifteen years by the raids of a dissident *malam*, Jibrilla. The eastern towns, inhabited by the Tera, were threatened by Fadr el-Allah of Bornu. Few people lived in the south of the Emirate, a no-man's land between the Fulani and the unconquered tribes of the Tangale-Waja hills. In 1903 the British defeated Jibrilla's people, who had given refuge to the Sultan Attahiru of Sokoto. This battle of Burmi is still remembered as a historical landmark by Gombe men, for after that

24

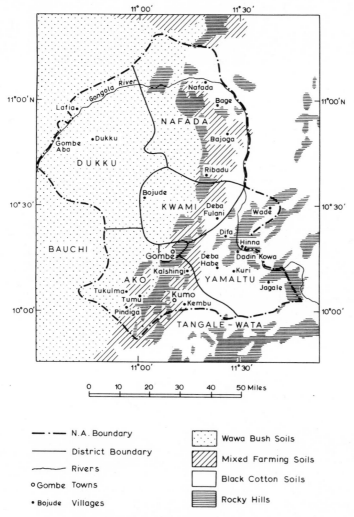

FIGURE 1 *Gombe Emirate*

there was peace. Within a few years even the inhabitants of Tangale-Waja had been compelled to cease raiding.

By 1916, from when the first detailed breakdown of population survives, there had been some recovery from the disorders, and the population had risen to 162,000. The average density was still only 27 per square mile. Most people still lived in the two northern districts and in Kwami (Table 1 and Map 1), clustered in walled towns near the River Gongola [2]. There were other important settlements on the rather poor Wawa bush soils within the bend of the river, dependent for their water on ponds excavated by slave labour from natural clay basins. Most towns were simply the fortified dwelling places of farmers and herders, who grew just enough guinea

District	1916	1931	Annual % change 1916-31	1952	Annual % change 1931-52	1963	Annual % change 1952-63
South							
Ako	32,120	58,244	+4·0	94,826	+2·3	175,904	+5·6
Yamaltu	21,278	31,474	+2·6	68,894	+3·75	142,558	+6·6
Gombe Town	–	3,243	–	18,483	+8·6	47,265	+8·5
Kwami	19,762	30,420	+2·9	55,934	+2·9	79,113	+3·1
North							
Nafada	50,179	45,153	–1·1	76,280	+2·5	97,063	+2·1
Dukku	38,003	29,335	–1·7	43,913	+1·9	88,992 (53,500)*	+6·4 (+2·0)*
Emirate Total	161,882	202,989	+1·45	358,330	+2·7	630,895 (595,000)*	+5·2

N.B.   Three Gombe villages were temporarily included in Bornu Province, 1926-1936. The 1931 total is the census total for the Emirate, plus these three villages. However, I was unable to trace in the 1931 alphabetical list of villages 2 Yamaltu villages and 1 Dukku village, total population c. 5,000, possibly owing to a change of name. The 1931 District totals for Dukku and Yamaltu are therefore slightly understated, and the District totals as given do not add up to the Emirate total. Till 1936 Ako District included both Yamaltu District and Gombe Town. Kwami was formed in 1952 from the southern parts of Nafada and Dukku. The dates in the above table are for years when village totals survive, and the population has in all cases been grouped according to the 1963 boundaries.

Sources
1916   District Officer, Nafada, *Report for Half Year ended December 1916.* Mss. Afr. 834, Colonial Records Project, Oxford.
1931   *Census of Nigeria, 1931,* Lagos, 1933.
1952   *Population Census of Nigeria, 1952-3,* Lagos, Federal Office of Statistics, n.d.
1963   *Administrative Population of Northern Nigeria.* Lagos, Federal Census Board, mimeo, 1965.
*   Estimate, based on the belief that the 1963 Dukku figure was inflated. (See ref 2).

TABLE 1   *Population totals by district, Gombe Emirate, 1916-63*

corn and millet for their own subsistence. The only food-demanding town was Nafada, which the British had made the capital, whose 6,000 people included a military garrison, traders and administrators. The Niger Company had a station at Nafada, and bought gum arabic, gutta percha and skins from the Emirate, while Hausa traders despatched cattle, skins and craft goods along the Kano-Bornu caravan route which passed through the northern Gongola towns. Caneo traders from the Niger-Benue confluence took sheep and goats south. However, trade was of very minor importance compared with subsistence farming [3].

The population and economy, c. 1963-68

Table 1 shows that, by 1963, the population had quadrupled and that the great majority now lived in the four southern districts, which had large areas of good soils, consisting of either fertile loams (Mixed Farming soils in Map 1) or heavy clays (Black Cotton soils). Though most farmers still cultivated staple grains for family consumption, the greater part of the produce from their farms, which were larger than in the previous period, was sold. In the most advanced district, Ako, most of the land was cultivated by the ox-plough, and over half the cultivated land was under cotton [4]. In 1965-6 the farmers of the Emirate sold 17,000 tons of cotton and 6,000 tons of groundnuts to the Marketing Board, and an unrecorded but very substantial tonnage of foodstuffs, including groundnuts, together with 17,000 cattle, to other Nigerian markets [5].

Stages of growth

Surviving Native Administration population records suggest there were two main periods of population growth. The first was from approximately 1907 until 1933. Until 1919 the population grew in all districts, as people displaced by fighting returned to their old homes, or took up land in Ako, which was no longer unsafe through raiding. In 1919 the capital was moved south from Nafada to a new site, Gombe Town. This led to emigration from the two northern districts, which lost political and commercial importance; but the population of the Emirate as a whole continued to grow slowly because of continued immigration into Ako. Marketing centres developed in the south for cattle, hides and skins, and ground-nuts, produced on the rich soils. Sales of groundnuts to the UAC rose from less than 50 tons in 1923 to over 6,000 tons in 1936-7 [6].

The second period of immigration started in the mid 1940's, when a new Gombe-Jos road, combined with a rise in food prices, made it profitable to sell grains as well as cattle to the tin-mines round Jos. Sales of grains to places outside the Emirate rose from almost none before 1939 to an estimated 30,000 tons in 1955-6 [7]. Growth accelerated during the 1950's, when the Marketing Board price for cotton in Gombe was in the range 5.8d to 6.0d per lb, and sales to the Board rose from 250 tons in 1948-9 to an average of 15,000 tons p.a. by 1960 [8]. Immigrants flocked in to join southern Gombe farmers in cultivating large acreages of cotton and corn with the help of the ox-plough. In consequence, there was an immigration of traders, to buy from and sell to the farmers. Between 1952 and 1963 Gombe town grew from 18,000 to 47,000 people. Many other administrative 'villages' and 'hamlets' grew into country market town, the biggest of which, Kumo, had 10-20,000 people in its urban wards [9]. However, urbanisation is not the main subject of this paper, and we will now examine five types of rural population movement which took place. The first three were most charact-eristic of the period up to 1933, the last two of the period after 1945.

Settlement by semi-settled Fulani farmers and herders

The main type of immigrant into southern Gombe up to the 1930's was the semi-settled Fulani farmer or farmer herder.

Typically, the Fulani were seeking virgin soil because 'the land was tired' in their former home, though their move might also have been prompted by oppressive administration. They generally travelled on foot with their families, herds and belongings, in groups, coming from the northern districts of Gombe, or from nearby Emirates such as Bauchi and Katagum. A wave of immigrants reached the Pindiga area of Ako between 1910-12, and many of these passed on to Kumo, in the same district, or into adjacent areas of Yamaltu District, in the 1920's. There was a later inflow into the Tukulma-Pindiga area in the 1950's. Many farmers can recollect that their fathers moved every few years. However, there was so much good land for grazing and farming in Ako that many stayed and built permanent compounds, herding and cultivating shifting farms in the vicinity.

By the 1950's the supply of virgin land in Ako was diminishing as the area under cotton and other crops increased. Shifting farmers and herders could either move again to emptier land, or stay and change their techniques. While some Fulani did move on again at this point, most stayed. They began 'kraaling' their fields, rotating crops, buying fertiliser, etc., to keep the land under permanent cultivation. Some gave up their herds to concentrate entirely on cotton and corn production. However, many families with herds retained them, selling increasing numbers of beasts to the expanding meat market. Some of the largest and most progressive farmers of Ako District are the sons of semi-settled Fulani who arrived in the 1920's and 1930's [10].

The descent of hill tribes to the plains

The pacification also made it safe for some Tangale-Waja farmers to cultivate wet-season farms in the Gombe plains, and later, to move down their homesteads. The process led to some disputes with the Fulani moving into the same area from the north and west. However, Burunde, the Fulani Galadima of Ako, then District Head of the joint Ako-Yamaltu District, knew that the British expected him to maintain the peace, and generally he did so. By 1967-8 tribesmen from Tangale-Waja were well integrated inhabitants of several Gombe villages, having adopted the social, and often religious, practices of their neighbours, along with new methods of farming. The father of one of them, interviewed near Kumo in 1967, had been a subsistence hill peasant with little use for money, growing guinea-corn, beans and groundnuts for foods, turning his surplus grain into beer, and exchanging goats for cloth to pay his taxes. His son was a farmer who cultivated and sold cotton, rice and a variety of fruits and vegetables in addition to his father's crops. He had used part of his profits to buy nine extra fields, and a plough and ox team, and put aside money after every harvest to buy fertiliser and hire labour in the next farming season. He earned, in consequence, a substantial cash income.

Emigration from Nafada and Dukku

In 1919 the garrison left Nafada, and the capital was moved to a new site, Gombe town. In 1923 the Niger Company (UAC) moved south also, to Dadin Kowa. At the same time, a new road via Potiskum attracted trade away from the old Bornu-Gongola-Kano caravan route. Many Fulani also moved, to be nearer new centres of political influence, or near the new marketing points. The Bolewa inhabitants seem on the whole to have stayed in their traditional homes, though sometimes moving from a walled town to a new hamlet in the nearby bush.

Meanwhile, the water supply also deteriorated. When the Emir and his chief office-holders moved to new Gombe, some farmers of slave status took the opportunity to move and to establish their own farms where they would be under no obligation to hand over part of their harvests to their owner. Often, not enough people were left to carry out the annual removal of silt from the pond on which the slave settlement had depended. With the owner away, herdsmen who had previously been compelled to carry water to their beasts allowed their cattle to trample the edges. As the ponds silted up, more people were forced to seek better watered land elsewhere.

In 1948 the Emir was anxious to induce semi-settled Fulani to stay permanently in the Wawa bush, as they were doing in Ako. He succeeded in interesting the Chief Commissioner of the Northern Provinces in the restoration of the old, pond system, and in 1953 £225,000 was granted from the Colonial Development and Welfare Fund for the mechanical excavation of new ponds. However, the Wawa bush soils were unsuitable for cotton. By this time, cotton was proving so profitable on the heavier soils of southern Gombe that no sensible immigrant could have considered farming on the Wawa bush soils so long as there was vacant cotton land a few miles away. The ponds again suffered from lack of interest, lack of maintenance and cattle damage [11]. The population of Nafada and Dukku increased in the period 1952-63 from the excess of births over deaths, but there is no evidence of much immigration by new settlers.

Immigration by settled Fulani, Hausa and Kanuri farmers

Since 1945 the majority of immigrants have been farmers already accustomed to farming from a permanent base. Though some have come from adjacent Emirates, many have travelled hundreds of miles by lorry, bringing with them their wives and children, to help clear and work the new farm. The majority went to Yamaltu District, by the 1950's the new frontier of settlement. The development of this area will be illustrated by the hamlet of Kuri [12].

In 1950 the leader of a group of thirty immigrants asked the Tera head of the Deba Habe for permission to become citizens of his area. He was shown land at Kuri, where Tera farmers had recently abandoned bush fields. The leader was recognised as Hamlet Head, and allocated abandoned farms and bush land amongst his followers. Settlers who had brought cattle with them sent them to the Wawa bush in the care of Fulani, until further clearing should reduce the incidence of tsetse infection. The new settlers soon sent for friends and relatives in Sokoto, Katsina and the Niger Republic. These did not see the chief of Deba Habe, but went straight to Kuri, where the Hamlet Head allocated them land. During 1957 and 1958 five new groups of settlers arrived, unconnected with the original ones, and formed their own settlements a mile or two from Kuri, under subhamlet heads who helped the Hamlet Head to collect tax. Settlers arriving in the 1960's joined one of the existing nuclei, and often had to buy land, as there was no more unclaimed bush.

The first settlers had travelled an old Gombe-Yola road, which was neglected after 1953, when work began on a new route. In 1960 the old road was reconstructed to a point some miles beyond Kuri, to Kurjelli, a hamlet of twenty people where no tracks crossed, where the Agricultural Department decided to locate a cotton market. The improved road brought a new influx of settlers: Kurjelli received 300 people in 1960-62, and had probably 1,500 inhabitants in 1968 [13]; Kuri had expanded to 1,000 people in 1962 and to 1,700 in 1968 [14]. The road also enabled the Hamlet Head of Kuri to get a market going. By 1968 thirty lorries were visiting its weekly market, and substantial quantities of grain, cattle, and hides and skins were being sold [15]. In 1964 a cotton market was established, which regularly bought 600 to 1,100 tons of cotton each year [16], without detracting from Kuri's fame as a grain market. By 1967, 64 Kuri farmers, about a quarter of the total number of family heads, had bought ploughs and oxen [17]. It can be estimated that hoe-using farmers had spent about £150 to establish their farms, and plough owners about £250 on equipping a larger acreage [18]. This capital cost includes the value of family labour employed to clear the bush, for Kuri was always a labour-hungry area where labour had a price [19]. Most settlers brought some capital with them, in cash or goods; they acquired some necessities, such as temporary accommodation, food prior to their first harvest, seed, etc., as loans or gifts from friends, relatives, or the Village or Hamlet Head; they earned money for current living expenses while establishing the new farm by working part of their time for other people; and they reinvested their profits to buy equipment, livestock, extra land, hired labour, etc. The new and prosperous villages of southern Gombe have been created by a combination of thrift and hard work.

New villages were also created by existing Gombe farmers. By the 1950's many Ako farmers were finding it difficult to obtain as much land as they wanted near the older settlements. Some farmers moved their compounds out to one of their bush fields, and expanded their holding from this new centre. In this way new hamlets and isolated compounds sprang up, until most of the cultivable land in Ako was taken up. The Tera seem to have been somewhat more reluctant to move out of their traditional villages, preferring to farm distant fields from a wet-season camp; but, by the 1960's, they too were forming new permanent hamlets [20].

Labour migration

Before 1950 most labour migration was out of Gombe, many young Tera men seeking work in the tin-mines. From about 1950 they have tended to stay at home instead, to earn their cash from cotton and guinea corn sales [21]. As the use of the plough spread in Ako and Yamaltu, the demand for weeding and harvesting labour on the enlarged farms grew. Wage rates rose considerably above Government minimum levels in the 1950's, and migrant labour was attracted from three sources: Tangale-Waja men, especially from those tribes where the cultivation of the home-fields was traditionally women's work; farmers from Bauchi Emirate, who could spare a week or two for work in Gombe between weedings on their own smaller farms; and farmers from the far north, who came for the cotton and guinea corn harvests when they had harvested their own millet and groundnuts. Labour was also attracted for marketing services, and for the construction and improvement of the homes of prosperous Gombe farmers [22].

Economic influences on migration

It is clear that economic factors had an important influence on the direction of population movements. People left areas where subsistence demanded most labour (because of declining fertility, deteriorating water supplies, etc.) for areas where subsistence could be obtained more easily. From very early on they seem also to have chosen their new homes in areas where there was an opportunity of making profitable sales, because of a conjunction of suitable soils and accessible markets. Ako attracted settlers in the 1920's, when its loams (Mixed Farming soils in Map 1) could be used to rear cattle for sale to Jos and the Eastern Region, and to grow groundnuts for sale down the river Gongola, via Dadin Kowa. Settlers ceased to come in the 1930's, when groundnut and cattle prices fell. Immigration started again in the 1940's and 1950's when the new road and the new cotton prices made corn and cotton production profitable both on the Ako loams and on the black cotton soils of Yamaltu; and it again fell off somewhat when cotton prices fell in 1962-68. The same soil types extended northwards into eastern Nafada District. However, prices were always higher in markets such as Gombe, Kumo and Dadin Kowa, which had the best access, both to the other regions of Nigeria, and to the ports, so Nafada was less attractive to immigrants than southern Gombe [23].

Political influences on migration

However, political factors also affected the direction of migration. The establishment of a new political authority capable of maintaining the peace opened up Ako for settlement. The siting of administrative headquarters was important, for, partly because of the administrative roads which linked them with other centres, and partly because they set off an urban demand for food and services, they tended to acquire the most active market in the locality [24]. The British did not transfer the Emirate headquarters from Nafada to new Gombe with the deliberate intention of attracting people into the underpopulated area of southern Gombe, though this was, in fact, the result [25]. By contrast, the Galadima Burunde appears to have left his old clan headquarters in Ako village (which was too near the Emir's new capital to secure him an independent political base) with the deliberate intention of founding a new political and commercial centre from which he could colonise a new area. He found the site at Kumo about 1921, drove off some Tangale farmers, and sent his sons out to gather in Fulani settlers from Ako village, the Pindiga area, northern Gombe and Bauchi Emirate. He promised the new settlers freedom from the greedy exactions of office holders, and even remission of official tax [26]. In 1936, under his son, Kumo became the official headquarters of Ako District. Both the Emir and the Galadima took care to foster the markets of their respective towns.

Many Village Heads, like the Emir and the Galadima, wanted to increase their prestige by having more people under their jurisdiction. Tera as well as Fulani Heads willingly made land available to Hausa and Fulani settlers, and often helped them with temporary accommodation, loans of food or seed, etc [27].

The push-pull mechanism of oppressive taxation or administration can easily be seen. Many immigrants were escaping from oppressive District Heads in Bauchi Emirate [28]. The reputation of the Emir of Gombe and the Galadima of Ako for benevolence was an attracting force. Some measures of the colonial administration caused emigration from Gombe: the call-up of labour for the Port Harcourt railway in 1926 [29], high taxes combined with low groundnut prices in 1938-39 [30], and the call-up of labour for tin mining, and corn requisitioning, in 1940-43 [31].

Religious and cultural influences on migration

The colonial administration was always nervous lest villagers should resent newcomers farming on 'their' land, and cause a breach of the peace [32]. In fact, this seldom occurred, except for one or two Fulani-Tangale fights. The process was peaceful, partly because of the general respect for the authority of title-holders, who welcomed immigrants, and partly because, initially at least, there was so much land. A degree of religious and cultural unity across the north of Nigeria also made it easy for Fulani, Hausa and Kanuri people to find acceptance. The only pagan, or recently pagan, people to settle in Gombe rural areas came from the familar, adjacent area of Tangale-Waja. Non-Moslem people from distant areas did not generally settle in Gombe villages (though culturally different traders, and artisans from the south did settle in Gombe and Kumo towns), and the originally non-Moslem indigenous inhabitants, the Tera and the Bolewa, seldom left their homelands with the intention of farming permanently in another area.

   Religion was also important in drawing people into Gombe. Many men came to Gombe for the first time on pilgrimage to the holy hill of Bima (near Dadin Kowa), or to study with one of the many *malams* who had settled near Bima. They subsequently decided they could prosper more in Gombe than in their home areas [33]. Once settled, we have seen how they sent home news which attracted more immigrants.

Population density, land tenure, and farming methods

Before 1940 land was so freely available in Gombe Emirate that shifting cultivation was the norm, except for fields conveniently near their towns which Fulani farmers might keep permanently cultivated by 'kraaling'. Land was still plentiful in 1968 in most parts of Dukku, and there land was still not allocated by the Village Head, but farmers freely cleared more land in the bush every few years as their older fields deteriorated. No-one cared what happened to the fields they abandoned.

   We can see this situation changing in Yamaltu District about 1945-50. Tera chiefs, who traditionally did not allocate land, began to do so when immigrants approached them for permission to settle.

As the land filled up, Tera farmers found it more difficult to find new bush land. They cultivated their fields for longer periods, finally keeping them under permanent cultivation. To maintain yields, they adopted ridge-making instead of planting on the flat, and the rotation of crops. By 1968 they were making more use of fertiliser on their older fields, though not on the newer ones which still retained the stored fertility of virgin bush. Land was no longer part-cleared, but was laboriously stumped, so that the ox-plough could be used. It also acquired a value, and by 1970 the sale of land was fully recognised in Gombe courts. Intensive cultivation had gone one stage further in Ako District, where population density had risen by 1963 to 200 per square mile (as against 140 in Yamaltu and less than 60 in Dukku). Ako farmers were the most substantial users of fertiliser and manure in the Emirate. Immigration had thus helped to change both attitudes to land tenure, and farming techniques [34].

Acknowledgements

I am grateful to the Overseas Development Administration for permission to use material from the report prepared for them [1]. I must thank many people in Gombe Emirate for hospitality and information. I also owe much to staff of Ahmadu Bello University, Zaria, especially to members of the Institute for Agricultural Research, for advice and help in collecting material, 1967 and 1968, and to Professor P.T. Bauer and Professor F.J. Fisher of the London School of Economics, for advice during the analysis and writing up of the results.

Notes

[1] This paper uses material from a fuller study of Gombe Emirate: TIFFEN, Mary. *The Enterprising Peasant: A study of the agents of, and constraints on, agricultural development in North Eastern State, Nigeria*, Research Scheme R. 2123, Overseas Development Administration, London, 1972. This report was based on interviews in Gombe in 1967 and 1968 with 192 farmers, 16 Village Heads, District Heads, Councillors and traders. It also made extensive use of files in the Nigerian National Archives, Kaduna (abbreviated as *Kaduna* in this paper).

[2] Population data, and its likely accuracy for the dates given in Table 1, is discussed in TIFFEN, *op. cit.*, Appendix III, pp. 407-9. To summarise, the 1916 breakdown followed a series of detailed Assessments, 1911 and 1912, and is likely to be at least as accurate as the 1931 Census, also based on the N.A. tax count. The 1952 Census was an improvement on the 1931 one, and some of the apparent growth 1931-52 is due to better counting. The 1963 Census results were inflated for political reasons. As other sources confirm that there was considerable immigration 1952-63 into Ako, Yamaltu and Gombe town, the large annual growth rates for these Districts are credible. The 1963 figure for Dukku is suspect, because there was no confirmatory evidence of immigration to explain the high average

annual rate of increase of 6.4%. Like Nafada, its population probably grew only from an excess of births over deaths. The natural increase in Dukku District is not likely to have been greater than in Nafada District, as the population of Dukku is on the whole poorer (i.e. less well nourished) than that of Nafada, and also suffers from a greater scarcity of water, which must have some effect on hygiene standards. A likely rate of population increase 1952-63 is therefore 2 per cent per annum.

[3] CARLYLE, T.F. Appendix, 'Nafada Economic and Trade', *Central Province Quarterly Report, June 1913*, SNP.588p 1913, and CARLYLE T.F. 'Gombe Division Intelligence Report', *Bauchi Province Annual Report*, 1916, SNP. 737; 1916, Kaduna.

[4] KOLHATKHAR, V.Y. *Spot check surveys in Gombe, Hadejia and Kontagora Divisions*, FAO Socio-Economic Survey of Peasant Agriculture in Northern Nigeria, 1964. First draft submitted to the Ministry of Agriculture, Kaduna, p. 10.

[5] Cotton: returns of Gombe Emirate markets taken from *Seed Cotton Purchases, 1965-66*, Produce Inspection Division, Ministry of Agriculture, Kano.
Groundnuts: Returns from Produce Inspection Office, Gombe.
Cattle: Annual Report, 1965-66, Northern Nigerian Livestock and Meat Authority, Kaduna.
The extensive trade in foodstuffs, including groundnuts, is discussed in TIFFEN, *op. cit.*, pp. 135-37 and 148-50.

[6] 26 tons in their first season at Dadin Kowa in 1924, cited in *Annual Report, Bauchi Province, 1928*, SNP 8990, Kaduna. The 1936-37 figure is from Annual Report, Gombe Division, 1937, Bauchi Provincial Office file 1297, Kaduna.

[7] *Seed Cotton Purchases, op. cit.*

[8] Nigerian Railway Corporation, *Traffic Survey in Zaria, Bauchi* and Bornu Provinces, Zaria, 1955, p. 47 and *Bauchi-Bornu Railway Extensions, Supplementary Traffic Survey Report*, Ebutte Metta, 1956, p.47.

[9] As the 1963 census did not give a breakdown by ward, the urban population of Kumo has been guessed by the proportion of N.A. taxpayers in the urban wards in 1967-68.

[10] This section is based on interviews with farmers and with the Village Head of Pindiga and the Galadima of Ako. The immigration was also mentioned in LONSDALE, P. *Ako District, Gombe Division, Assessment Report, 1912*, Ministry of Local Government file 43202, Kaduna; E.S. PEMBLE-TON, *Gombe Division Quarterly Report, March 1923*, Mss. Afr. S. 834, Colonial Records Project, Oxford, and by KRZYWON, A.M. *Monthly. Reports, Cotton Seed Multiplication Officer, April, 1954*, Institute for Agricultural Research, Zaria.

[11] *Production Development in Gombe*, SNP 47825, Kaduna; *Provincial Development Committees, Bauchi Province*, Department of Agriculture file 2412, Kaduna; information from Urban Doma, Councillor for National Resources, Gombe, a man old enough to remember the old ponds.

[12] This section is based on interviews with the Village Head of Deba Habe, the Hamlet Head of Kuri, and six Kuri farmers.

[13] WOODROOFE, R.B. 'The development of a Gombe Village, 1960-62', *Newsletter*, Ministry of Agriculture, Kaduna, No. 46-47, June-July 1962. The population of Kurjelli in 1968 is only a guess from its apparent size.

[14] The Hamlet Head of Kuri, for 1968 population. He said it was 1,000 in 1962–ECONOMIST INTELLIGENCE UNIT et al. *Road Survey in Northern Nigeria*, Mimeo, London, 1964, Vol II, p. 9.

[15] ECONOMIST INTELLIGENCE UNIT et al. *Northern States Road*

Development Survey, Mimeo, London 1969, Vol III, p. 56-57.

[16] *Seed Cotton Purchases, op. cit.*

[17] From a count of plough owners made by the Bauchi Agricultural Office, 1967.

[18] The basis of these estimates is explained in TIFFEN, *op. cit.*, pp. 313-315. It is assumed that the average hoe farm was ten acres, the average plough farm over fifteen acres.

[19] In Dec. 1952 the District Officer was unable to recruit road labour in the Kuri area at the government rate of 1s.6d per day because local farmers were paying 2s.6d to 3s. per day for land clearance—*Jos-Yola Road*, SNP K 2437, Vol. II, Kaduna.

[20] This paragraph is based on information from the Galadima of Ako, and the Tera Village Heads of Hinna and Wade.

[21] The migration to the mines was already some years old in 1913— CARLYLE, 'Nafada Economic', *op.cit.* By 1926 it was described as regular and large—*Gwani District*, Bauchi Provincial Office file 735, Kaduna. MAIDEN, R.L. *Report of the Cotton Co-ordinating Officer No. 72, 3.12. 1953*, Institute for Agricultural Research, Zaria, was one of those who noticed it was stopping in the early 1950's.

[22] Information from the Galadima of Ako and Village Heads in Ako and Yamaltu. For wages in 1952 see ref. 19. VIGO, A.H.S. *A survey of agricultural credit in the northern provinces of Nigeria*, Ministry of Social Welfare and Co-operatives, Kaduna, 1958, p. 40, noted Kumo farmers were paying 3s.6d to 5s. for a 4 or 5 hour day, compared with the then government rate of 2s.4d for a longer day.

[23] In early January 1968, a bundle of guinea corn could be sold for 3s. in Kumo and Dadin Kowa, but only 1s.6d. in Nafada. For the price hierarchy between Gombe markets see TIFFEN, op.cit. pp. 86-92.

[24] This is a general rule. Exceptionally the market in the Provincial Headquarters, Bauchi town, is not as active as those of Gombe and Kumo, towns with less administrative importance.

[25] *Divisional Headquarters, suggested move from Nafada*, SNP 56p 1918, Kaduna, mentions only administrative and military reasons.

[26] The Galadima disliked the headquarters the British had appointed for the combined Ako-Yamaltu District because it was a Tera town, Deba Habe, not suitable for a Fulani clan base. The history of Kumo has been pieced together from interviews with the present Galadima, son of the founder of Kumo, with the Village Head of Pindiga, and with farmers. I also made use of some essays by students from Kumo, lent me by Dr. Victor Low. E. S. PEMBLETON, *op. cit.* mentions a Tangale attack on Kumo in 1923, but does not seem to have realised that this may have been a reprisal for an earlier fight. He also noted that the Galadima told him that people were emigrating from Pindiga to Bauchi Emirate—it is more probable, in fact, that the missing taxpayers had moved to Kumo, and were being excused tax.

[27] Interviews with farmers.

[28] *Annual Report, Bauchi Province, 1926*, SNP K101, Vol III, Kaduna.

[29] *Annual Report, Bauchi Province, 1939*, SNP 32079, Kaduna, noted that the population had fallen by nearly 17,000. The Resident commented that Gombe could bear the distinction of being one of the most highly taxed in the northern provinces 'while the price of groundnuts remained at more than £5 per ton, and in past years, the population has increased steadily. . . . It would now appear that many of those who were attracted to Gombe in prosperous years have returned whence they came.'

[30] Village Head, Pindiga.

[31] Village Head of Deba Habe, Hamlet Head of Kuri and WOOD, W. M. *Tera Notebooks*, c. 1947, typed extracts taken by H. D. Gunn from the Gombe Divisional Office, in 1951, and deposited in the International African Institute, London.

[32] For instance, the District Officer noted in 1922 that the Fulani migration southwards was all to the good economically, 'but no natives like encroachment on their land'—*Annual Report*, Bauchi Province, 1922, SNP 58 1923. This led to work in surveying and delineating the boundary between the Emirate and Tangale-Waja.

[33] Very apparent from interviews with farmers.

[34] This section is based on interviews with Village Heads, and on references to farming practices in some contemporary reports, especially WOOD, *op. cit.*, pp. 1-3, p. 22 and Pt. II, p. 9, for the change in Tera practice, c. 1947. More detail is given in TIFFEN, *op. cit.*, pp. 235-241.

Population and Colonial Policy

Elizabeth Hook, in considering the influence of population density on colonial policy, was more concerned with the effects of low population densities than of 'population pressure' in the more usual sense. The colonial governments generally shared this concern—the 'empty wastes of Africa' were a favourite feature of the imperialist fiction of the Rider Haggard type, though little accurate knowledge was available; estimates of population, often misleading, were based on head-counts by District Officers and 'informed guesses' based on tax lists. Density of population was recognised as of crucial importance—people were regarded as an economic asset as important as, and closely related to, agricultural and mineral resources.

Whatever the original motives for colonisation, development was essential to offset the cost of obtaining and running new colonies. First came the establishment of law and order and of an administration—much easier where the population was relatively dense and closely settled; in the Cameroons, the Germans adopted a deliberate policy of concentrating certain peoples into cohesive groups which could be more effectively controlled [1].

The next necessity was transport to 'open up' a colony to development; and in the early colonial period this meant railways. While it was reasonable to connect densely populated and potentially profitable areas by this expensive and inflexible system, it was much more difficult to justify the building of lines through sparsely-populated areas which offered little hope of economic exploitation. In Tanganyika, where small islands of dense population were surrounded by vast stretches of almost uninhabited bush [2], Clement Gilman claimed for the route he chose for the railway that it connected 'more areas of closer settlement than any other feasible route between coast and lake [3]. In Ghana, despite Governor Guggisberg's enthusiasm, the railway was never extended to the north through the thinly-populated middle belt.

Scarcity of people meant scarcity of labour. Even with a large population, it was not always easy to persuade people to go to work; in sparsely-populated areas where there was plenty of land, there was little incentive to undertake uncongenial and poorly-rewarded wage-labour. Peasant agriculture could only form the basis of profitable export trade with fairly high densities in intensively-farmed areas; mineral resources could only be worked with a good pool of local labour. Everything pointed to more successful development being associated with an area with higher population density. Uneven densities also created serious problems.

In Kenya, with what was believed to be a very low population density and no mineral resources, the strategically necessary railway had to be made to pay. It was agreed from the beginning, both in London and in the Colony, that some policy to bring settlers to the country was going to be essential. The local population was thought to be too small and too backward to form the basis for any sort of development [4]. In fact, density had been under-estimated [5], but numbers were very low at the turn of the century after a series of disasters—famine, disease, slave-raiding; many areas which had formerly been occupied appeared to be empty. In the 1890s, it was thought that Indian settlement would be the answer; many Indians were imported to work on building the railway, and East Africa strengthened its already close trade links with India. East Africa, it was suggested, would provide India with the same kind of outlet that America had provided for Europe [6]. But some areas, believed to be unoccupied, were climatically suitable for white settlement. Sir Charles Eliot, appointed Governor of the East Africa Protectorate in 1900, urged the Foreign Office to encourage white settlement. All the later problems of land settlement, labour conditions and 'native rights' sprang from that decision made by the 'man on the spot' and accepted without question by his superiors in Britain—the decision to try to solve the problems of under-population by importing aliens to lead development.

Eliot advocated the paramountcy of European interests; he was even against the establishment of native reserves—he did not wish to see the Africans preserved in their 'barbarity' [7]. Later governors generally followed in his path and were firm supporters of the white settlers. On the other hand, the District officials, whose views rarely reached London, became the defenders of African rights.

If the whole pattern of development policy in Kenya sprang from the low population densities of the 1890s, it was the very lack of resources in Tanganyika which led to the resettlement schemes of the 1930s. Underpopulation was associated with the tsetse fly which made large stretches of bushland impossible for human habitation; the population was too small and too scattered to keep the bush cleared and the fly at bay. Concentration into villages enabled the people to clear small inhabitable oases in the bush. It was an inexpensive policy, and one which had the attraction of being regenerative: when bush had been cleared, the water-table usually rose, creating better living and farming conditions and leading to a consequent increase in population and the clearing of larger areas.

Many of the problems arising from low population density, and not least the problem of tsetse fly, must have faced the people of Africa before colonial rule; they were, however, not burdened with the urgent need to develop in order to pay for colonial rule itself.

Notes

This section is a summary, by Marion Johnson, of a paper written by Elizabeth Hook.

[1]   W. B. Morgan and J. C. Pugh, *West Africa*, London, 1969, p. 727
[2]   C. Leusbuscher, *Tanganyika Territory*, London, 1944, p. 23
[3]   C. Gilman, in the *Geographical Review*, July 1936, p. 372
[4]   M. P. K. Sorrenson, *Origins of European Settlement in Kenya* London 1968, Appendix 2
[5]   Sir Charles Eliot based his estimate of the Kikuyu population on observation of the sparser southern groups near the railway. See C. C. Wrigley, 'Kenya, the patterns of economic life, 1902-45', in *History of East Africa, Vol II*, Harlow, Chilver and Smith (eds), Oxford, 1970, p. 213
[6]   Sir Harry Johnston, *Colonisation of Africa by Alien Races*, London 1899, p. 281
[7]   Sir Charles Eliot, *The East African Protectorate*, London, 1905

Another valuable reference is Kuczinski, *A Demographic Survey of the British Colonial Empire*, London, 1948.

Linguistic and
Anthropological Aspects

Introduction

T. D. P. Dalby

There can be no adequate study of the relationship between man and the land, in a specific environment, without an adequate study of the human societies involved and of their inter-relationships. In order for anthropologists and linguists to make such a contribution, however, it will be necessary for them—without in any way abandoning their traditional areas and methods of research—to think more strategically as far as Africa itself is concerned. Both social anthropology and linguistics operate within a complex framework of theory, and both disciplines are concerned with the continuous re-examination, testing and extension of this framework. As a continent, Africa has provided much of the social and linguistic data necessary for this theoretical work, within both disciplines, and it is therefore appropriate that both disciplines should contribute their experience and energies to the examination of some of Africa's current problems. In the recent words of a social anthropologist, 'there is no reason why we should continue to draw academic nourishment from poor countries without giving them something which they value in return' [1].

In the session of the Conference devoted to linguistic and anthropological aspects, under the joint chairmanship of a linguist and an anthropologist [2], it was possible to consider four complementary papers. Two of these, based on West African experience, presented some of the methodological considerations involved in defining and distinguishing between the concepts of 'language', 'ethnicity' and 'population' (Edwin Ardener), and between 'language' and 'culture' (Paul Hair). The second and third papers, based on East African research, presented case-studies of the social relationships existing between ethnically and linguistically distinct populations in a rural environment (Paul Spencer) and in an urban environment (David Parkin, whose paper was presented at the Conference *in absentia*) [3].

No discussion, and certainly no interdisciplinary discussion, will get far without a clarification of terminology, and the contributors

43

to this session posed—and endeavoured to answer—a number of basic problems of definition. These included the questions 'what is—i.e. what do we understand by—a 'population' (Ardener), an 'ethnolinguistic unit' (Hair), or 'expansion' (Spencer)?' In each of these papers, we were warned of the dangers of feed-back from an over-simplified interpretation of these and other related concepts. There is, of course, also the basic question of 'what is a "language"?', but in general it was agreed that purely linguistic distinctions are more readily quantifiable and definable than cultural, ethnic and other categories. Language thus provides us with a starting-point, both for the diachronic and synchronic study of populations. It is now firmly accepted, however, by members—hopefully by all members—of relevant disciplines that 'language, racial and cultural traits are independent variables' [4]. Ardener raises the problem of taxonomic scales, and the variable criteria on which these may be based, but we have yet to establish procedures for the more scientific classification of populations, or rather—faced with some of the excesses and ambiguities of classification in the past—with their 'declassification'. Ardener emphasises the fact that 'human populations ascribed to particular ethnic entities do not necessarily represent demographic units with a purely demographic past and future', and he introduces the important concept of 'hollow categories' of population, especially on the borders of two larger, interacting groups—as illustrated by the 'Kole', between the Efik and the Duala, and apparently also by Spencer's 'Ariaal', between the Rendille and the Samburu. Hair makes the related point that 'cultural and genetic drift' may occur without significant ethnolinguistic displacement, and he is almost certainly right in supposing that the extent of such drift may have been underestimated in the past (not only involving the influx of captives and slaves he mentions, but also the superimposition of ruling minorities [5]. It thus became clear that little scientific use could be made of a term such as 'tribe', quite apart from the fact that it has acquired offensive overtones—although Hair, with scepticism, clearly feels that preference for terms like 'ethnolinguistic unit' reflects a mere love of scientific-surrounding polysyllables. It does not, of course, matter what terms are actually used, so long as we define them clearly; this is sometimes easier if we start with a new term, rather than add yet another definition to an already ambiguous item.

The most important point, made collectively and independently by the papers in question, is that we are dealing in most cases, not with an 'empty world' into which so-called 'populations' may move or expand, but rather with a complex network of inter-relationships which—except in times of great upheaval or disaster—provide a very slowly changing chess-board of linguistic and ethnic domains, across which cultural and biological exchanges and movements can, and do, take place. The permanent nature of the physical environment, the more or less permanent nature of the rural economics practicable in each area (fluctuating within certain climatic and technological limits), and the interlocking social systems established in response to these, form the network which holds the squares of the chessboard in place. Hence we have the 'ethnolinguistic continuity' traced historically by Hair on the coasts of West and South-East Africa, where the sea—at the edge of the chessboard—forms the most intransigent barrier of all (cf. the Celtic 'continuity' on the coasts of Western Europe), and also the long-term balance, described by Spencer, between such populations as the Rendille and Samburu, in spite of their contrasting aspirations of 'restriction' and 'expansion'. Put another way, 'migration'—a favourite theme of historians—may, in many cases, have been more a case of 'diffusion', comparable to a relay-race [6]; and 'expansion'—a favourite theme of anthropologists—has perhaps often been an 'ebb and flow' process, amounting ultimately to running on the spot.

Whereas the social effects of climatic disasters, like the forerunners of the 1972/74 drought in the Sahel region of West Africa, have tended to rectify themselves with time, modern urban development has created 'holes' in the established chess-board, into which linguistic and ethnic elements have been drawn from all directions. Urbanisation is probably the most important source of demographic 'upheaval' in Africa since the introduction of iron to the sub-Saharan continent some two millenia ago. Yet even here, as Parkin showed, urban interelationships between populations of diverse origin often continue traditional inter-relationships and attitudes established in the rural environment. It becomes only a matter of time before the 'holes' are bridged over by a new network of inter-social and inter-linguistic relationships ('inter-linguistic' in the sense of the balance achieved between neighbouring and co-occuring languages, rather than in the sense of 'genetic' relationships among languages).

Parkin's work in the field of socio-linguistics, in which he had collaborated closely with the late Professor Wilfred Whiteley, himself both a linguist *and* an anthropologist, raised the important question of future interdisciplinary research. Although Parkin's research has a strong—and essential—quantitative basis, it does not neglect the qualitative element, the need for which Ardener has rightly emphasised. Parkin's study of inter-social and inter-linguistic relationships, and of the factors involved in the establishment of these in an urban environment, are an indication of the future contribution which socio-linguistics can make to population studies in Africa. As yet, socio-linguistic studies have been concerned primarily, although not exclusively, with urban situations. There is a need for the extension of these studies into the traditional rural environment and into the historical field, with the increasing involvement of linguistically-aware anthropologists and historians. Above all, there is a need for African linguists to concern themselves more with 'strategic' studies, in addition to the study and description of individual languages and literatures, and to look increasingly at the contemporary and historical interaction of neighbouring languages and their speakers. A particular contribution can be made in this area by indigenous African linguists, especially where they already have two or more relevant languages at their command.

It would be sad if the majority of African research students in the linguistic field were to continue to concern themselves primarily or exclusively with purely descriptive studies. With the application of modern linguistic science, it is possible for competent grammatical and phonological descriptions to be undertaken by non-African scholars—with the help of good informants—without even visiting the relevant area of Africa. Detailed socio-linguistic work cannot be undertaken on such a basis, however, and demands a detailed knowledge of the social and environmental, as well as of the linguistic, background of an area. It should perhaps be noted, on the other hand, that there is a danger of socio-linguistics developing as a discipline in its own right, with socio-linguists talking only to other socio-linguists, and—although this is certainly not apparent in Parkin's work—with the development of its own 'protective' jargon. Such a tendency needs to be resisted.

On the wider front, the disciplines involved need to work together increasingly on the identification of the patterns and processes involved in the establishment and maintenance of inter-social and inter-linguistic relationships in Africa, and on the exemplification through case-studies of the types and scales of such relationships. What factors, for example, determine the positive or negative relationships and attitudes existing between neighbouring speakers of different languages, often independently of the presence or absence of any close 'genetic' relationship between the languages involved? There is a need, in fact, for the results of more descriptive ethnography—including cultural ethnography and the ethnography of speech—and it is to be hoped that we may reduce the prejudice towards ethnography as such, engendered by its often purely 'cataloguing' nature and by some of the excesses of earlier comparative ethnography. Above all, however, it is important that we should not confine ourselves—despite our primary concern with Africa—to examples and case-studies drawn from Africa alone. This is, of course, the danger of interdisciplinary studies organised on a regional basis, and we should perhaps bear in mind Hair's admonition that 'the curse of African studies is its limitation to Africa'. If our work is to be of value, not only in achieving closer collaboration among the disciplines, but also in helping to consider some of the major social and developmental problems facing modern Africa, then we need to be aware, not only of the work of our Africanist colleagues in other disciplines, but also—through them—of parallel research being carried out by those disciplines in other parts of the world.

Notes

[1]   Paul Devitt, 'Notes on some social aspects of drought in pastoral areas of Africa: an opportunity for a radical rethink', paper presented to the Symposium on Drought in Africa, Centre for African Studies, S.O.A.S., London, 19-20 July 1973.

[2]   The task of compiling this introduction has fallen to the linguist alone, since the anthropologist concerned is himself the author of the first of the four papers considered at this session of the Conference.

[3]   David Parkin's paper was regrettably not available for publication.

[4]   C.F. Shula Marks and A. Atmore, 'The problem of the Nguni, in David Dalby (ed.), *Language and History in Africa*, London, 1970, p. 127.

[5]   In the geographical area Hair discusses—Sierra Leone—, there is evidence that cultural and genetic drift in the direction of Manding has occurred among certain Temne-speaking and other non-Manding groups, through the introduction of Manding rulers and of Manding-influenced forms of Islam.

[6]   See, for instance, the section on Population Movement (pp. 9-11).

Language, Ethnicity, and Population

E. W. Ardener

I

It may seem difficult at first sight to understand exactly the relationship between the three terms: 'language', 'ethnicity', and 'population' in a conference at which the focus is primarily on the third [1]. We are, of course, used to some doubts about the precise application of the first two in African circumstances. For example, as far as 'language' is concerned, even a simple list (let alone a classification) of linguistic units leads to hoary problems of 'language' versus 'dialect', 'cluster', 'family', and the like, or to discussions of criteria of 'genetic' or 'typological' or other sorts. With 'tribe' or 'ethnicity', discussion turns on the overlap with 'race', 'culture', or 'language' itself (however ultimately delineated). We are less used to doubts about the third term 'population'. As is common in human studies, we confuse different ideas. Thus we imagine that population is a reality, 'infrastructural' to the other two. Population measures have all the earmarks of objectivity and, for many, the reality of the term 'population' is itself an expression of the various indices used by demographers: birth, death, fertility, and nuptiality rates, and enumerations and samplings of various kinds.

Yet what is a population? What is, in each case, the unit to which the demographic measures relate? In a study of the Bakweri of Cameroon, some years ago, for example, a central question began to emerge. Were the Bakweri a declining population? Now the Bakweri tend to think that those of their number who live in modern centres are not quite 'real' Bakweri. The Bakweri picture of themselves made a clear distinction between those inside their village fences (leading a 'Bakweri way of life' as it were) and those outside them. The modern centres (*par excellence* outside the fence) were ethnically mixed, cosmopolitan, un-Bakweri. There was a sense then in which, if the rural heartland was losing population, the Bakweri were also declining *in toto*. The definition of the target population as rural, in

48

an area notorious for a vast 'multitribal' migration to an adjacent plantation industry, moved the question of Bakweri 'decline' out of the realm of demography into that of ideas. For the rural population was not, as it stood, a self-perpetrating population. Demographically it was marked by 'distorted' age-structures and sex ratios—and probably fertility patterns too [2].

This did not prevent us from usefully wearing out a demographic armoury on the mensurational aspects of the problem, and learning a great deal of value thereby. The most valuable lesson was that, in the discussion of the dynamics of a population, your unit—'the population'—is not merely subject to a statistical determination on the part of the observer; it is also dependent on the subjective definition of that population by the human beings concerned. Over time, therefore, population series are continually affected by changing definitions on the part of both the measurers and the measured. This factor has received less general emphasis than it deserves, in part because of the dogmatic, even ideological, definitions of populations that accompanied the development of the nineteenth and twentieth century nation states.

II

In Africa, the assumption that ethnicities were entities of the type that would yield a 'population' has always been too easily made, in both linguistic and biological studies. For that reason the figures for 'tribal' membership and for language-speakers are really even more difficult to evaluate than we usually suspect them to be. The extreme north-west corner of the Bantu-speaking area (I adhere for the present to be the boundary according to Guthrie, 1948) illustrates this problem with remarkable clarity. We are presented with some two dozen entities, usually called 'tribes', but which also form the elements of the linguistic classification of the area. These entities are marked by very small individual populations from 300 or less to about 30,000, with 6,000 or so being the mean. They are surrounded by 'groups' of quite another scale: Efik, Ekoi, Bamileke, and so on. What are we to make of discrepancies of this sort? We are in a difficult area of analysis, which belongs to a field of wider interest than our more limited regional concerns. The classification of human groups will exhibit features common to the classifying of all phenomena. Some part of the question of the particular scale of the north-western Bantu ethnicities lies in the criteria of the Bantu classification itself—determined, if you like, in armchairs in Europe.

First, then, the scholars. It is easy to start with the recognition that the tribal and linguistic classifications were not independently arrived at. Even so, in what sense is it true that the speakers of Nigerian 'Ekoid' languages are more linguistically homogeneous than the West Cameroon group of Bantu speakers? We may answer this in different ways, but we should note that any scholarly or scientific classification occupies a specific taxonomic space. Its confines are to some extent coercive and they must be taken into account when problems of relationship within the space are being examined.

The conventional units which make up the taxonomy of the Bantu languages are defined, on the face of it, by fairly clearly determinable criteria [e.g. Guthrie, 1948]. The north-west Bantu entities belong, of course, to this taxonomy. If these criteria are strictly applied we shall not be surprised that the taxonomic space of the Bantu classification does not correspond with that independently set up for the West African languages, since the latter notoriously depends on a much less rigorous set (even a mixture) of criteria, and belong on a different plane of analysis from that which is feasible in Bantu studies [Ardener, 1971, 218-19].

Secondly, the 'people'. We have to consider here the nature of self-classification or self-identification. For the 'people' themselves play the part of theoreticians in this field. Here we touch on the close match of the classifying process with the workings of language itself. It has frequently been noted that the Bantu languages have 'overdetermined', as it were, precisely along the axis of classification. The smallest differentiation of humanity can immediately be linguistically labelled, with a *ba*-form, homologous with that used for the largest ethnic entities. The Bantu taxonomy is continuously self-amending.

In the interaction between insider and outsider, the Bantuizing tendency has aided the differentiation and discrimination of units. The multiplication of 'separate' Bantu languages was even an overt aim of nineteenth-century scholars. For the north-western Bantu area, it is a fact that many of the divisions now in existence lean on classifications in which the scholar-turned-administrator or the administrator-turned-scholar (German, British, and French) played a not insignificant part. There was a feedback to the people, so easily achieved through interpreters and others, to confuse the matter further. After all, one of the more inaccessible 'populations' of the zone is quite content to be called, and to call itself, 'Ngolo-Batanga', a hyphenated form which owes its existence to classifying for the convenience of scholars and foreigners [3] —thus joining the select but expanding company in which are found 'Anglo-Saxon', 'Serbo-Croat', and some others.

The Bantuizing tendency itself belongs to that well-documented domain of structure in which language and reality are intermingled. It is also something of a special case of the more complex phenomenon of 'taxonomic scale'. This is underlined when we consider the neighbouring Ekoi case. The intervention of British-style, ethnically minded, Native Administrations had given, by the 'thirties of this century, a local reality to general classifications whose autochthonous basis was originally limited and contradictory. The search for one Ekoi ethnicity, rather than a series of ethnicities, must be brought into relation with the particular scale of the main elements of the southern Nigerian ethnic space. Dominated as it was by the entities labelled Yoruba, Edo, Ibo, and Ibibio, it became virtually determined that 'Ekoi' would be set up homologously with these—despite the possibility of establishing several Ekoi 'tribes' [Talbot, 1926; Crabb, 1965].

The effect of two essentially different taxonomic spaces in this zone upon tribal divisions can be seen in the usage of the German and British administrations. The former, 'Bantuizing' in tendency, used three 'ethnic' names to divide up the relatively small Ekoi-speaking area which overlapped into its territory. On the other hand, when West Cameroon came under British administrators, some of the latter (e.g. Talbot), being more at home on the Nigerian scale, classified the whole 'Bantu' group together, for population purposes. This did not become general, but the ethnic 'diversity' of the area always remained a source of classifying malaise to them.

In the colonial period, then, the scale of the units in the prevailing ethnic taxonomies was far from uniform. The accepted scale was, in a sense, a result of arbitration between the foreigners and the politically important groups. The Yoruba and Bini kingdoms set the scale for southern Nigeria, but this was itself set in some ways by the imperial scale of the Fulani-conquered north. It should not be forgotten that the still unsuccessful search for Ekoi unity was preceded by the Ibo case, the successful outcome of whose progress from label to population was not self-evident. It is by continuous series of such contrasts and oppositions (to which, I repeat, both foreigners and Africans contributed) that many (and in principle all) populations have defined themselves.

Much of the discomfort of West Cameroonians in the Federation of Nigeria derived from the discrepancy between their 'Bantuizing' taxonomic scale and that of the Federation as a whole. This led to the paradox, noted at the time, of the growth of a new 'Kamerun' ethnicity of Nigerian scale, covering this 'artificial' political unit—which actually, despite its internal diversity, was, while the taxonomic constraints existed, one of the most homogeneous-looking of the units of the Federation. The Bantuizing scale of the new Cameroon state clearly suits West Cameroon better at present. The West Cameroon area nevertheless still preserves elements of the newer and broader 'ethnicity' generated by the Nigerian phase of their experience [Ardener 1967, 293-9].

The position of minority peoples in a zone of 'large populations' is thus more complicated than it seems. I wish to bring out of the discussion so far these points, as they relate to the African situation. I think they have more general validity.

1)   The ethnic classification is a reflex of self-identification.
2)   Onomastic (or naming) propensities are closely involved in this, and thus have more than a purely linguistic interest.
3)   Identification by others is an important feature in the establishment of self-identification.
4)   The taxonomic space in which self-identification occurs is of overriding importance.
5)   The effect of foreign classification, 'scientific' and lay, is far from neutral in the establishment of such a space.

III

'Tribes are not permanent crystalline structures, belonging to one "stage" of historical or social development . . . the process of self-classification never ceases' [4]. There is a true sense in which the human populations ascribed to some of these entities do not therefore represent demographic units with purely demographic pasts or futures.

Take an entity such as the Kole, one of the labelled units on the border of the Bantu and Efik linguistic domains. This was ascribed a population in 1953 of hundreds. The Kole, or some of them, speak a dialect of Duala, and are traditionally offshoots of the latter people, who live some 100 miles down the coast. Something corresponding to the Kole entity has been attested for 130 years, and on some interpretations of the evidence it could be 200, even 300 years old [5]. This small population always seems to be on the brink of extinction. What is meant by the demographic continuity of populations of this sort? Do we assume they are all the rump remnants of larger groups in the past? For various reasons, the evidence for ethnolinguistic continuity on this coast tends to suggest the opposite—that we are dealing with populations bumping along in exiguous numbers over fifty or a hundred or even several hundred years. With populations of millions, extrapolations back and forward in time using demographic indices may not generate truth, but they contain plausibility. With small hunting and gathering bands an ecological balance is at least a hypothesis (although Douglas, 1966, has called it into question). The populations of the type to which I refer are not at this elementary technological level. In the Kole case, it may well be that the whole dynamic of the 'population' is linguistic or sociolinguistic.

The Kole environmental interest is a border interest—between the Efik and Duala trading zones. The 'Kole' coast probably always had a mixed population. Kole may have always used a trading dialect, whose structure may reflect several neighbouring Bantu languages. Kole, as identifiable people under that label, were probably those members of the commercial group who maintained some connections with the Duala and perhaps with the intervening Isubu. The category Kole may have been filled according to different criteria at different times. Perhaps sometimes, the Kole were mostly Efik. Perhaps sometimes the Kole speech was learnt by all in the zone. Perhaps sometimes it was spoken by nobody of social importance. In all these coastal areas the expansion and contraction of slave or client communities, and their relationships to their masters and hosts, must also be borne in mind. In a case like this the dynamics of a 'population' with a certain label over the centuries are not the dynamics of cohorts, and of fertility or mortality rates. They are the dynamics of an economic, social, and linguistic situation.

Who, or what, however, determines the preservation of the classification itself? We can easily hypothesize a situation in which everyone can point to a Kole, but no one calls himself Kole. Labels of this sort are fixed to what may be termed 'hollow categories'. In the actual case, the Efik no doubt maintained the category of 'border coastal Bantu peoples' without much concern for the exact constituents of the category. The Bantu-speaking Duala, Isubu, and others might equally have maintained the category of 'those like us, nearest the Efik'. I suspect that the Kole were, in part, a hollow category like this. They were fixed as an 'ethnic group' in the British administrative system. No wonder many were puzzled by the tiny number of 'linguistic' Kole among a welter of Efik and other migrants. No wonder too that linguistic Kole itself was so hard to pin down, a language of aberrant idiolects. Perhaps it had never been any different?

In order to summarize the population characteristics of a hollow category, we may express the matter so: since the category is filled according to non-demographic criteria, the population's survival or extinction, growth or decline, age-structure or fertility, are not determined in demographic space.

A close congener of the hollow category is the entity maintained by continuous replenishment from a home area. Thus the ethnic map of Cameroon contains stable, growing or declining concentrations of Ibo, Bamileke, Hausa (and the like), which are demographically not necessarily self-perpetuating. This type of unit is familiar now in Africa, as well as in most of the urbanized world. Such concentrations were, however, also known in the past. Nomadic groups such as the Fulani, or economically defined groups such as the Aro among the Ibo, and others elsewhere shared some of the features of such continuously concentrated but demographically unstable groups.

Their close connection with hollow categories lies in their

tendency to *become* hollow. Thus the supposed Bali settlers on the Cameroon Plateau are now, in their main settlement, an entity which under close examination turns out to look like a representative sample of all of their neighbours. Their present dominant language is a kind of average Cameroon Bantoid. In northern Cameroon the category 'Fulbe' has become 'hollow' in this way. In various places and times the categories 'Norman', 'Pict', 'Jew', 'Gypsy', 'Irishman', and many others may have become, or be becoming hollow—a mere smile surviving from the vanished Cheshire cat. Thus not only can a hollow category become a 'population', but a 'population' can also become a hollow category. Indeed, this process need never stop: the category may become a population again. Certain peculiar features in the supposed continuity of certain ethnic, even 'national', groups may well be elucidated in this way.

It is essential to make this effort to separate the concept of 'population' from those of language and ethnicity. In the past the separation has been urged in biological terms. A biological population, it has been pointed out, may coincide in its history with the affiliations of its language or of its culture. I am not repeating this truth, or truism. For we are not able to be so confident about the concept of a biological population. We are concerned with continuities whose processes are only in part biological. Fulbe, Jews, and (as we know) Britons are created by definition as much as by procreation. We are dealing with 'structures' of a clearly recognized type whose transformations may be documented in statistics, but whose dynamics lie outside the field of statistical extrapolation. I have made this assertion of principle without the important modifications and qualifications in order to highlight its importance in African studies. We may, in the West or in the global context, avert our eyes from these contradictions. Our largest units of human classification have reached such a scale that population dynamics now form the tail that violently wags the human dog. This is not so even with smaller western units or subunits. It was rarely so with African ethnicities.

IV

I have kept these remarks brief. I have not alluded more than sketchily to the topographical, ecological, economic, and political elements which enter into identification and self-identification. Ultimately, among the things that society 'is' or 'is like', it 'is' or 'is like' identification. The entities set up may be based upon divisions in empirical reality, or may be set up on reality by the structuring processes of the human mind in society. In such statements 'reality' is, however, frequently only a compendium of 'positivistic' measures and approximations. We experience the structures themselves as reality: they generate events, not merely our experience of events [6]. Anthropologists would argue, I think, that this process is analogous to language, possibly subsuming language, rather than a process of language. But all agree that language acquires a position of critical empirical importance in its study.

For population studies, the most impressive advances have occurred in the study of entities of a macrodemographic scale to which statistical and mensurational indices are central. Nevertheless, *changes* in these indices come back to the differentiation of entities ('minorities', 'classes', 'sects', 'ideologies') within the mass population which redefine or restructure population 'behaviour' and thus, the population. This differentiating process is of exactly the kind which, in our more parochial field of interest, is associated with the waxing and waning of 'ethnicities' and the like. I have used only two or three elementary formulations ('the taxonomic space', 'taxonomic scale' and 'hollow category'), but the basic approach is a small part of recent movements which restore scientific validity to the mentalistic framework within which human societies shape and create events. Thereby, population studies themselves may be given back some of the intuitive life and colour that their subject matter deserves.

Notes

[1]   This paper was first published in the *Journal of the Anthropological Society of Oxford*, 3.3.1972, 125-32.
[2]   See Ardener *1962, 1972a.*
[3]   To distinguish them from the distant Batanga of the South Cameroon coast.
[4]   Ardener *1967*: 298.
[5]   Under the name of 'Romby'—Ardener *1968, 1972b.*
[6]   For a full scale treatment of this problem see Ardener *1974.*

References

Ardener, E. (1962) *Divorce and Fertility: an African Study,* London.
(1967) 'The Nature of the Reunification of Cameroon', in A. Hazlewood (ed.), *African Integration and Disintegration.* OUP and R.I.I.A., London.
(1968) 'Documentary and Linguistic Evidence for the Rise of the Trading Polities between Rio del Rey and Cameroon 1500-1650', in I.M. Lewis (ed.) *History and Social Anthropology,* London.
(1971) 'Social Anthropology and the Historicity of Historical Linguistics', in E. Ardener (ed.), *Social Anthropology and Language.* ASA 10. London.
(1972a) 'Belief and the Problem of Women', in J. La Fontaine (ed.) *The Interpretation of Ritual,* London.
(1972b) Introduction and Commentary to J. Clarke: *Specimens of Dialects,* Berwick-on-Tweed 1848. Reprinted, Gregg Press.
(1974) 'Population and 'Tribal Communities' '. Wolfson Lecture delivered at Oxford on 6th February, 1973, to be published 1974.

Crabb, D.W. (1965) *Ekoid Bantu Languages of Ogoja*, Cambridge.
Douglas, M. (1966) 'Population Control in Primitive Groups', *British Journal of Sociology*, 17, 3.
Guthrie, M. (1948) *The Classification of the Bantu Languages*, London.
Talbot, P.A. (1926) *The Peoples of Southern Nigeria*, Oxford.

Scarcity and growth in two African societies

P. Spencer

Published monographs on traditional East African societies frequently present models of expansion. The Nyakyusa chiefdoms systematically expanded and formally divided into two autonomous halves once every generation [1]. The recent history of Buganda is presented in terms of a constantly expanding conquest state [2]. The two were a dispersed ethnic group whose expansion took on different guises in various parts of East Africa [3]. The basic model of the Lugbara is of a local cluster based on a shallow lineage that grows, and divides after the death of the elder [4]. The Arusha are analysed in terms of a society that has constantly been expanding since its inception in about 1840, at first up the slopes of Mount Meru and then out onto the plains as the younger men asserted a degree of autonomy from their fathers [5]. The Karimojong-speaking peoples are seen as having derived from possibly a single ancestral group [6]. To these I might add the Samburu for whom the model presented was of large polygamous families, and growing herds of cattle that were eventually divided between a number of sons [7].

Two points must be stressed in order to appreciate these processes of growth. In the first place, not all societies were expanding into an empty world. An expanding state such as Buganda absorbed surrounding people without necessarily entailing overall population increase. The inception and expansion of the Arusha (and for that matter the Gogo [8]) is partly expressed in terms of the assimilation of different alien groups. A recurrent theme throughout the area is of lineages and clans who claim ultimate descent from some alien ancestor. Dispersed and defeated minorities tended to be absorbed into more successful and viable groups. Where women were taken over by their captors, there was, in effect, a transfer of their child-bearing capacities between groups, but not necessarily an increase in the total population.

Secondly, these models of expansion were often traditional ideals in which prevailed the notion that growth was propitious and

57

sustained life, whereas the absence of growth spelt death and extinction. They were normative achievements to which people aspired, but they were not necessarily norms in an observable statistical sense. Inevitably these models of growth have drawn the attention of anthropologists who are especially concerned to understand the philosophies that underlie patterns of behaviour. Thus Wilson presents a vivid account of the process whereby Nyakyusa chiefdoms divided once every generation and merely notes the anomalous possibility of no permanent division occurring when a chiefdom was too small and weak; but her genealogies of chiefly families suggests that permanent divisions were relatively infrequent [9]. Middleton was able to explore the dynamics of lineage expansion among the Lugbara by selecting a family cluster on the point of fission; but the general shortage of land suggests that, at the time of study, expansion could only occur at the expense of other less successful groups that would, in effect, be forced to contract. In a number of studies it has been noted that, over time, lineages tend to coalesce ancestors that were not prominently placed at the points of genealogical growth; through this process the apparent rate of increase in genealogies is accelerated [10]. In a rather similar way, oral histories tend to stress periods of successful expansion in greater detail than periods of contraction: Bunyoro's recent losses were Buganda's gains, but in their oral history, the Banyoro tended to stress their earlier successes [11].

In other words, in searching the literature on East African traditional societies for evidence of demographic growth, one should not automatically assume that the social models of expansion held as ideals by the people themselves and explored and elaborated by anthropologists, are necessarily the same as the process of population expansion. Rather, they should be seen as relevant factors—often highly relevant—that only acquire a true perspective when one has equally valid data on the less prominent minorities who were defeated, dispersed, absorbed or who only achieved partial success. One depressing feature of the literature is that frequently one knows that the ideal of growth was not generally attained, but there is insufficient data recorded to discern even a rough perspective. Occasional figures and even tables do not provide a comprehensive demographic picture, even though this could substantiate and even shed new light on the social models.

Clearly, not all ethnographic accounts are of situations of growth and expansion. One that deserves mention is of the Sonjo of Tanzania [12]. Here, one had an irrigation economy where the supply of water in an otherwise arid and hostile area limited the opportunities for growth. Each Sonjo village and its irrigation activities were governed autonomously by a council of elders. There were a fixed number of places on the council and a fixed number of other men with substantial rights in the irrigation system. In contrast to most other East African societies, there was no ideal of becoming a founder of an expanding lineage: a man with too large a family might even sell one of his wives and her children to the neighbouring Masai, and no attempt would be made to assert his rights over any children of a divorced wife. The Sonjo preference for limiting the sizes of their families was linked to an economic system that had no room to expand, just as the numbers of title holders were not allowed to expand. Here, then, one has an example of restriction rather than expansion, in which the social ideals were linked to the economic realities.

The Rendille and Samburu of Northern Kenya are interesting in this context since one (the Rendille) is an example similar to the Sonjo, in that economic factors appear to inhibit growth; and the other (the Samburu) follow the more prevalent ideal of growth. This paper outlines ways in which the two societies have a symbiotic relationship through the complementary nature of their economic and demographic needs. Both are pastoral nomads who do not practise any form of agriculture [13].

Culturally, the Rendille are closer to the Somali, from whom they claim ultimate descent, than to the Samburu; and the Samburu are very close to the Masai and identify themselves within the same ethnic group. Their languages belong to different basic groups (Cushitic and Nilo-Hamitic respectively) and are mutually unintelligible. The Rendille, with their camel economy, prefer the land to the east of Lake Rudolf which is too waterless for cattle; and the Samburu, with their cattle economy, prefer the land to the south of the lake which is too disease-ridden for camels. To this extent the two tribes live apart and have little day-to-day interaction. Only to the south-east of the lake, which is less than ideal for either the camels or the cattle, are they to some extent interspersed, and here are concentrated a special group of Rendille whom I refer to as the Ariaal Rendille as distinct from their northern neighbours, the Rendille proper. Altogether there are an estimated 8,000 Rendille proper, 5,500 Ariaal Rendille and 50,000 Samburu.

In terms of their day-to-day activities, the Rendille camel economy and the Samburu cattle economy are mutually exclusive. While this is consistent with the geographical, social and linguistic barriers between the two tribes, it must be emphasised that the political alliance between them and the interplay of their longer term needs has persisted for a number of generations. Apart from vague notions of ultimate descent from different ethnic groups, their oral histories do not reach back to a time when the two tribes were independent of one another.

In order to appreciate the demographic balance between the two societies and the role of the Ariaal Rendille, it is useful first to compare the Samburu and the Rendille proper and to show how ecological differences appear to influence their rates of growth.

Expressed quite simply, cattle management under the Samburu is a going concern, whereas camel management under the Rendille is not. This may be due partly to the local terrain, to the pastoral competence of the people or the characteristics of the stock. The precise balance between these is uncertain. Cattle under Samburu management give enough milk for much of the year to satisfy human needs. Herding is time-consuming but not arduous, and may be carried out by any active boys or men. However, the milk supply of cattle is affected by long treks searching for browse and water, and this encourages the Samburu to live in small mobile settlements that can exploit the land as opportunities arise and lessen the demands on the cattle. It is essentially seen as a benign, rewarding economy. Given a degree of luck and good management, a man can double the size of his herd in five years, and a really poor young man of 30 can become unusually wealthy before he is 60. This is the model of growth and expansion before every Samburu. It tends to overlook the harsh droughts that every ten years or so decimate herds and serve to restrict ultimate growth. Thus, while the realities of growth appear to have a saw-tooth profile in which there is a steady increase in herds and a sudden catastrophe every ten years or so, the Samburu themselves see the possibilities of uninterrupted growth as an ideal to be achieved leading to more wives, more children and yet more cattle.

Camels under Rendille management contrast in each of these respects. Their great advantage lies in the abundant quantities of milk they provide and their ability to survive the worst droughts. The terrain is unsuitable for riding the camels, and the limitations in herding are not the endurance of the stock but of the herdsmen. This considerably restricts the age-range of men fit enough to undertake the task, and hence the numbers available. The main problem of the camel economy is its stunted rate of growth. This is partly because camels only calve at half the rate of cattle, partly because of their proneness to a number of prevalent diseases, especially anthrax and trypanosomiasis, and partly it seems because the heavy demands on the herdsmen limit the sizes of the herds that they can successfully manage. The constant concern of Rendille is to maintain the size of their camel herds at all costs, since they have no guarantee that any losses will in the fullness of time be replaced. In contrast to the Samburu, they do not have an optimistic attitude towards the prospects of their economy; rather they are generally concerned about events that seem almost outside their control.

Corresponding to this stunted growth of their herds, the Rendille have a number of practices that, in effect, stunt their own population growth. A principal that overrides all others is that the precious camel herd should in no circumstances be split. A man should ideally have only one wife and his herd should be entirely inherited by his eldest son. Younger sons are given only a few camels with which to marry. A few exceptionally rich men would take on second wives, and have a number of sons, but their customs repeatedly draw attention to the first marriage, the senior son, and maintaining the herd intact. There are a number of customs that limit the number of children a woman may have. They tend to be married later than Samburu girls, and some daughters of men belonging to certain age-sets cannot marry until they are in their thirties. First-born twins, children of unmarried girls, younger sons born on moonless Wednesdays, and sons born after the circumcision of their eldest brother would be killed at birth. These practices serve to limit the reproductive capacity of Rendille women and to limit the population growth of the tribe as a whole. Indeed, it is said that the practice of delaying the age of marriage was previously extended to the daughters of other age-sets, but it was relaxed when the Rendille found that, as a tribe, they faced a serious dwindling in numbers.

Evidently, one cannot have a situation in which one tribe and its economy expands indefinitely while the other remains static, and over the longer period, Samburu growth may well be largely illusory (they lost nearly all their cattle in the 1880's). Nevertheless, one has here a relationship and an ecological balance that appears to have persisted for an indefinite number of generations. The Samburu observe only two of these customs—killing first-born twins and the children of unmarried girls at birth. Otherwise they are geared to a general expansion of their population, marrying girls when they are younger and preferring large families. The average polygamy rate is 1.5 wives a Samburu elder as against 1.1 wives among the Rendille, and the Samburu have a set of customs prescribing the way in which their cattle herds should be divided between wives and between the sons of these wives. Both societies have sheep and goats in addition to their large stock, but these play essentially different roles. For the Samburu they are held as reserves for the dry season when the milk from their cattle diminishes. For the Rendille, they are cultivated by younger sons who are denied an adequate share of the family's camel herd. While it is harder to eke out a living from these small stocks, they do at least afford a measure of independence, and very occasionally it is possible to trade a flock for a camel.

Despite their political alliance, personal relations between the Rendille and Samburu tend to be distant. The Samburu see the Rendille as a dour, unpredictable people whose preference for monogamy is as incomprehensible as their language (but they admire the respect shown by their womenfolk). The Rendille see the Samburu as showing an irresponsible lack of concern for their herds, and lacking control over either womenfolk or their young men. It is a contrast between a society facing serious economic problems on the one hand, and a more carefree way of life on the other. Clearly, we have here an ethnic boundary, and now that I have outlined the two societies and some of their major social and economic differences, I would like to explore this boundary further. This entails the Ariaal Rendille, the lesser segment of the Rendille tribe who to some extent live interspersed with the most easterly Samburu, although still economically self-contained and separate.

Many members of the Ariaal are either immigrants from the Rendille proper or first and second generation descendents of such immigrants, retaining the culture and exogamous restrictions of their former Rendille clans. The typical history of such families is of impoverished younger sons who left the Rendille proper and built up camel herds of their own by breeding and trading sheep and goats.

Each Ariaal settlement is, however, affiliated to a Samburu clan and, in due course, the immigrants follow a number of Samburu age-set customs while retaining their Rendille language and camel economy. The principal link with the Samburu is through other immigrants to the Ariaal who claim descent, have cattle-owning kinsmen among the Samburu, retain their Samburu age-set practices and clan affiliations, but who have adopted the Rendille language and Rendille customs associated with the camel economy. Thus, over time, immigrant families from both economies share the same settlements and come to share similar ways of life. To the casual observer they are Rendille in the fullest sense.

The typical history of Ariaal families who claim ultimate Samburu descent is of Samburu ancestors who fortuitously gained camels in warfare and decided to turn to the camel economy while retaining rights in their cattle herds. These ancestors and their descendents have tended to be polygamists, bridging the gulf between the two tribes. In such a case, a man's first wife would be a Rendille girl living in the Ariaal settlement with his camels; and his other wives would live in a Samburu settlement in the vicinity and look after his cattle. In his Ariaal home, this man is an Ariaal, speaking Rendille and observing Ariaal Rendille customs; and in his Samburu home, when he visits it, he is a Samburu, speaking Samburu and observing Samburu customs. The distinction between the two tribes is as slender as that. It is between ways of life rather than between individual people.

His eldest son in the Ariaal settlement, following Rendille customs, inherits the bulk of his camel herd and has some cattle allotted to him from the Samburu herd. He is thus in a position to follow his father in being an Ariaal Rendille in one settlement and a Samburu in another. As a Rendille he will, in his turn, try to ensure that the camel herd is not divided between sons; and as a Samburu he will aim to increase his cattle herd and family depending on it. The younger sons in the Ariaal settlement are in a more robust position than other Rendille in that, once it is clear to them that the camel economy holds few prospects, they are in a position to transfer their entire energies to the cattle economy. At this point, in effect they are emigrating and becoming full-time Samburu.

The following genealogy is one of a number recorded in which an Ariaal lineage progressively shed those that could not be contained within the camel economy. The light shading in the diagram indicates the camel-owning Ariaal members of the lineage, and the boundary represents points at which members became Samburu.

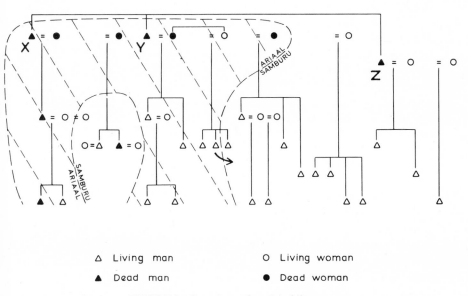

| △ | Living man | ○ | Living woman |
| ▲ | Dead man | ● | Dead woman |

FIGURE 1   *Genealogy of an Ariaal lineage*

In this lineage, X and Y were Samburu brothers who gained camels in warfare and took on camel husbandry in addition to cattle. Their younger brother Z did not capture any camels and he remained in the cattle economy. X and Y both departed from Rendille custom in trying to marry a number of wives in the camel economy. However X's second wife and Y's third wife were allotted so few camels that their sons have since migrated to the Samburu cattle economy. The youngest son of Y's second wife migrated to the cattle economy some time ago and his elder brother was expected to follow him in 1960.

The shape of this genealogy is of particular interest. Taken as a whole, it represents the Samburu ideal of growth, with 21 living adult males descended from the father of X, Y and Z. The shaded area shows altogether less growth, with only six men descended from two ancestors and the possibility of further migrations. Bearing in mind that, through the fortunes of war this was originally an exceptionally well endowed lineage, it becomes evident how, in time, the camel-owning sector becomes progressively closer to the Rendille expectation in which, relatively speaking, there is only a stunted growth. In another recorded instance, the Ariaal lineage founded by a Samburu who gained camels in warfare effectively died out as the last impoverished descendent migrated to the Samburu cattle economy.

These chequered histories of ex-Samburu Ariaal lineages substantiate the general theme of this section, but they do not account for the less fortunate Rendille with no ready *entrée* to Samburu society. Nevertheless, the cattle economy is a generally easy one where newcomers can be contained and, regardless of the linguistic and cultural barriers, considerable numbers of Rendille proper do migrate. Perhaps one-third of the Samburu claim ultimate Rendille descent, and they assume that their ancestors were squeezed out of the Rendille economy at an earlier time. It is a logical inference, for this is precisely what is happening today. With every generation there are new Rendille arrivals seeking out their close and distant agnatic kinsmen who migrated in previous generations and settled down among the Samburu.

The extensive immigration of Rendille men to the cattle economy is matched by an even more extensive marriage of Rendille girls to the Samburu, so that the Rendille are, in a sense, losing women as well. The following table shows the extent to which this is occurring. The general pattern is quite consistent with the fact that the Rendille customs of later marriage for men and monogamy create a surplus of marriageable women, while the Samburu custom of insatiable polygamy creates a shortage of marriageable women.

tribe of husband	tribe of wife			sample base
	Rendille	Samburu	other	
Rendille proper	98%	1%	1%	121 (100%)
Samburu	15%	83%	2%	149 (100%)
hypothetical distribution of random marriage	21%	79%	—	

TABLE 1   *Intermarriage between Rendille and Sanburu*

A number of points emerge from this table. In the first place, the small number of outside marriages clearly demonstrates the extent to which the Samburu and Rendille together form a relatively closed endogamous group. Secondly, each tribe, and especially the Rendille, appears at first sight to be relatively endogamous with few intermarriages. However, this is somewhat deceptive since the apparent pattern is distorted by the numerical preponderance of the Samburu. The final row of figures indicates the effects of this disparity: *if* Samburu men were to marry girls at random without regard for their tribal affiliation, then 79% of these wives would be Samburu, simply because there are so many more Samburu girls; and only 21% would be Rendille. The figures would, of course, be the same for Rendille men practicing random marriage. Seen from this point of view, the degree of endogamy of Rendille men (first row) becomes even more striking, contrasting as it does with the final row. However, the figures for Samburu marriage (second row) take on a new significance: the degree of male endogamy appears to be altogether less significant than the extent to which the Samburu men approximate to a pattern of random marriage. The implication is that the marriage market for Rendille women is almost as wide open to them as for their own Samburu women.

I will not attempt here to explain fully the economic circulation of rights over camels on the one hand, and cattle on the other, that accompanies this dual process of male migration and female marriage to the Samburu. It should be noted, however, that stockless immigrant Rendille men with kinswomen married to Samburu have a strong claim to Samburu cattle, and that this may often provide them with the nucleus of a new herd. Equally, their kinsmen still among the Rendille may welcome such marriages in the knowledge that this is increasing the Rendille stake in Samburu herds which one day they or their sons may wish to exploit.

Here then, one has a balance of interests between two very different groups of peoples with diverse languages, cultures and ecological problems. Coalescence into one undifferentiated group has never appealed to them, since the management of cattle and camels pose such different problems, and herding them together would be disadvantageous to both. Total divergence with a severing of all contact would cut across numerous ties of kinship caused by migration and intermarriage, and would in addition deprive the Rendille of their vital overflow for surplus population, and the Samburu of their reservoir for further wives. As things are, each economy retains its attractions: the abundance of milk in the camel economy offsets the rigours of herding and the problems of stunted growth for a large number of Rendille, just as the attractive possibilities of growth of cattle herds offsets the lesser yield of cattle for those who wish to migrate.

By way of conclusion, I consider the relevance of this paper for various models that have been put forward concerning the social context of scarcity and growth. In effect I would like to synthesise two basic approaches which consider the causes of growth on the one hand, and the effects of growth on the other.

With regard to the *effects* of population growth, there has been an awareness of the need for restraint that goes back at least to Malthus. Richard Wilkinson is probably the latest in a line of ecologically-oriented authors who have tended to assume that the most primitive societies live in an idyllic state by restricting their population to a size well within their available resources. Progress, he suggests, stems from population growth which leads to scarcity and need, and creates the demand to develop new technologies [14]. One point should be conceded at once: hunting and gathering societies, to which Wilkinson refers, are on the whole less concerned with growth than other more technologically advanced societies. But one can still question whether they have any more profound an insight into their ecological dilemma or the needs for population restraint than most other primitive societies or, for that matter, than the modern man in the street. If one can generalise from the Rendille example, it would be to suggest that a situation in which a society perceives the need for restraint is a rather tense one, and far from idyllic. It seems more pertinent to note that hunting and gathering societies tend to be relegated to a lower status by their more sophisticated neighbours, and their lack of ambition for growth is shared by other under-privileged groups elsewhere.

As a useful example of an approach which considers the *causes* of growth and advances the argument by one stage, one may consider a review of the problem by Mary Douglas. She focuses her attention on four societies, including the Rendille, where customary practices have restricted population growth. It is not, she suggests, purely a matter of demographic foresight that leads such groups to maintain a certain size in relation to their resources. Rather it should be seen as a process in which scarcity is socially defined and closely related to values of status and prestige: population growth would diminish the amount of prestige vested in each individual [15]. In other words, one should not look simply at available food resources, techniques and manpower, but one should focus on the social construction that is put on these. To this she adds an ominous corollary—that one would expect a population explosion at periods of rapid social change when notions of prestige and population restraint become irrelevant and are discarded.

Here, there is a shift in emphasis from biological survival to social survival, and scarce luxury goods that are biologically irrelevant acquire a new significance. However, Douglas has selected her examples carefully and one can reasonably question how widely applicable this model is. Among the Samburu, for instance, and many other African societies, the concern for growth and large families is closely associated with notions of prestige, and is sustained by the wider society. It follows that, in a situation of rapid change in which the popular notions of prestige are discarded, infertile men might be less anxious to seek out friends to impregnate their wives, and there might be less concern for the welfare of sick children. This would lead to less and not more growth. But my argument still acknowledges that considerations of prestige may well be related causally to population growth.

A striking feature of these models of social change as a result of growth (Wilkinson) and as a cause of growth (Douglas) is that they reflect arguments put forward a century earlier by Darwin. On the one hand, like Wilkinson, Darwin saw progress in terms of a response to growth, and suggested that population increase intensifies the struggle for existence, leading to the emergence of more intelligent beings and higher forms of civilisation. 'Had he (man) not been subjected during primeval times to natural selection, assuredly he would never have attained his present rank'. On the other hand, like Douglas, Darwin also related population restriction and growth to different configurations of society: civilisations on a plateau of moral excellence and foresight. tended to restrict their growth, while decadent streams increased in numbers to the point of poverty, ignorance and a more barbarous confrontation with the struggle for existence [16].

Given these two points of view relating growth to social change, what relevance do the Rendille have for either? I suggest that the most pertinent aspect lies in the position of the Ariaal, whose inception is said to have stemmed from ecological pressures of growth and the abandonment of Rendille prejudices against small stock. The enigmatic success of the Ariaal who have reversed their fortunes, even with camels in a poorer area, may be regarded as a short step in the direction of progress. This would support Wilkinson's thesis.

With regard to Douglas's concern for the causes of growth, one can cite the same example. The Rendille restricted their own potentiality for growth partly through the exclusive social value they placed on camels, restricting prestige to those who could maintain their independence without resort to other types of stock. They had a social investment in a way of life that did not exploit the environment to the full. Those who were squeezed out of the society faced a situation of crisis. They overcame this by modifying their prejudices, leading to a fuller exploitation of the environment and considerable growth, if not exactly a population explosion.

However, both approaches to the analysis envisage a single cause and a single effect; whereas the actual process—if one accepts the Ariaal oral tradition as a historical truth—would have been more complex, with a cumulative chain reaction of cause and effect that Myrdal has described as the principal of circular and cumulative causation [17]. Originally, it is said, a small group of impoverished Rendille set up on their own with only small stock; they then attracted some younger kinsmen and bred this stock in order to trade with the Somali for camels. This was successful, and more Rendille followed. This, in turn, inspired some Samburu who had gained camels in warfare to join the new sub-tribe. With each new migration, the paths between the Rendille proper, the Ariaal and the Samburu were developed, leading in time to an established network. Success bred success and led to sustained growth. It could, of course, be argued that this is essentially a mythological charter that validates the current pattern of migration between the tribes, and not an accurate reflection of historical processes. It is worth noting, therefore, that a similar process in reverse is said to have occurred within living memory: all the Samburu families of the most successful Ariaal clan (Ilturia) became cumulatively frustrated with the limitations of camel husbandry and a trickle back to the cattle economy led to a mass exodus. Failure had bred failure in an equally self-fulfilling way.

As Petersen has pointed out in discussing population migration in another context, the key to understanding such processes is not just population, but aspiration [18]. Ambitions fulfilled provide motivation for further ambition and a wider acceptance of change; this is true not only for migration, but also for local adaptation. In East Africa, this cumulative process has been well documented for the Nyakyusa (mentioned at the beginning of this chapter), whose entry into the cash economy through the introduction of new and infectious ideas of economic growth led to rapid change. The population increase during the critical period of change was relatively slight, but the escalating demand on land caused by new economic and technological possibilities created a considerable problem that was perceived as one of over-population [19]. Thus, contrary to Wilkinson's thesis, 'progress' caused population pressure and not the reverse.

In short, rather than seek the causes of population growth or the effects, one should perhaps first clarify the processes of cumulative change whereby new perceptions of opportunity, of population pressures and ecological problems become established; and one should fully recognise the social content of these. Beyond a level of basic subsistence, *need* is socially defined and demand can become insatiable.

The infectious philosophy of growth which most of us share to some extent—whether in a traditional East African context or in a national or international economy—creates scarcity and grips us in an ecological trap in which increasing population is only one important factor. Pressure on resources by the more privileged drives the less privileged into the marginal areas of existence, where their presence creates a local crisis. This may be experienced in urban areas as the swelling ranks of unemployed and undernourished; in the more affluent rural areas as an increase in the number of unwanted dependents and vagrants; and in the remoter and less fertile rural areas as an increasingly external pressure on land which reduces the freedom for mobility and hence the viability of the traditional modes of existence.

It is with this in mind, that I would suggest that the prime importance of over-population is not because it is, in itself, the most radical cause of our ecological dilemma, but because it is the most obvious index of need. As growth reaches its limits, so we are more likely to be aware of those for whom provision does not exist, and we define this as a population problem elsewhere rather than as a problem for ideological introspection.

Notes

[1]   Wilson, 1951 p. 23
[2]   Fallers, 1964
[3]   Southall, 1952; 1956
[4]   Middleton, 1960 pp. 214-5
[5]   Gulliver, 1963 pp. 10-12, 73
[6]   Gulliver, 1952 p. 5
[7]   Spencer, 1965 Ch 3
[8]   Rigby, 1969 p. 65f
[9]   Wilson, 1951, 1959 (genealogies facing p. 3 and p. 27), Chasley 1968 presents a less expansive reinterpretation of the Nykymon system.
[10] e.g. Gulliver 1955 p. 113f
[11] Beattie, 1971 p. 58
[12] Gray, 1963
[13] A fuller account of the Rendille and their relationship with the Samburu is given in Spencer 1973
[14] Wilkinson 1973. Wilkinson's notion that it is *we* who are relatively poor and trapped by ecological pressures should be viewed in the context of the current Malthusian concern for the limits of growth and the depletion of world resources. His perception of primitive societies in a Garden of Eden is perhaps a reflection of the view that *they* at least are innocent of our present dilemma.
[15] Douglas 1966
[16] Darwin 1871 p. 212-9. In relation to the rise and fall of civilisations, Darwin emphasises that progress is not an invariable rule.
[17] Myrdal 1957 ch 2. Reprinted in Dalton 1971
[18] Petersen 1958
[19] Gulliver gives a graphic description of this process in relation to the cumulative desire for more land for cash cropping (1958 p. 14) and for labour migration (1957 p. 57), and shows how in one area the society was radically transformed over a period of only one decade. The population increase in this area was only a marginal factor amounting to about one percent a year.

Bibliography

Beattie, J. (1971) *The Nyoro State*, Oxford
Charsley, S.R. (1969) *The Princes of Nyakyusa* Nairobi

Darwin, C. (1922) *The Descent of Man*, London

Douglas, M. (1966) 'Population control in primitive groups' *Brit J. Sociology*, Vol. 17, no. 3

Fallers, L.A. (1964) *The King's Men*, Oxford

Gray, R.F. (1963) *The Sonjo of Tanganyika*, Oxford

Gulliver, P.H. (1952) 'The Karamojong Cluster' *Africa*

Gulliver, P.H. (1955) *The Family Herds*, London

Gulliver, P.H. (1957) 'Nyakyusa Labour Migration', *Rhodes Livingstone Journal*

Gulliver, P.H. (1958) *Land Tenure and Social Change among the Nyakyusa*, Kampala

Gulliver, P.H. (1963) *Social Control in an African Society*, London

Middleton, J. (1960) *Lugbara Religion*, Oxford, p. 214-5

Myrdal, G. (1971) 'The principle of circular and cumulative causation', in Dalton G., *Economic Development and Social Change*, New York

Petersen, W. (1958) 'A general typology of migration', *American Sociological Review*

Rigby, P. (1969) *Cattle and Kinship among the Gogo*, Cornell

Southall, A.W. (1952) *Lineage Formation among the Two*, Oxford

Southall, A.W. (1956) *Alur Society*, Cambridge

Spencer, P. (1965) *The Samburu*, London

Spencer, P. (1973) *Nomads in Alliance*, Oxford

Wilkinson, R.G. (1973) *Poverty and Progress*, London

Wilson, M. (1951) *Good Company*, Oxford

Wilson, M. (1959) *Communal Rituals among the Nyakyusa*, Oxford

From language to culture: some problems in the systematic analysis of the ethnohistorical records of the Sierra Leone region

P. E. H. Hair

In 1964, a meeting of social scientists in the University of Khartoum persuaded me to read to them a brief paper on the pre-1700 distribution of ethnolinguistic units on the Guinea coast. The comments I received, particularly from the then Head of the Department of Anthropology, Ian Cunnison, encouraged me to pursue the research and to produce, over the next five years, a saga of some 120 pages of printed text and notes [1]. Professor Cunnison was struck by the ethnolinguistic continuity I claimed to demonstrate, which contrasted with the lack of continuity his own researches a decade earlier had shown to have been the case in parts of Central Africa. Quite justly, he also pointed to his own researches as evidence that anti-historicism on the part of anthropologists had never been general—for, in my opening remarks, I had dilated on the aversion of anthropologists to historical sources, thinking especially of the studied neglect of the rich sources on Guinea in a number of the earlier volumes of the Ethnographic Survey of Africa. Today, not only has this theoretical anti-historicism almost totally evaporated, but respect for the disciplinary procedures employed on each side is being renewed by anthropologists and historians. True, there are one or two senior anthropologists who write discursions on the past without much regard for the elementary cautions of historical inquiry: reference to sources in their original language, rather than in translation; reference to earliest statements of information, rather than to later corrupt copies; reference to manuscript originals, rather than to printed versions. But, on the other hand, a 1968 paper by Edwin Ardener on Cameroon coast ethnohistory, in the care and caution which it displayed in the analysis of multi-lingual historical sources, put to shame most of the professional African historians who had previously dabbled in 'tribal origins' [2]. A theme of this present paper is that the study of historical migrations in Africa demands sound and systematic historical inquiry. In my own ethnolinguistic papers, I have endeavoured to bring to bear on pre-colonial African history the systematic methods of procedure normal in other fields of history, and in particular the step-by-step critical examination of the full range of available written sources. I am deeply in debt to an editor who allowed me to quote at length sources in a variety of languages, producing more pages of notes than of text. The commonsense and dullish conclusions of this pedantic exercise may well turn out to be more meaningful than the thrilling speculations engendered by the sloppier methodology so prevalent in contemporary African historical research. In the end, our knowledge of Africa in the past, of migrations or of what I term 'ethnolinguistic continuity', can be no fuller or more precise than the sources permit; and it would seem that, in many instances, the sources do not allow us to make confident assertions or draw incisive conclusions.

Nevertheless, in these papers I have argued that the available written sources, and these alone, do permit us to list, with a measure of confidence, the ethnolinguistic units on the Guinea coast in the sixteenth and seventeenth centuries; and, further, to relate these individually and almost without exception, to present-day ethno-linguistic units occupying approximately the same geographical location. My argument for ethnolinguistic continuity is based essentially on the study of early vocabularies. I now have a few additions and corrections to insert in my detailed discussion, [3] but I stick to my conclusion that, *in terms of the linguistic evidence,* there is little support for the view that in the last five centuries the peoples of the Guinea coast have experienced significant migratory movements. Since publishing these conclusions regarding the Guinea coast, I have turned to another area of Africa, and have tried to perform the same exercise on the sources relating to the South-East coast. With guidance from Mr David Rycroft of S.O.A.S., I have been looking at the early vocabularies of Natal and South Mozambique, which are vocabularies of Bantu languages. Though the research is far from being finished (partly because many of the Portuguese sources lack sound editing and have to be studied *ab initio*), and despite the obvious difficulty that it is much more difficult to distinguish between two neighbouring Bantu languages than it is to distinguish between almost any two neighbouring Guinea coast languages, it begins to look as if the conclusions will be much the same. I seem to find earlier forms of the two languages spoken on that coast today, Zulu and Ronga; though the vocabularies also contain a number of Swahili terms, apparently contributed by Portuguese and Afro-Portuguese speakers who had acquired them on the Swahili coast [4]. Thus, the linguistic evidence will probably come to suggest, more or less strongly, that on this coast too there has been a major element of ethnolinguistic continuity for 400 years.

A fundamental assumption of these researches is that concentra-tion on the linguistic evidence provides a sound and rigorous first stage in the investigation of ethnohistory. It is generally accepted that language, culture, and genetic stock are, to some extent, independent variables in history. Each may vary without direct relation to another. Though I do not wish to commit myself to the view that language and culture (that is, both material culture and socio-ideological structure) are quite as separate as the contrast of the two terms in my title might imply, it is a convenient practical procedure to abstract the linguistic variable from the historical evidence, by collecting the early vocabulary and studying that first. Those who have attempted to deal with all variables at once have frequently achieved this only by skimping on the sources; and they have, as a result, produced muddy history, no part of which is firm enough to afford a sure stepping stone for further inquiry. My attempt at rigorous inquiry by concentration on the linguistic evidence immediately raises two questions. Is it genuinely rigorous? And how do we go on to study another variable, culture, attempting to be at least as rigorous?

To date, there has been a disappointing lack of critical assault on my ethnolinguistic papers. Broadly, the only comment has come in certain papers given at the 1972 Conference on Manding Studies at S.O.A.S., London—some of which unfortunately represented a reversion back to inspirational dipping in the sources. These comments were limited to one small part of my study, that relating to Sierra Leone, and principally to my handling of one historical episode, the Mane invasions. As it happens, this was the one part of my study where I relaxed my rigour and deliberately included a little speculation, announced as such; and I would not care for my methods to be judged solely on my inquiry into the earlier history of the Mende [5]. However, since this episode is perhaps the best-documented alleged migration in Guinea history, and since I have considered it as a possible exception to my conclusion regarding ethnolinguistic continuity, the matter can bear further discussion. Much of what I go on to say will be with special reference to the history of the Mane invasion(s) of Sierra Leone in the mid sixteenth century.

Lacking critical comment from others on the methodology of my study, I have prepared my own critique:-

a)   The early vocabularies which document the thirty or so Guinea coast ethnolinguistic units are in a few cases too brief to carry statistical significance.

b)   Identifications are occasionally less rigorous than they should have been.

c)   A point insufficiently stressed in the first paper was the number of 'wander-words' in the early vocabularies (compare what was stated above about Swahili terms appearing in vocabularies which purported to be of native speech in Natal and Mozam-bique). I conclude that collectors of vocabularies often operated through creole languages, or through pidgins, or through a basic Common-African vocabulary. Further, the historical extent of African bi-lingualism and multi-lingualism needs urgent study. Regular use of a second language must have led to borrowing and to shared vocabulary in earlier centuries: these certainly occurred in the Sierra Leone area, between the Mande and Mel languages. By underestimating 'wander-words' and common vocabulary, I made it seem that almost any word in an early vocabulary could be confidently assigned to one and only one language.

d)   Early vocabularies seldom give details of the geographical and social range of the language of the informant. Some of the anomalous or unidentified terms may belong to regional or caste dialects which have not yet been documented (and may even be extinct). For instance, Gail Stewart, in the course of her scholarly examination of the early texts in the Vai script [6], has pointed to anomalies which she tends to ascribe, either to errors in their transcription by non-Vai, or to historical changes in the script; but they may instead record genuine speech anomalies, possibly of an undocumented regional dialect. The early vocabularies will need to be studied again, for comparison against dialect forms, preferably in the field.

I hope that these criticisms of my method are only marginally damaging. I remain impressed by the following points:-

i)   The languages of the Guinea coasts—and, I now add, even the closely-related Bantu languages of the South-East—are discrete in vocabulary to the extent that the majority of small numbers of terms can be assigned with reasonable confidence to one language or to another. Although a language may contain dialects which vary greatly, to a point approaching non-interintelligibility; though a language may share a portion of its lexical stock with its neighbours, by recent borrowing; and though many individual speakers may be multi-lingual, yet there exist clear language boundaries, to be traced in speech and on the ground, with only very slight blurring.

ii)   While the early vocabularies provide some evidence of language change, they give more evidence of continuity. There is no reasonable doubt that the languages of the early vocabularies are close ancestral forms of the present-day languages, at least in their broad features. As regards their detail, it has to be recollected that the early vocabularies document only a small proportion of total vocabulary, and that they record almost nothing of grammar and syntax, or of tone. From the point of view of the historical linguist, changes in 'detail' may be of overwhelming interest. But from the point of view of the historian, broad continuity is more important, because it enables him to identify a human group in the past, and to direct his researchs to other possible links between the early and the later speakers of a language.

iii) The early ethnolinguistic units display geographical as well as linguistic continuity with the later units. The list of languages does not change, and individual languages continue to be spoken in approximately the same areas. This geographical continuity over a period of three, four, or five centuries has been demonstrated, with fair rigour.

But what exactly is an 'ethnolinguistic unit'? (The tiresome term was coined for practical reasons, to mollify readers and editors who quivered at the word 'tribe' but loved polysyllables; later, it found its semantic niche.) In my first paper, I defined ethnolinguistic units as 'substantial groups of people ('tribes') traditionally defined by their use of a distinct language as a mother-tongue'. The term connotes both the totality of speakers of a language and the area they occupy but, despite these concrete connotations, it is basically abstract, since it considers the human beings involved in only one aspect of their being, their speech. Hence, in my first paper I was very careful to stress that the continuity I had deduced from the linguistic evidence was an abstract ethnolinguistic continuity. 'In the particulars of name, geographical location and language, the ethno-linguistic units displayed continuity. It cannot, of course, be assumed from this that the cultural or genetic-stock content of the units displayed similar continuity.' But, history is, of course, about human beings in the round. We want to know about their cultural and genetic, as well as their linguistic, devolution. In my first paper I could offer only the following thought. ('It is schematically conceivable that our units were taken over by new human stock equipped with different ways of life during the centuries of ethnolinguistic continuity; but perhaps not very likely in practice.') In my bones I still feel that this statement points the right way, though I would accept that it may underestimate the amount of cultural and genetic drift into an area which can occur without significant ethnolinguistic change or displacement (for instance, when captive children or women, or dispersed slaves or refugees, arriving in small numbers, abandon their former habits and speech).

By demonstrating ethnolinguistic continuity, the systematic analysis of the written sources, beginning with their linguistic material, has given some understanding of the African past. Can that understanding now be broadened by an extension of the analysis to cultural material? Can we similarly investigate the extent and rate of cultural change in the given area during recent centuries? (Culture, like language, cannot remain totally unchanged over a long period, and therefore continuity means minimal change.) The records of the Mane invasions of Sierra Leone, undoubtedly the most dramatically recounted 'migration' in Guinea Coast history, should provide a test case. Large hypotheses have been constructed out of this piece of history. 'The Mane invasions constitute a typical episode in the spread of the influence of the Mande in West Africa, which is recognised as one of the most important themes in the history of West Africa.' Dr Rodney has listed the cultural changes which he believes were brought about among the Temne and Bullom of Sierra Leone by the Mane invasions [7]. I have already expressed reservations about several of these alleged changes [8], and I can substantiate some of my reservations from recent researchs in connection with the annotation of the Sierra Leone sections of the early Portuguese texts on Upper Guinea (editions of which will be appearing shortly under the general editorship of A. Teixeira da Mota). I believe that I now have under my hand virtually every scrap of written documentation on the early history of the Sierra Leone region, and I am hopeful that translations and editions will soon make all this material available to scholars. Here then is an area of African history where we can begin to look seriously into a corpus of extant written sources for evidence of cultural change. But how do we investigate cultural change, systematically and rigorously? Rodney's hasty and over-simple conclusions (though perhaps excusable in a thesis which covered an enormous field and opened up many interesting topics) show, to my mind, the dangers in any less cautionary procedure.

Let me outline a few points in relation to the Mane (i.e. Manding) conquest of the coastal peoples of Sierra Leone, especially the Temne.

a)   The sources are not in agreement over the character of the invasions. Portuguese sources stress the element of migration in the invasion, the cultural difference between the Manes and the natives, and the cultural impact of the Mane. But the Portuguese writers collected their information some considerable time after the invasions (30-60 years), they were clearly over-impressed by dramatic and horrific events, and their evidence on unrelated points shows them to have been men of limited judgement and a somewhat 'medieval' cast of mind (for instance, in their acceptance of the notion that the invaders of Sierra Leone were the same people as the contemporary invaders of Mozambique, the Congo and Ethiopia). Dutch sources, though no earlier, were more hard-headed, laying stress on the political vassalage of Sierra Leone, and implying that the conquest was only part of a traditional pattern of local political relations and military agression. The Portuguese interpretation, with its emphasis on massive cultural change, needs to be taken with a grain of salt; not least since the very earliest Portuguese sources, reporting on the Temne *before* the invasions, give a picture which, despite its limited range and precision, matches in many points the picture given by later Portuguese sources *after* the invasions and after the alleged Manding cultural impact. Rodney and some other historians have followed the Portuguese uncritically in assuming that invasions so dramatically-recounted must have brought cultural revolution, and in looking for evidence of change while overlooking more obvious evidence of continuity.

b) One unpublished Portuguese source (Álvares 1616) contains much vernacular vocabulary. From this and other sources I have collected over 100 terms, almost all of which turn out to be Temne (that is, they are identifiable in terms of modern Temne). I have long searched for a term in an early source which was unambiguously Mane/Manding, but in vain until recently—when I came upon six terms in Alvares for war-medicines which appear to be genuinely Manding (and not even Vai). This removes a doubt that I have long entertained as to whether the so-called Mane invasions in fact contained any Manding at all: I now accept that there were Manding-speakers present, as well as Vai-speakers and speakers of non-Mande languages. However this appears to be the only Mane vocabulary documented. Other vocabulary said to be Mane is actually Temne. The Portuguese sources are not very specific on the point, but their failure to state otherwise, plus the evidence of the vocabulary, suggests to me that very little Manding was being spoken in Sierra Leone, that is, in Temneland, by the 1600s, only half a century after the invasions.

c) I conclude from a general view of the sources, and from the linguistic evidence, that there must be a measure of doubt as to whether the Mane invasions were, in fact, an event of lasting significance for Sierra Leone. Had the invasions involved the migration of large populations, there would have been a high probability of massive cultural change. But the apparent failure of the Mane to maintain their language suggests that the Mane migration was one of very limited numbers [9]. (It might, however, be worth considering whether the counter-migration of peoples fleeing from the conquest was not sufficiently large to have a cultural impact on neighbouring areas.) Thus, I see the Mane invasions as being more likely to have brought about the lesser cultural changes which may or may not follow political conquest than to have brought about the massive changes which regularly accompany large-scale migration.

I have sketched two opposite views of the cultural impact of the Mane in order to show why historians of early Sierra Leone are obliged to face up to the problem of measuring cultural change, not by inference from general considerations, but by systematic study of the recorded changes in individual items of culture. I therefore come to the practical problem which inspired this paper, and also to the methodological problem which underlies the practical difficulty. The early Portuguese sources which have recently become available to me are rich in references to items of contemporary African cultures in Sierra Leone, items of both material culture and socio-ideological behaviour (e.g., nose-rings, house furnishings, judicial ordeals, circumcision rites, 'secret societies'). In the forthcoming editions, I aim to provide notes on each item, and I have followed the obvious procedure of seeking out references to these items in later writings. Thus, I am, in a sense, trying to do for cultural items what I did formerly for lexical items: I am trying to compare historical references with modern or more recent references, in order to categorize each item. I originally hoped that, by doing this, I would discover whether specific later items derived from Mane or 'native' sources, and this I naively thought would enable me to assess the cultural effect of the invasions. But this exercise with cultural items has proved to be more difficult and less conclusive than the earlier exercise with lexical items—as I should always have realised.

There are two minor difficulties. Just as there were defects in the documentation of the modern languages, many of them having no adequate dictionary, so there are defects in the documentation of the modern cultures of the Sierra Leone region (which extends from modern Sierra Leone into Liberia and Guinée). On the Bullom, there is almost nothing, while the Temne, the Vai and the Baga have received only a limited amount of modern anthropological inquiry. The second minor difficulty is that the early sources often fail to distinguish between Mane and 'native' items of culture. Some of this was due to incompetence in recording, but a more fundamental explanation may be that the two cultures were not easily distinguishable [10].

This introduces a major difficulty, which I suspect may be the basic difficulty in the analysis of cultural devolution. I have stressed above the discreteness of African languages, which makes the categorisation of early vocabularies possible, even when these are brief and scrappy. But the culture of a society is less discrete than its language. Culture is more diffuse than language. A cultural item will often be shared by speakers of many languages; a series of cultural items may be unique to a single group yet the items in the series may be found, singly or in combinations covering less than the whole series, in many neighbouring groups. Hence, cultures shade into each other in a way which languages do not—indeed, to an extent which makes it impossible to map them as languages are mapped. Each cultural item may have its own geographical range. Unfortunately, in most cases the exact range of a cultural item in modern Africa is only partially known; and the range of the same or corresponding item four or five centuries ago is, of course, not known at all. Even when the modern range is known, it cannot be assumed that this is any close guide to the range in earlier centuries, since this would be to beg the very question we set out to investigate, the possibility of cultural shifts and cultural migration. This lack of knowledge about the diachronic ranges of cultural items is part of the essential obscurity of the African past, and those who fail to recognise the difficulty cannot expect their shortcutting arguments about cultural history to have logical and scientific validity.

It is extremely dangerous to draw conclusions regarding cultural similarities from casual and virtually random documentation of items—and even the corpus of sources on early Sierra Leone is no better than this. Rodney argues that the Mane must have been Mandingo, because Portuguese sources record that the Mane in Sierra Leone and the Mandingo on the Gambia each used the same weapon, a short bow [11]. The argument is a weak one, unless it can be shown that other implicated parties (Temne, Vai, Susu, Kru, etc.) did not use the weapon, or better still, that throughout West Africa only the Mandingo used it. But it is even more dangerous to draw historical conclusions from random diachronic documentation of cultural items. Rodney argues that the war-fence was a Mane innovation in Sierra Leone because it was mentioned in connection with the invaders, and was not mentioned in pre-invasion accounts [12]. This argument would begin to carry conviction only if it could be shown that the war-fence in Guinea has never been documented except among the Manding and among peoples with whom they have been in contact. It is, of course, much more likely that the war-fence existed in Sierra Leone before the invasions, but escaped documentation in the thin Portuguese sources of that period.

Since our knowledge of the range of cultural items, not only in the past but even today, is very limited, it seems to me that we cannot proceed in the same brisk way as I did with lexical items. Unlike words, cultural items cannot be assigned to one and only one unit in time and space. Instead, we must be content to proceed more soberly, collecting and listing, but eschewing generalisations and far-flung historical conclusions. The first step is to assemble all references in historical sources to specific cultural items. Before I attempt any conclusions about the cultural history of Sierra Leone, I would like to consult a corpus of cultural information on other parts of Guinea. For the purposes of my annotation, I may have to be content with listing all sources referring to the cultural item in question over a wide geographical range, without drawing conclusions about identity or continuity. Before I can comment intelligently on the derivation of Temne cultural items, I will need to know a great deal about neighbouring and possibly related cultures: those, for instance, of the Baga (Guinée), Manding (Guinée and Mali), Susu (Guinée), Vai and Kru (Liberia), to go no further afield. Since I have grave doubts whether the historical documentation on these other peoples can match that on the Temne, I suspect that we shall never be able to see the Temne of earlier centuries within their precise cultural context, and we shall therefore never be certain about their 'cultural origins'.

Yet there is one way in which we can use our historical material to proceed to some limited conclusions about cultural devolution. When presenting the argument about the war-fence mentioned above, Rodney cited the vernacular name given in Portuguese sources, *atabanca*. Though the war-fence was allegedly a Mane innovation in Sierre Leone, and though *atabanca* was alleged to be a Mane term (and it may be allowed that it might have derived from a Manding term), in fact the shape of the word suggests fairly strongly that it was a Temne term c.1600. I do not argue that this is proof that the war-fence was not a Mane innovation; I do make the more limited assertion that this indicates that, c.1600, the war-fence was an accepted part of Temne culture, since it had a Temne name. Similarly, other cultural items can be categorized in relation to their documented vernacular terminology. We have seen that very many of the cultural items cited in the Portuguese sources are given a vernacular name which turns out to be a Temne term. We can advance our study of early Temne vocabulary from linguistic analysis to semantic analysis. We can study earlier Temne culture by listing those items which appear in earlier Temne speech. While the Portuguese sources distinguish between Mane and 'native' cultural items, where the terms are all Temne, we can disregard the dubious distinction. Working from the early vocabularies in this way, we will not be drawn into the muddy discussion about origins, but will simply be studying the culture items for which, in c.1600, Temne speech needed to have terms.

With assistance from Dr A.K. Turay, I have compiled a list of early seventeenth century Temne terms relating to a fairly wide range of social life. They indicate a considerable measure of continuity in Temne life, though no precise assessment of that continuity is possible. Here are a few examples, mainly of short phrases illuminating non-material aspects of Temne culture. The words as given in the early Portuguese sources are followed by the corresponding words in modern Temne.

1)   *cru cola camu*, 'God, here is your cola, give me health, wealth, rice, let me kill animals, may nothing make me mourn' (a

prayer); *kuru, kɔla kamu* 'God, your cola' (a prayer always said before offerings).

2) *raca sonco raca,* 'money from money, property from property' (a saying); *rəka rəsɔŋ kɔ rəka,* 'something gives him something' (i.e. you never get anything for nothing).

3) *fache boga oni* (a saying about iron and its value); *ɛfat ɛboka wuni,* 'iron takes care of a man' (a popular saying).

4) *bogoto,* 'an association for farmwork'; *kəbɔthɔ,* 'mutual self-help society' (e.g. in agriculture).

5) *ramu rarongosa,* (name of a dog, meaning not supplied); *ramu rəroŋkətha* '[you know] yours to be bitter' (i.e. one only recognises one's own troubles [dogs are still commonly given a popular saying as a name].

6) *onibama offcru o summa,* (what the pagans say when a storm comes); *wuni bana ɔfi, kuru ɔsuma,* 'an important person will die, God is unhappy' (at times of flood and storm, similar remarks are still made).

7) *Benle* and *Togma* among the Temne, *Poro* among the Mane, *Cimo* among the Susu, are four secret societies whose rites are described; *rə-Gbeŋle* among the Temne, *Thoma* now only among the Bullom, *Pɔrɔ* among the Temne and Mende, *Simo* among the Susu, are the major modern societies [13].

Lest it be thought that I am claiming that it is possible to deduce from the sources a cultural continuity comparable to the ethnolinguistic continuity I have claimed to have existed, I add here one recorded cultural discontinuity. The activities of the Benle/Ragbenle society recorded by Álvares (1616) do not correspond to those of the modern society in several respects, one of them a striking respect. One function of the modern Ragbenle is to put to death chiefs who appear to be mortally ill, but, according to Álvares, in his day this service was performed on all members of the society. Presumably information about society activities was no easier to obtain in the 1600's than it is today, so Álvares may have been merely wrong. But it is possible that ritual murder was a more widespread feature of Temne culture in earlier centuries [14].

In this paper, I have raised doubts about that interpretation of the Mane invasions which presents them as a large-scale ethnic migration, producing massive cultural changes [15]. After going through all the evidence, I am primarily impressed by the lacunae and contradictions in it, and hence I am still undecided about many aspects of the episode. As I noted above, I have only recently been convinced that the invaders included Manding-speakers as well as Vai-speakers (the difference between the two languages may, admittedly, have been very small at that period). My indecision may be due to an oversceptical mind, and further mulling over the evidence may lead me to gain a clearer picture. But the fuzziness may instead be due to the thinness of the evidence, and hence to the basic problem of assessing cultural change on thin evidence which I have raised. If this is so, it may be that, not only in the case of the Mane invasions but in the case of other alleged migrations in West African history, the uncommitted and cautious historian must suspend judgement on both the nature of the event and its consequences. What I am confident about is that the comprehensive and rigorous examination of sources in a systematic way, without consideration of whether the results add up to a thesis or produce seminal conclusions, is the only sound way of proceeding in African as in other history; and that, in the case of the Mane invasions, this procedure does not produce the clear and simple picture of migration and cultural change alluded to above.

Notes

[1] 'Ethnolinguistic continuity on the Guinea coast', *Journal of African History*, 8, 1967, pp. 247-268; 'An ethnolinguistic inventory of the Upper/Lower Guinea coast before 1700', *African Language Review*, 6, 1967, pp. 32-70: 7, 1968, pp. 47-73: 8, 1969 [appeared 1971], pp. 225-256. See also 'The earliest vocabularies of Cameroons Bantu', *African Studies*, 28, 1969, pp. 49-54; 'The contribution of early linguistic material to the history of West Africa', in D. DALBY (ed.), *Language and History in Africa*, 1970, pp. 50-63.

[2] E. ARDENER, 'Documentary and linguistic evidence for the rise of the trading polities between the Rio del Rey and Cameroons 1500-1650', in I.M. LEWIS (ed.), *History and social anthropology*, 1968, pp. 81-126. This article analyses the same vocabularies of Cameroons Bantu as my own article (cited in note 1), but more fully and correctly, and it draws attention to an important point I overlooked: that some terms in Efik were included. A note by M.W.D. JEFFREYS in *African Studies*, 20, 1970, pp. 55-6, criticising my article, ignores Ardener's and exaggerates the Efik component.

[3] Especially these. The *Lebu* around Cape Verde were first noted in an unpublished Portuguese text (Dornelas 1625) under the name 'Bilebos'. The *Limba* were first noted in 1582 (E.G.R. TAYLOR, *The troublesome voyage of Captain Edward Fenton*, 1959, p. 108). Another unpublished Portuguese text (Álvares 1616) twice lists the term 'Coras' in relation to soldiers serving a section of the Mane in the inland Sierra Leone kingdom of Mitombo, and elsewhere it notes that 'after Cape Mount follow the Coras, people of the hinterland, hill-people . . . the land stretches on to Mecca': the last reference may indicate that these are the earliest references to the *Koranko* (Kora-nko). (For knowledge of these Portuguese texts I am indebted to A. Teixeira da Mota, who is editing them for publication.) The article by E. Ardener (cited in note 2) gives early *Efik/Ibibio* terms.

[4] In discussion on this paper at the conference, Dr Shula Marks suggested a more complex peopling of the coast, substantiated by wider evidence; and she instanced the role of the 'Lala' (as argued in S. MARKS and A. ATMORE, 'The problem of the Nguni: an examination of the ethnic and

linguistic situation in South Africa before the Mfecane', in DALBY, *op.cit.*, pp. 120-132). The 'Lala' hypothesis is derived from Bryant, a writer whose historicising is treated with some indulgence in the paper cited. Until the early Portuguese sources have been systematically studied and analysed, evidence of the kind brought forward by Bryant is difficult to evaluate, as the paper admits (p. 128). On the subject of early Bantu vocabularies, I should like to draw attention to the fact that the early vocabularies of Zambesia/Rhodesia are fairly substantial, and include a large number of what appear to be earlier-Shona terms. The intensive study of these vocabularies is urgently recommended to scholars expert in this field.

[5] See my 1968 paper, pp. 54-57. Useful criticism appeared in M.H. HILL, 'Speculations on linguistic and cultural history in Sierra Leone', a paper presented to the 1972 Conference of Manding Studies in London. The present paper does not discuss the theory that the Mende were in some sense the product of the Mane invasions. I can now confirm that the unpublished Portuguese texts throw almost no additional light on Mende 'origins'. They seldom mention the interior region South-West of the Sierra Leone Peninsula, and contain only a handful of casual and problematical references to the inhabitants.

[6] In a paper, 'The early Vai script as found in the Book of Ndole', presented to the Manding Conference.

[7] W. RODNEY, *A history of the Upper Guinea coast; 1545 to 1800*, 1970, pp. 58-70. I shall be criticising certain aspects of Rodney's account of the Mane invasions, but it is to be noted that it represents a marked advance on the previous account, in P. KUP, *A history of Sierra Leone 1400-1787*, 1961, chapter 4.

[8] My 1968 article, p. 60, note 7.

[9] The existence in modern Temne of borrowings from Manding cannot be assumed to be a result of the invasions. The Manding and the Temne have been in contact since, and it is possible that there were earlier contacts before, the Mane invasions. See A.K. TURAY, 'Manding and Susu words in Temne', a paper presented to the Manding Conference, and also a chapter in the author's University of London Ph.D. thesis, 1971.

[10] The early sources offer inconsistent comments on this point. Álvares, for instance, speaks of the Mane settling in Sierra Leone 'in order to maintain the existence of the group, 75 years ago, years spent in peace during which they have taken over all the customs of the natives'.

[11] RODNEY, *op.cit.*, p. 41—but five pages later, it is noted that the Susu had the same weapons as the Mane.

[12] *ibid.*, p. 61

[13] Álvares' account of the Benle pre-dates by some decades the earliest account of Sande, the female society corresponding to Poro. This raises doubts about the accepted view that similarities between Ragbenle and Poro/Sande were due to the former evolving in imitation of the latter.

[14] Rodney, who used Álvares, does not mention this feature of Benle, possibly because it would contrast with his thesis of progressive degeneration of Guinea cultures following contacts with whites and capitalism.

[15] 'A whole material culture collapsed under Mane pressure', *ibid.*, p. 64.

Demographic and
Biomedical Aspects

Introduction: Bio-social factors in African demography

W. Brass

There is an inherent danger in the use of terms like 'African Demography' which has not always been avoided in the past; an initial warning is valuable because it should serve as a note of caution throughout the succeeding comments. The danger lies in the assumption of homogeneity of population characteristics and determinants throughout the continent (even if certain exceptions are made for peoples of relatively recent immigrant stock). There are similarities among the different countries and areas, which it is convenient to stress in a broad review. But often, just as in Europe, it is the particular, specific features of a population which are of most interest and importance in a study made for a defined purpose. The naïve idea that the peoples of Africa are largely living in a primitive state of unrestrained 'natural' mortality and fertility has long disappeared from serious thinking, although it sometimes re-emerges in surprising places. In fact, it is now accepted that social factors have been an influential, perhaps even dominating, determinant of population growth and structure for thousands of years.

A discussion of African demographic characteristics can only be useful if it is constrained by a fair assessment of the extent and certainty of our knowledge. Here, two completely opposed misconceptions are only too common. At one extreme there is the belief that published statistics of population numbers, classifications by categories, growth and vital rates can be taken at their face value, that is to say, that they have the same validity as corresponding information for Europe or (say) Latin America. The other view is that the measures are all simply crude guesses and that we have only the most general impression of levels, little better in quality than those of the early explorers. The truth lies somewhere between the two positions. For some African populations the basic demographic characteristics are established with very reasonable precision; for others they are little more than informed speculations. Unfortunately, because of the indirect and sophisticated means by which the better results are achieved, a familiarity with specialized techniques is needed to arrive at a balanced judgement.

The outstanding improvement in our knowledge has come over the past fifteen years, although there was pioneering work in the ten years before that. Progress has been such that, although initially it was the most backward region in this respect, the basic demography of large parts of Africa is now established to a degree of confidence which exceeds that of many more developed areas. The advance has been mainly due to three factors.

a)   There has been an accumulation of reasonably good 'stock' or 'profile' data of the structure of populations at fixed times, by the organization of modern censuses or census-type sample enquiries. (Although the distinction between the two categories has many implications for the detailed value of the data, these are not important for the present broad purposes). By a modern census is meant one in which certain biological and socio-economic characteristics are recorded *separately* for each individual. For a limited number of countries there is now more than one such census, making it possible to study the pattern of population change.

b)   Research and experimentation in developing regions everywhere, but pre-eminently in Africa, have produced a special range of questions designed to provide, from censuses and sample surveys, measures of the outcome of past fertility and mortality (children born and died, survival of parents and of spouse etc). These can be used to overcome the universal lacunae in the registration of vital events.

c)   In step with the advances in the collection of data, stimulating these and being stimulated by them, there has been the invention of new techniques of analysis to exploit the records. In particular these have included methods for the detection and correction of the errors of omission and misstatement which are the primary problem in achieving accuracy, and for the translation of unconventional indices into the traditional measures of fertility and mortality.

Ayeni deals with several of these matters in his paper, particularly in the context of public health issues. Even since his paper was written, some useful techniques for the estimation of adult mortality by indirect means have been devised.

In his contribution to the volume, Hill reviews the knowledge that has been gained of the basic demographic measures of Africa, almost entirely from the three types of development outlined above. As he points out, we have reasonable estimates, for much of the continent, of population size, age distribution, fertility level and child mortality, although not always for current periods. The reservation is significant because of the rapid change with time in some of these quantities for many of the populations and sub-groups. Information on adult mortality is poor. Because of this, the lack in most instances of two good censuses and the intrinsic inaccuracy in the calculation of a value which is the difference between two larger quantities (births and deaths), the estimates of growth rate are, in general, crude. Projections into the future must, everywhere, be treated with great caution and be taken as illustrative, rather than plausible, forecasts of likely population sizes. It follows from these remarks that any assessment of trends must be extremely tentative and qualitative. The evidence that there have been substantial falls in childhood mortality in many areas is convincing. As Hill points out, there are some indications of increased fertility and certainly none of appreciable reductions. Growth rates are certainly increasing, but to what extent and how fast is doubtful.

Although the improvement in basic measurements, despite the reservations, has been encouraging, the present picture and the prospects of any advance in understanding of the determinants of population change are less cheering. There have been few of the more intensive studies, relating demographic measures to social and economic indicators, which are required for such an enlargement of the scope of explanation. The difficulties of defining and collecting the right data of the required accuracy are formidable. In the particular field of health, a major obstacle is the lack of information on the quantitative impact of the diseases causing death and morbidity. Until health services reach a level where few seriously ill persons remain unexamined by a doctor, the vital statistics will be inadequate for establishing disease trends. In these conditions, any cogent explanation of changes in mortality is impossible. Africa falls short of reaching the required standard of health services, and movements toward it are at a slow pace. Despite the difficulties, however, the bits and pieces of survey and qualitative evidence available must be put together to provide as well defined outlines from the mosaic as can be achieved. The contribution by Ajaegbu and Mann is an attempt to examine in this way the implications of health levels for African populations. In their study of migration, Gould and Prothero refer to the gaps in understanding of the determinants of mobility. There has been useful progress in the measurement of the migration contribution to population change, mainly through the use of census records, but not much towards the clarification of the volume and nature of the complex streams of movement, of which this is an aspect, and which they attempt to classify.

Although our knowledge of the underlying influences on population structure and change is so limited, there has been some pioneering research in Africa. In addition findings from other parts of the world make it possible, in some cases, for the scarce materials to be re-interpreted without too extreme a reliance on assumptions. It is then permissible to give a tentative outline of the bio-social features, including health and nutrition, which are, at least, intermediate factors in population dynamics. Since deductions must be made from signs rather than from a completed map, the conclusions are liable to modification. Because of brevity these remarks are made more dogmatically than they would be in a fuller exposition.

As pointed out by Hill, the average level of fertility is high. A reasonable estimate makes it about 6.5 children born per woman during the reproductive period (unmarried and sterile women are included in the averaging). Variations among communities are substantial; even if a small number of cases of very low fertility are excluded (see later), mean values are commonly found of from 5 to 8 children per woman.

The factors which push fertility upwards are the early and almost universal marriage of women, low sterility of couples and the negligible extent of deliberate, individual planning of families. The mean age of mating of women is low, not because of a very early start to marriage, but because of its almost entire concentration in the 15-19 years age group. In general, only a few percent are single beyond 20. This is possible, in a socio-economic situation where men often marry at later ages, because of polygamy. Fertility of women in polygamous marriages may be lower than for monogamous unions, but the difference, if any, is slight and is far outweighed by the increase in the mean number of children per woman which results from the earlier marriage. Typically, only some 4-5% of women fail to conceive; since part of this must be due to male infertility, complete sterility of women is extremely low. It may be noted that there is no evidence that African fecundity, that is *potential* for bearing children, is higher than among other groups, for example Europeans; in fact, a case can be made that it is lower because of poorer health. The definition of family planning has been worded carefully to cover only those cases where contraception is used with the aim of restricting family size to a particular level or postponing the next birth; Caldwell has estimated that less than 1% of Africans use modern contraceptive techniques. It does not refer to social and natural biological controls or the avoidance of particular live births for other reasons, for example by induced abortion.

The factors which tend to restrain fertility include the frequency of marriage dissolutions from mortality, particularly of older husbands in polygamous unions; in some communities there is also a high incidence of divorce. The effects are reduced, however, by the extent of remarriage. The length of the period during which the woman is exposed to the risk of child-bearing is also shortened by early sterility. Within the child-bearing age range, the major influence is the long period of breast-feeding, which causes a post-partum lowering of pregnancy rates and during which there may be social restrictions on intercourse. The proportion of pregnancies which end in a live birth is substantially reduced by foetal mortality; although there is no satisfactory measure of this for Africa, it seems a plausible inference that the health conditions favour a high loss. The influence of early sterility and long breast-feeding are particularly important. Many surveys in Africa have indicated that, even where fertility is high, the age at which married women bear their last child is, on average, considerably lower than in historical European communities and in certain North American religious groups which are opposed to contraception. The mean differential in the exposed to risk period may be as much as seven or eight years. Despite doubts about age recording, the overall weight of the evidence is heavy. Speculatively, the most likely cause of the relative reduction is poor health and nutrition. Within the child-bearing period, the average birth interval of two and a half to three years is reasonably consistent with the findings (mainly from Asia and the Pacific) that breast-feeding of eighteen months or more adds some eleven months to the expected time of the next pregnancy, assuming no contraception; the variability among women is large, however. Thus, studies by Morley and others of lactation and birth intervals have shown a substantially greater 'waiting time' with long breast-feeding. The suggested cause is prohibitions on intercourse with a nursing mother, but other factors such as health cannot be ruled out.

It is firmly established that there are population pockets of moderate to low fertility widely dispersed in tropical Africa—for example in Zaïre, the Cameroons, Uganda and Tanzania—although their effect on the overall average level of children born per woman is small. Romaniuk has made a thorough study of the Zaïre data and has shown conclusively that there is a strong association between low fertility in an area and a high incidence of gonorrhoea. Further investigations (Azefor, Rubin and others) have supported this finding in general but have shown the problems of proving that this disease is the only or primary determinant. High sterility rates and a low number of pregnancies per mother are not always associated in the same population, and it is by no means clear that the prevalence of gonorrhoea is a good predictor of fertility level in all circumstances. In the communities with much lower fertility, there are also social disruptions caused by frequent divorce and casual unions. A possible hypothesis is that sterility from the disease causes changes in partners in an attempt to achieve the desired offspring and that, in some populations, this can initiate a process of breakdown in the marital system.

Apart from the limited impact of venereal disease, the major constraints on African fertility are probably poor nutrition and long breast-feeding, with the second of these intimately linked to the first, both in its causes and effects. The strength of these restraints is being reduced, particularly in the urban and more developed areas. The movement from breast-feeding to artificial foods has been documented by nutritionists who are worried about the dangers to child health. There are thus pressures towards higher fertility and, as Hill points out, the observations support the view that the trend is in this direction. Unless offset by a faster spread of family planning, birth rates will rise above the present high level.

Information on the death rates in African populations is scantier and less reliable than that on birth rates. It rarely averages less than 20 per thousand and may be greater than 40 in groups of substantial size. A recently developed estimation technique has given higher values than were previously arrived at. Not only are variations from area to area large, but also from year to year in the same population. A number of surveys which have been carried out immediately following epidemic periods, for example in communities of Mali and Kenya, have given retrospective estimates of child mortality beyond anything that could be undergone regularly without the disappearance of the population.

One of the most striking features of African mortality is the heavy incidence of deaths in the second and third years of life relative to the normally high rates in the first. Claims have even been made for a higher loss in the second than in the first year. It seems likely that these instances were aberrant, but it is common for fewer children to die under one than between the first and the fifth birthdays, in striking contrast to the pattern in developed countries. The same feature appears in high mortality populations in other parts of the world, but Africa is the most extreme. Recent research has strongly suggested that the explanatory cause of death is gastro-enteritis, a non-specific outcome of poor nutrition, combined with infectious and parasitic diseases such as measles and malaria. There are data which indicate that the excess mortality in the second and third year is less in East than West Africa, and this may be an important element in the higher child loss in the West which Hill mentions. Ultimately the variations probably come from environmental differences. The critical period in the appearance of the deviant mortality characteristics is near weaning, although the widely held view that it comes because the child is switched from the breast to less nourishing and hygienic solid foods has been challenged by Cantrelle. His careful studies in Senegal support the thesis that an equally important factor is the quantitative inadequacy of the mother's milk for the growing child towards the end of the long lactation. Surveys have also shown a sharp retardation of physical growth rates (heights and weights) around this time, after a satisfactory development from birth, and it is claimed that this may be the genesis of the weight-height deficiencies at later ages referred to by Ajaegbu and Mann.

The biggest gap in knowledge is of adult mortality; retrospective reports of deaths in a preceeding period have sometimes given impossible results and are always highly suspect. Even here, however, careful, intensive field work, usually with repeated surveys of the same households, and new techniques of estimation from indirect measures are beginning to increase the range of acceptable statistics. Nevertheless these are still for spots rather than wide areas. Most of the adult mortality indices are still obtained by extrapolation from the better established child death rates. This can be misleading since there are a number of high mortality countries in other parts of the world where the relationship between child and adult death incidences deviates greatly from the average. The fact that in Africa the relation has been close to average in nearly all the examples where more reliable estimates can be made encourages the belief that the broad picture of mortality is correct, although there may be considerable errors for some individual populations. Despite the necessary reservations, there are strong indications from various measures that the mortality differences between males and females do not have the same pattern as in developed countries. In general the sex differences in death rates in childhood appear to be small with only a slight male excess. In conjunction with the low sex ratio at birth (about 103 males per 100 females) this prompts interesting speculations about the extent to which the biological inferiority of the young male is displayed in foetal rather than infant deaths. The striking discrepancy, however, is in the pointers to the higher mortality of adult females compared to males. This is not confined to the reproductive period but extends into old age. The excess female mortality during the most fertile ages in Asian countries such as India has usually been attributed to the direct and indirect effects of frequent maternities, but it is not so obvious that their influence would continue well beyond this period. It is difficult not to associate the higher death rates of the older females with the studies which have shown substantial falls in mean weights of women aged over 40 years compared with the modest decreases for men. Again nutrition may be a primary determinant, with the woman past the reproductive period taking a place at the end of the queue in conditions of food shortage.

Population growth rates in Africa are high; an overall increase of about 2½% per year is a reasonable estimate. But there are enormous variations by country and community from around zero to perhaps 3½%. The interesting questions concern the nature of the variability and the potential for the future. Since deliberate family planning is so rare, a positive association between population growth and economic development would be expected. This obvious generalization seems to be broadly correct. The higher birth rates and lower death rates tend to occur in the more prosperous populations. Improved health, perhaps mainly due to better nutrition, increases fertility by reducing widowhood and foetal mortality as well as, possibly, in less obvious ways such as raising the age at menopause. The lessening of the practice of long breast-feeding is also a factor, although as yet it is unlikely to have had much effect except in larger towns. Better nutrition may also be the major contribution to the falling mortality, although education in health and hygiene, and particularly in child care, is of great weight. Natural growth is very high in the larger towns because fertility is at least as great as in the villages and mortality is lower. The youthful age distribution also favours higher birth rates and lower death rates than would occur with a more stable age composition. It is worth noting, therefore, that, although in-migration to towns is large, the component of internal growth is comparable in size. Thus the social and health problems of urban migrants discussed by Gould and Prothero must be seen in relation to the rapid expansion in the number of town dwellers born to the environment. This is likely to be a factor which contributes to the effects of social division and the pace of change, increasing the stresses on the migrant.

If economic standards continue to rise, there will be strong pressures towards higher growth rates from increased fertility and lower mortality, for the reasons indicated in the discussion of variability among areas. The offsetting influences of later marriage and family limitation have, as yet, had little impact, and cannot be expected to do so for some time to come. The potential for future population growth in Africa is greater than in any other major region of the world. The United Nations' forecasts and the systematic projections by Frejka, which explore the outcomes of a wide range of possible assumptions, agree on the inevitability, short of catastrophe, of massive population increases over the next half-century. Even falls in fertility far faster than at present seem possible would not alter this prospect because of the momentum from the high birth rates of the past. The size of the population in Africa is expected to be at least double the present 380 million by the end of the century, and to reach 1000 million in forty to fifty years time.

Population mobility in tropical Africa

W. T. S. Gould and R. M. Prothero

Introduction

Population mobility is diverse and complex, its study relevant to the interests of all the human sciences (Kosinski and Prothero, 1974) [1]. Any one of a variety of aspects relating to how and why people move and the impact of their movements upon source and destination areas might be discussed. With the need to be selective, this paper concentrates upon the nature and variety of population mobility in tropical Africa, these being of general interest and of practical relevance.

Much of the mobility which is studied by economists, sociologists and geographers is of an aggregate nature. Data represent in composite form movements which are seemingly specific in space (from one place to another) and in time (over some given period). However it is an obvious fact, though one to which little attention is given, that the majority of actual movements which are combined in the aggregate are neither spatially or temporally so specific. Movements between one area and another over a given period of time which appear as conventional census data represent a multitude of movements which have in fact occurred. Some of these will have been movements within, and some between, census enumeration areas. There are short-distance and repeated movements which occur that are difficult, if not impossible, to measure by conventional methods of enumeration. There is the need to appreciate the complex reality of total mobility, and to understand something of the various components which contribute to 'migration', as such movements are usually called, and in terms of which they are conventionally measured.

A typology of mobility in tropical Africa.

The working typology outlined here has been formulated to facilitate the study of population mobility in a continent of rapid social and economic change, where problems of urban and rural development and interaction are of major importance. Space and time are the essential dimensions of its framework.

Space may be considered in two respects:

a)   *Distance* may be measured in linear terms, in social and economic terms or as within or between administrative units. The last of these may, for example, differentiate the distance continuum through successively larger units of interaction, from the smallest in the administrative hierarchy through to the national and international scales. Differentiation of this sort is clearly more satisfactory than measures of a distance continuum where 'short' and 'long' are relative terms which may prove impossible to apply in comparative analysis.

b)   *Direction* may be most satisfactorily considered in terms of rural/urban relationships. 'Rural' and 'urban' represent the ends of a continuum, and problems of differentiation may arise. For example, it may be difficult in practice to distinguish the extent to which a rural market is an urban place or the extent to which a large agricultural settlement is rural. However, in most instances it is possible to make an acceptable differentiation.

Direction rather than distance has been used in the typology here. Physical distance is difficult to measure and, in Africa, data for administrative units, particularly small ones, are for the most part limited in amount. There is the further problem of how migrants perceive distance and this is generally unknown.

Time may also be considered in two respects.

a)   In *historical* terms [Prothero 1968]:
    i)   movements that took place formerly but which have now ceased;
    ii)   movements that have been continued from the past to the present day;
    iii)   movements that have developed in recent times, i.e. within the present century.

b)   In *contemporary* terms as measured by the periodicity of the movements which may involve a continuum from repeated movements of a few minutes duration within a limited area to a permanent move from one place to another over some distance.

The concern here is with contemporary mobility, though it is important to recognise that, even at the present time, the relative importance of various types of mobility is changing over quite short periods.

The basic framework for the typology considers space in four categories of rural/urban relationships, and time in terms of the span of each movement, generally but not invariably increasing from left to right (Table 1).

Population mobility in Africa

SPACE	TIME					
	Circulation				*Migration*	
	Daily	Periodic	Seasonal	Long term	Irregular	Permanent
Rural-rural						
Rural-urban						
Urban-rural						
Urban-urban						

TABLE 1   *Typology of population mobility: schema*

Fundamental to the dimension of time are distinctions made between *mobility, migration* and *circulation. Mobility* is a sufficiently broad concept to be applicable to all population movements, from the one extreme of those which are repeated daily, to the other of a definitive, inter-continental movement over several thousand miles. Migration is sometimes used to include all types of movement [Jackson 1969], but should be recognised to be more limited in scope, and to exclude specifically such movements as those of seasonal workers, tourists, etc [Lee 1966].

Migration may be defined in a strictly operational sense as movements revealed in official statistics—as in the official definition used by the United Nations. This definition has no rigorous conceptual basis, but rather is one of convenience. However, the use of more theoretically-based definitions may be limited in practice as a consequence of the need to depend upon official statistics. Most definitions of migration include reference to permanent change of residence, movements which are not of this nature being of a rhythmic or oscillatory nature. Movements where there is no permanent change can be most suitably designated by the term *circulation* to include 'a great variety of movements, usually short-term, repetitive or cyclical in character, but all having in common the lack of any declared intention of a permanent or long-standing change of residence' [Zelinsky 1971, p. 266].

The principal difference between migration and circulation lies in the permanence of the former and the non-permanence of the latter; but 'permanent' has been, and may be, defined in different ways, so that the distinction may be blurred (e.g. 'the period of time implied by the term *permanent* cannot be generalised in all instances of migration, but has to be considered individually in each specific case' [Mangalam 1968, p. 8].). Hence the United Nations' definition of migration as those movements lasting more than one year has been generally ignored in practice in African studies involving field investigation and data collection, but has been followed by statisticians and formal demographers using official census data. Other discussions of permanence have considered the mover's economic and social commitments to his destination compared with those to his home area (e.g. Van Velsen 1963).

If there is an intention on the part of the individual or group of individuals who are moving to return to their place of origin, and if, before leaving in the first place, this is clear, then the movement may be considered as circulation rather than migration. However, where movers know only the timing or the direction of future movements, or neither of these, their movements may be considered as migration. This distinction between circulation and migration is not directly related to the duration of each movement, for some circulatory movements may last longer than migratory ones, but to the possible long-term changes in the distribution of population that result from movement. In circulation changes in the distribution of population in the long-term are small, whereas in migration changes in the long-term are large.

CIRCULATION

Circulatory movements have been divided according to the length of their cycle into four main groups.

Daily circulation includes the great variety of intra-rural and intra-urban movements that are sufficiently commonplace to require no detailed description. Daily intra-urban movements have become an increasingly important component of African mobility in recent years, being associated with the rapid growth of towns and the development of various forms of transport.

Periodic circulation may involve absence from home for periods ranging from one night (e.g. to visit a relative or a market) to one year, though it is more usual for periodic circulation to involve absences of shorter duration than seasonal circulation.

Seasonal circulation is a particular type of periodic movement, the period being defined by marked seasonality in the physical/economic environment. Seasonal circulation does not include local movements with a high seasonal incidence, (e.g. movements of farmers to market their produce), but movements which involve individuals or groups being absent from their permanent homes during particular seasons of the year. Movements of this nature are particularly important in West Africa.

Long-term circulation involves absence from home for longer than one year. It includes important groups of wage labourers and traders who, despite long absences, maintain close socio-economic links with their home areas with the objective of eventually returning to them. Such movements occur throughout tropical Africa, but are particularly characteristic of east and central Africa.

MIGRATION

The presence or absence of intended permanent elements in movement is the basis for distinguishing between migration and circulation. However, different interpretations of permanency give rise to two types of migration.

Permanent migration, in the conventional use of the term (i.e. definitive movements with no propensity to return to the home area), is relatively uncommon in tropical Africa, though less so now than was the case in the past. Movements which fall into this sub-category are, for example, 'downhill movements' in parts of West Africa and elsewhere [Gleave 1966], movements to new settlement schemes [Chambers 1969], residential changes within cities [Roussel *et al* 1968; Knoop 1971; Brand 1972].

Irregular migration is not wholly permanent in that further movement is likely in the future but neither the term nor direction of such movements are known. This sub-category includes the movements of nomads and the movements of refugees displaced by political events or natural disasters such as floods or drought.

All population movements in tropical Africa may be accommodated in one of the six major time categories outlined and, within the framework of the typology, each of these has a spatial dimension.

Application of the typology

Applying the spatial-temporal dimensions outlined, movements may be assigned within the typology as illustrated in Table 2 and as elaborated in the following examples. The latter are differentiated on a broad two-fold basis between movements, the motivation for which is primarily either economic or non-economic.

MOBILITY ASSOCIATED WITH CULTIVATION

Cultivators move daily from their permanent settlements to their fields, and then return (*daily circulation*) [Ojo 1970, 1973]; or, if fields are at some distance, they may move away to them and occupy temporary dwellings for a few days or for even longer during periods of maximum agricultural activity (*periodic circulation*) [Grossman 1972; Hunter 1967]; or, movements may take place to specialised areas for cultivation (e.g. by irrigation) during a particular period of

	Circulation				Migration	
	Daily	*Periodic*	*Seasonal*	*Long-term*	*Irregular*	*Permanent*
Rural-rural	Cultivators Hunters Traders (rural markets)	Cultivators Hunters	Pastoralists Labourers Cultivators	Labourers	Pastoralists Gatherers Shifting cultivators Refugees	Spontaneous colonizers Sponsored settlers
Rural-urban	Commuters Cultivators to market	Pilgrims Labourers	Labourers	Labourers	Refugees Drought victims	Labourers
Urban-rural	Cultivators	Traders	Labourers Cultivators	Traders	Labourers Refugees	Retirement
Urban-urban	Intra-urban commuters	Pilgrims Traders	Traders	Traders Civil servants	Refugees (elite groups)	Residential change

TABLE 2   *Typology of population mobility: African examples*

the year (*seasonal circulation*) [Prothero 1957; Udo 1964]. Shifting cultivators who move their settlements with the lands which they cultivate are involved in *irregular migration* [Allan 1965; de Schlippe 1956]; and people who settle in previously empty or newly acquired land are involved in *permanent migration* [Chambers 1969]. In addition to these rural/rural movements, seasonal cultivation may involve urban/rural movements, as among the Yoruba in Western Nigeria [Mabogunje 1962; Oluwasanmi 1967].

MOBILITY ASSOCIATED WITH PASTORALISM [Dyson-Hudson 1972; Johnson 1969]

Various types of movements by pastoralists illustrate clearly the distinction between *circulation* and *migration*. Where nomads move according to the day-to-day availability of pasture for their animals and where they do not know precisely when and where their next move will be, this constitutes *irregular migration* ('grande nomadisme'). This is in contrast to the seasonal movement of pastoralists, whose daily rhythm is similar to that of nomads but whose movements overall have a regular and discernible pattern in space and time—those who live in areas where the availability of resources at different seasons is, in general, known [Stenning 1957]. These movements are therefore relatively predictable, and will include an annual return to a home in which some of the group may remain throughout the year, and which is in a definite area even if not in a permanent settlement. Such movements are *seasonal circulation* since they involve no permanent change of residence. Transhumant pastoralists moving between different altitudinal zones fall within this category [Gulliver 1969].

MOBILITY ASSOCIATED WITH FISHING [Bradley 1968; de Surgy 1965; Hill 1970; Rouch 1950]

Sea, river or lake fishing involve fishermen in *daily circulation*, with these activities occasionally extending over several days (*periodic circulation*). There is also *seasonal circulation* related to changes in water level of rivers and lakes. A more specialised example of *seasonal circulation* associated with fishing involves agriculturalists who fish in the dry season, when the scope for cultivation is limited and when fish may supplement the farmer's diet and supply an additional source of income.

MOBILITY ASSOCIATED WITH LABOURERS

The largest mobile group, other than of people involved in daily movements, is made up of those who move from their home areas for economic gain, either in paid employment or to work on their own account. Movement of wage labour from home areas to employment centres is commonly referred to as 'labour migration', though

Mitchell [1969] suggests that it would be better described as 'labour circulation' in the Rhodesian case with which he was concerned. Certainly a large component of labour movement in Africa and in other parts of the developing world involves the individual returning to his home area sooner or later, and often several times in his employment career. The majority of these labourers are involved in *long-term circulation*. They move either as individuals or, increasingly as a more stabilised work force evolves, with their families. Usually a labourer functions as part of a larger group with a relatively permanent and identifiable ethnic, social and economic structure in the work area [Cohen 1969]. Though individuals in the group may change, it tends to remain identifiable; while some members return home others arrive and, as times goes on, individuals, like the group, become more permanent as their average length of stay at work increases. These individuals may retain a place in the social structure of their home communities, but the long-term effect of their absences may result in a decline in the economic life of the home communities.

In direct contrast to such long-term circulation, the *seasonal circulation* of wage labourers, which is common within and from the savannah lands of West Africa, has no such detrimental long-term effects [Goddard *et al* 1971; Prothero 1957; Rouch 1957]. Workers leave their home areas after the harvest and move to dry season work areas; they then return home for the onset of the next wet season to resume their activities as farmers. In this way they not only retain their place in the social structure of their home areas, as is also the case in long-term circulation, but they maintain their function in the economic structure of these areas.

Most of these labour movements are spontaneous in character, in contrast to the time-specific contract labour system which operates within the Republic of South Africa [WNLA 1959; Wilson 1973].

Seasonal circulation and long-term circulation of labourers include both rural/rural and rural/urban movements. Rural/rural movements are clearly of greater significance in seasonal circulation than they are in long-term circulation, the former taking advantage of demands for agricultural labour in work areas at times of the year when there are few or no agricultural opportunities in home areas (Barbour 1965). Seasonal circulation of labourers also occurs to mines and towns in West Africa [Peil 1972].

Less widespread labour mobility may be identified in the seasonal movements of urban workers to rural employment at peak harvest periods, as in the movements of West Africans living in towns in Sudan to areas of cotton cultivation [Davies 1964]. This sort of movement may not be seasonal, however, and may involve a permanent change of residence. Rural/urban migrants may become disillusioned with urban life and move from the towns to rural areas other than their places of origin. Other urban/rural mobility includes the compulsory expulsion of urban unemployed back to home areas, compulsory or semi-compulsory movements to official settlement schemes, and the retirement of urban workers back to rural areas from which they came and with which they may have retained some contact, though tenuous, throughout their lives in town.

MOBILITY ASSOCIATED WITH TRADE [Bohannan and Dalton 1964].

Trading is primarily a function of central places. In the case of rural markets, where traders operate over relatively short distances, their movements are generally within the category of *daily circulation* or *periodic circulation* [Hodder 1961; Jackson 1973]. Urban trading takes on different forms in different parts of tropical Africa, and even within the same area different types of movements may be part of the overall pattern of trading. Some longer distance trading movements are circulation, traders operating from a permanent base and plying their trade over various spans of distance and time, on a periodic or seasonal basis [Cohen 1966]. Others establish a permanent base away from their home areas, though they retain kinship and other links with their home areas and return to them for retirement [Mabogunje 1972].

MOBILITY ASSOCIATED WITH PILGRIMS

The traditional movement of pilgrims over long distances in tropical Africa is mainly of Muslims from West Africa via Chad and Sudan to Saudi Arabia, but there are also numerous examples of more localised pilgrim mobility. Both such movements are circulation, though the time span may extend over the many years which some pilgrims take to work their way to Mecca and back again [Birks 1974]. The season of pilgrimage is fixed in the Islamic calendar but, as this is lunar-based, it varies with the seasons in West Africa. Modern transportation, by lorry and more especially by air, means that the *haj* may be completed within a much more limited time, and so these movements are becoming increasingly *periodic circulation* rather than *long-term circulation* as was the case in the past.

MOBILITY ASSOCIATED WITH REFUGEES [Gould 1974]

Movements of refugees, an element in population mobility in tropical Africa that has become more important recently, is migration rather than circulation, but migration which may or may not be permanent. Petersen [1958] distinguishes between refugees (permanent settlers) and émigrés (those who wish to return to their native land), but such a distinction is difficult to apply in practice. Refugees may therefore be placed in the category of *irregular migration*, since the pattern of their movements in the future is unknown.

Conclusion

This working typology has been devised primarily to facilitate more broadly-based research on population mobility in tropical Africa, and in particular to provide a framework for systematising existing knowledge. Spatial and temporal dimensions have been emphasised for these have tended to be neglected, much greater attention having been given to socio-economic factors in the causes and implications of mobility. Rural/urban movements, while of major importance in the processes of modernization, have tended to be emphasised at the expense of movements within rural areas, where the majority of population is located and will remain for the foreseeable future. Movements within rural areas require more attention with respect to the promotion of economic development and the provision of social amenities, particularly as resources are scarce. Economically motivated movements remain important, but mobility associated primarily with non-economic factors has proved to be of increasing political importance in contemporary Africa. Spatial and temporal dimensions should be integrated with the socio-economic and political aspects of mobility.

Note

The authors are involved in the African Mobility Project, Department of Geography, University of Liverpool, financed by the Social Science Research Council. A version of this paper with different emphases is to be published in Kosinski and Prothero [1974].

References

Allan, W. (1965) *The African husbandman*, Oliver and Boyd.
Barbour, K.M. (1965) Rural-rural migration in Africa, *Cahiers de l'institut de Science Economique Appliquée*, 5 (9), pp. 47-68.
Birks, J.S. (1974) Overland pilgrimage from West Africa, *in* Kosinski and Prothero.
Bohannan, P. and Dalton, G. (eds.) (1962) *Markets in Africa*, Northwestern U.P.
Bradley, D.J. (1968) The epidemiology of fishermen as migrants, *East African Medical Journal*, 45 (5), pp. 254-62.
Brand, R.R. (1972) The spatial organization of residential areas in Accra, Ghana, with particular reference to aspects of modernization, *Economic Geography*, 48 (2), pp. 284-98.
Chambers, R. (1969) *Settlement schemes in tropical Africa*, Routledge and Kegan Paul.
Cohen, A. (1966) Politics of the kola trade, *Africa*, 36 (1), pp. 18-36

Cohen, A. (1969) *Custom and politics in urban Africa: A study of Hausa migrants in Yoruba towns*, Routledge and Kegan Paul.

de Schlippe, P. (1956) *Shifting cultivation in Africa: the Zande system of agriculture*, Routledge and Kegan Paul.

de Surgy, A. (1965) *Les pêcheurs de Cote d'Ivoire*, C.N.R.S. (Paris).

Dyson-Hudson, N. (1972) The study of nomads, *Jnl. of Asian and African Studies*, 7 (1-2), pp. 2-29.

Davies, H.R.J. (1964) The West African in the economic geography of the Sudan, *Geography*, 49, pp. 222-35.

Gleave, M.B. (1966) Hill settlements and their abandonment in tropical Africa, *Transactions of the Institute of British Geographers*, 40, pp. 39-49.

Goddard, A.D., Fine, J.C. and Norman, D.W. (1971) *A socio-economic study of three villages in the Sokoto close-settled zone. Land and people.* Ahmadu Bello University, Institute for Agricultural Research, Samaru Miscellaneous Paper, 33.

Gould, W.T.S. (1974) Refugees in Tropical Africa, *International Migration Review* (Special issue on International Migrations in Africa).

Gould, W.T.S. and Prothero, R.M. (1974) Space and time in African population mobility, *in* Kosinski and Prothero.

Grossman, D. (1972) The roots and practice of migratory tenant farming: the case of Nikeland in Eastern Nigeria. *Journal of the Developing Areas*, 6 (2), pp. 163-84.

Gulliver, P.H. (1969) Nomadism among the pastoral Turkana of Kenya: its natural and social environment, *in* Rigby, P. (ed.), *Society and Social change in Eastern Africa*, Nkanga Editions (Kampala), pp. 30-41.

Hill, P. (1970) Ewe Seine fishermen, *in* Hill, P., *Studies in rural capitalism*, C.U.P., pp. 30-52.

Hodder, B.W. (1961) Rural periodic day markets in part of Yorubaland, *Transactions of the Institute of British Geographers*, 29, pp. 149-59.

Hunter, J.M. (1967) The social roots of dispersed settlement in Northern Ghana, *Annals of the Association of American Geographers*, 57 (2), pp. 338-49.

Jackson, J.A. (ed.) (1969) *Migration*, C.U.P.

Jackson, R. (1973) Economic rationality amongst African rural market traders, *Geografiska Annaler*, 54B (2), pp. 85-94.

Johnson, D.L. (1969) *The nature of nomadism: a comparative study of pastoral migrations in south-western Asia and Northern Africa*, University of Chicago, Department of Geography, Research Paper no. 118.

Knoop, H. (1971) The sex ratio of an African squatter settlement: an exercise in hypothesis building, *African Urban Notes*, 6, pp. 19-23.

Kosinski, L.A. and Prothero, R.M. (eds.) (1974) *People on the move*, Methuen.

Lee, E.S. (1966) A theory of migration, *Demography*, 3, pp. 47-57.

Mabogunje, A.L. (1962) *Yoruba towns*, Ibadan U.P.

Mabogunje, A.L. (1972) *Regional mobility and resource development in West Africa*, McGill/Queens U.P. (Toronto).

Mangalam, J.J. (1968) *Human migration*, University of Kentucky Press (Lexington).

Mitchell, J.C. (1969) Structural plurality, urbanization and labour circulation in Southern Rhodesia, *in* Jackson, pp. 156-80.

Ojo, G.J.A. (1970) Some observations on journey to agricultural work in Yorubaland, south-western Nigeria, *Economic Geography*, 46, pp. 459-71.

Ojo, G.J.A. (1973) Journey to agricultural work in Yorubaland, *Annals of the Association of American Geographers*, 63 (1), pp. 85-96.

Oluwasanmi, H.A. (1967) The agricultural environment, *in* Lloyd, P.C., Mabogunje, A.L., and Awe, B. (eds.) *The City of Ibadan*, C.U.P. pp. 37-33.

Peil, M. (1972) *The Ghanaian factory worker: industrial man in Africa*, C.U.P., African Studies Series, no. 5.

Petersen, W. (1968) Migration: Social aspects, *International Encyclopedia of Social Sciences*, 10, pp. 286-300.

Prothero, R.M. (1957) Migratory labour from north-western Nigeria, *Africa*, 27, pp. 251-66.

Prothero, R.M. (1968) Migration in tropical Africa, *in* Caldwell, J.C., and Okonjo, *The population of tropical Africa*, Longmans, pp. 250-62.

Rouch, J. (1950) Les Sorkawa, pêcheurs itinerants du moyen Niger, *Africa*, 20 (1), pp. 5-25.

Rouch, J. (1957) Migrations au Ghana, *Journal de la Société des Africanistes*, 24, pp. 33-196.

Roussel, L., Turlot, F., and Vaurs, R. (1968) La mobilité de la population urbaine en Afrique Noire: deux essays de mesure, Abidjan et Yaoundé, *Population*, 23 (3), pp. 333-52.

Stenning, D.J. (1957) Transhumance, migratory drift, migration: patterns of pastoral Fulani nomadism, *Journal of the Royal Anthropological Institute*, 87, pp. 57-73.

Udo, R.K. (1967) The migrant farmer of Eastern Nigeria, *Africa*, 34 (4), pp. 326-39.

Van Velsen, J. (1963) Some methodological problems of the study of labour migration, in *Urbanization in Africa*, University of Edinburgh, Centre of African Studies, pp. 34-42.

Wilson, F. (1973) *Labour in the South African gold mines, 1911-1969*, C.U.P.

Witwatersrand Native Labour Association, (1959). Organization of migrant labour in the South African mining industry, *Bulletin of the Inter-African Labour Institute*, 6 (3), pp. 41-48.

Zelinsky, W. (1971) The hypothesis of the mobility transition, *Geographical Review*, 61 (2), 219-49.

Population trends in Africa

K. H. Hill

Introduction

Information on populations in Africa has been collected by three main types of enquiry, these being administrative censuses based on tax registers, proper counts of the population, and small, carefully designed sample surveys. The most frequent sources of population data in tropical Africa are combinations of two of these methods. In English-speaking Africa, the population census has been combined with a built-in sample survey, the census to give an accurate population total, the sample survey to make possible the collection of more detailed information about the population at a reasonable cost. In French-speaking Africa, the sample survey has been combined with the administrative census, the surveys being small and often extremely detailed, and making possible more accurate estimates of total population than are normally available from tax registers. Information on population in Africa is still seriously deficient however. A few countries, the largest of them being Ethiopia, have never conducted a national census or sample survey, and thus have no reliable information about their populations at a national level at all; several other countries have failed to conduct enquiries at regular intervals (for instance no census has been conducted in the Sudan since 1956) and thus have no up to date population data; yet other countries, particularly those still under white minority regimes, are using out-dated and inaccurate techniques for enumerating their African populations. Nor is the conducting of a census just a question of holding an enquiry; even using carefully designed questionnaires and adequate supervision, the data collected will still show inaccuracies. Although it is possible to give a total number of persons with reasonable accuracy, any questions requiring a knowledge of age, dates, or numbers will result in errors because of the inability of a respondent in a non-numerate society to answer correctly. There are thus two fundamental problems facing the population analyst in Africa; the lack of data of any sort for large areas of the continent, and the errors inherent in the data which is available.

There has recently been a great upsurge in interest in population throughout the world, and this has resulted in a substantial improvement in the state of knowledge of Africa's population. For one thing, considerable sums of money have become available from external sources for those countries which could not afford to carry out censuses or population surveys, and thus the number of complete blanks is being reduced. Secondly, increasingly sophisticated methods of analysing inaccurate and incomplete data have been developed over the last decade, and these have made it possible to produce relatively reliable estimates of demographic parameters from data suffering from serious and systematic biases. The fruits of these developments are only now beginning to appear as better data for more countries. Unfortunately one result of this is that, although better figures are available for the current demographic situation, estimates made a decade ago can no longer be regarded as reliable, so that the detection of trends and changes is made very difficult.

Population growth for any area over any period will be equal to the number of births, less the number of deaths, plus the number of immigrants, minus the number of emigrants, during the period. Migration can be a very important factor for an area of a country, and exceptionally for a whole country, but it is of no importance when considering the population of the continent; the levels of fertility and mortality, on the other hand, are always important in determining growth; they will therefore be treated separately in the next two sections, and migration considered briefly in passing on to overall growth.

Fertility

The level of fertility is higher in Africa than in any other continent. The United Nations estimate for the crude birth rate, that is, births per thousand population per year, for Africa for the period 1965 to 1970, was 46; this compares with crude birth rates of 38 for Asia, the next highest after Africa, and 18 for Europe. The birth rate seems to be high throughout the continent; the five regions identified by the United Nations all have crude birth rates of over 40, varying from 41 for Southern Africa to 49 for Western Africa [U.N.O., 1970]. These figures are, of course, based on seriously deficient data, and should be regarded as relative indications of fertility levels only.

The apparent homogeneity of fertility levels in Africa is somewhat misleading. Estimates of the crude birth rate and total fertility rate (the mean number of children born to a woman passing through the reproductive period) have been made for many African countries, and often for separate areas within the countries, and these estimates show a degree of variation in the level of fertility which is remarkable. Recent reworking of data collected in the Republic of Zaïre in the late fifties has produced estimates of the crude birth rate varying from 21 births per thousand population for one area to 63 births per thousand population in another, with the total fertility rates being respectively 2.8 and 9.2 [Page & Coale, 1969]. Some of this variation may be the result of errors in the data, or sampling errors, but there is no doubt that, throughout Africa, there exist pockets of low fertility and high fertility, the reasons for which are only just beginning to be explored. It is only when aggregates of several countries are considered that the level of fertility appears to be much the same throughout the continent.

Estimates of the level of fertility of reasonable accuracy are such a recent thing in Africa that it is almost impossible to draw any firm conclusions about the trend of fertility levels. It seems unlikely, however, that overall levels of fertility have changed much during this century. In some areas, there is an increasing body of evidence to suggest that fertility has recently started to rise somewhat. The recent censuses of both Kenya and Uganda have suggested higher levels of fertility than the previous censuses; in the case of Uganda the total fertility rate is thought to have risen from 6.5 in 1959 to 7.1 in 1969, the crude birth rate rising from about 44 to 49. The explanation for this seems to be a reduction in the proportion of women who remain childless; evidence for this in Uganda, for instance, is that it is amongst women aged 25 to 29 that the lowest proportion childless occurs. Closely linked to this is the apparent increase in fertility in the low fertility pockets. Fertility might be expected to continue to rise as the differentials from one area to another are filled in and as the proportion of women childless due to medically treatable causes is reduced. There is as yet no evidence of fertility falling anywhere on the continent as the result of government policy or socio-economic pressures except in the island groups of Mauritius and the Seychelles, and perhaps also along the North African littoral. The only other clearly identified cases of falling fertility are amongst certain minority racial or social groups, the Asian population of East Africa being perhaps the most obvious example.

Mortality

Whereas the estimation of fertility in Africa is fraught with uncertainty, the estimation of the level of mortality is virtually impossible. Techniques have been developed during the last decade for estimating infant and child mortality to give plausible and consistent results [e.g. Brass, 1968]; this, in fact, goes a long way towards estimating the crude death rate (that is, deaths per thousand population per year) since in Africa deaths amongst children under five account for about half of the total deaths in any year. Little or nothing is known about the age pattern of mortality after childhood in Africa; the best that can be done is to assume a constant relationship between the levels of child and adult mortality, and to apply an age pattern of mortality similar to that recorded for other areas of the world (usually developed countries) having adequate statistics on deaths. Errors in age reporting, and the selective omission of deaths in surveys and registrations, mean that there is literally no reliable data on mortality patterns for any part of Africa against which to check the suitability of such age patterns of mortality; even the incidence of various diseases, the mortality patterns of which are known, cannot be estimated with any accuracy. The application of these age patterns of mortality to give estimates of adult mortality is thus essentially the best of a bad lot. Several systems of model life tables, as these standard patterns of mortality are called, have been developed, and the analyst has quite a wide range to choose from [Coale and Demeny 1966].

As with fertility, mortality is higher in Africa than in any other continent. The crude death rate estimated by the United Nations for the continent as a whole for the period 1965 to 1970 is 20, compared with a figure of 15 for Asia, and about 10 for America, Europe and Oceania [U.N.O., 1970]. Considerable variation in mortality levels from one region to another is suggested. Western and central Africa experience the higher mortality levels, with a crude death rate of 24, whereas northern and southern Africa experience the lower levels, with a crude death rate of 17, comparable to the higher mortality regions of Asia. The estimates are, of course, little better than informed guesses, since for large areas there is no information whatever; but there can be little doubt that the overall picture is correct.

The crude death rate is not a perfect measure of the level of mortality, since it is affected also by the age distribution of the population. The infant mortality rate (the number of deaths in the first year of life per thousand live births) and expectation of life at birth, are two widely used indices of mortality. It is in the incidence of infant mortality that African mortality is so much higher than in more developed areas of the world. The level for the continent as a whole is probably about 150, implying that 150 out of every 1,000 births will die in the first year of life. This compares with a rate for Europe of around 20. The infant mortality rate varies dramatically from one area to another; rates as high as 250 have been estimated for certain areas, for instance areas of Guinea in the mid fifties [Page, 1970], Upper Volta in the early sixties [Page, 1970], and Malawi in 1970 [personal communication]. On the other hand, rates of around

100 have been estimated for some countries, for example Botswana in 1971 [personal communication], and frequently for the better-developed areas within countries, for example a rate of 82 for West Mengo district, an area of 800,000 people including Kampala City, in Uganda, in 1969 [personal communication]. Part of the explanation of these differentials is the level of economic development, and the extent of provision of health services, education, water supplies, and so forth. Thus, in most countries of Africa, the infant mortality rate is lowest around the capital city or industrial centre. This also seems to explain some of the differentials between countries: Kenya's infant mortality is lower than Uganda's, which in turn is lower than Tanzania's, which in turn is lower than Malawi's. Some part of the country differentials does seem to be explained by natural factors, however: the low, wet forest areas of West Africa experience higher mortality levels than the higher and drier areas of Eastern and Southern Africa—the absence of malaria in high or dry areas may be an important factor. Expectation of life at birth is clearly closely connected with the level of infant mortality, and will fluctuate with it; this will be particularly so for estimates of expectation of life in Africa, where there is little or no information on adult mortality. The expectation of life at birth for Africa as a whole is between 40 and 45 years, which may be compared with a figure of 70 years for countries of Western Europe. The range of values for particular areas in Africa is from around 30 years for areas with the highest levels of mortality, to about 55 years for areas with low mortality.

Unlike fertility, there is a convincing body of evidence of a consistent trend in the level of mortality for most areas of Africa. In Uganda, for instance, the infant mortality rate has fallen from an estimated level of 200 in 1948 to 120 in 1969; similar falls have been recorded for Kenya, Tanzania, and other countries with estimates for a reasonable time span. On the basis of this evidence, it seems reasonable to suppose that mortality has also been falling in those areas for which no series of estimates exists. The decline in mortality has probably been going on for some considerable time, since early in the present century, although the pace of the decline has almost certainly been accelerating over recent years, so that now expectation of life at birth is rising at about a third of a year per year. The causes of the decline in mortality are not clearly established. Increased material wealth can hardly be a significant factor for whole populations, and increased provision of health and welfare services is unlikely to account for much of the improvement, given their still limited impact on the common man. A strong association has always been found, where the necessary data is available, between the educational standard of mothers and the mortality risk of the children, but whether it is the education that is the primary cause of the lower mortality, or whether both the education and the mortality are associated with some third variable such as wealth, is unclear. It seems possible that better education would result in a more balanced diet and better use of government facilities, and could therefore be the primary cause of the lower mortality levels.

Migration

The third component of population change is migration. Only in very exceptional circumstances is this a significant feature of population change at a continental level (migration from Europe to the Americas and Oceania and the slave trade in Africa would be the only possible cases), and it is rare for migration to be demographically significant at country level (although migrants might, for instance, make up a significant portion of the paid labour force). There are exceptions to this: for instance, nearly five per cent of the population enumerated in Uganda in 1969 is believed to have migrated into Uganda, either as refugees or from economic motives, during the ten years before the census. This is, however, an exceptional level of net migration. It is at the level of smaller areas, administrative sub-divisions of countries, that migration has a significant effect on population growth, age distribution, and sex structure. Migration to urban areas in particular, and, to a lesser extent, to better-developed rural areas is becoming increasingly apparent in Africa, and pressure on urban services is becoming a serious problem. Although the density of population is lower in Africa, at 11 persons per square kilometre, than in any other continent except Oceania, there are particular rural areas of extremely dense population, with densities up to 200 persons per square kilometre. This population pressure results in emigration to surrounding less densely populated rural areas, as well as to urban centres.

Population growth

Fertility and mortality are both higher for Africa than for any other continent; fertility is constant or rising slightly, mortality is falling fairly rapidly. The rate of natural increase of the population is determined by the balance of these two factors, the annual rate of natural increase per thousand being given by the difference between the crude birth rate and the crude death rate. The rate of natural increase, estimated by the United Nations to be 2.6 per cent per year for Africa for the period 1965 to 1970, is also the highest for any continent, the nearest challenger being Asia, with a growth rate of 2.3 per cent per year. Europe's population growth rate is estimated at 0.8 per cent per year, which will double the population over 87 years, compared with 27 years at 2.6 per cent per year. With falling mortality and constant or rising fertility, the rate of natural increase of Africa's population will rise over the next few decades until the trend of fertility is reversed. There is no signs that such a reversal is about to take place.

The variations in the levels of fertility and mortality from country to country and from region to region are naturally mirrored by variations in the rate of population growth. There is little doubt that the populations of all African countries are growing, the vast majority at rates of growth between two and three per cent per year. The only major countries reported by the United Nations to have population growth rates of less than one per cent are the Portuguese colonies, for which the estimates must be regarded as unreliable. The United Nations estimates show north Africa as having the highest rate of population growth (3.1 per cent per year for the region as a whole) and central Africa as having the lowest rate. (2.1 per cent per year). Rates of population growth do vary considerably: for East Africa, consisting of three rather similar countries, the latest estimates of the rates of natural increase of the population range from 3.3 per cent for Kenya, through 2.9 per cent for Uganda, to 2.6 per cent for Tanzania. Within Uganda, the rates of natural increase for the 20 administrative districts vary from a low of 1.9 per cent for a low fertility, high mortality area, to 3.6 per cent for a high fertility, lower mortality district. As development and the provision of social services spreads out, these marked differentials are likely to be considerably reduced.

The relatively high levels of fertility and mortality, and the rapid population growth rates found in Africa have a profound effect on the age structure of the population. About 45 per cent of the population of Africa is under the age of 15, and about 13 per cent over the age of 45. Any acceleration of the rate of growth will tend to increase the proportion under 15, and populations with 50 per cent of their members under 15 are not unknown. Age distributions can also be distorted by migration. Migrants, especially those seeking wage employment, tend to be young adult males; accordingly, net immigration increases the male proportion of the population and also the proportion of the population in the active age groups whereas the areas from which the migrants are drawn have a below-normal proportion male, and also a below average proportion in the active age groups.

The present trend of the level of mortality is likely to continue for the foreseeable future; mortality can decline at its estimated present rate till the end of the century, and still have increased the expectation of life at birth to only 55 years. In those areas where fertility is rising, it will, in all probability, level out over the next ten years at a new high point, but fertility is unlikely to fall to any great extent anywhere. These two factors together imply an accelerating rate of natural increase to the end of the present century. Migration is likely to continue to act as a safety valve for overpopulation pressure, and to even out local variations in population density. On a continental scale, however, migration is most unlikely to play a significant role, and Africa's burgeoning population, estimated at 344 million in 1970, must be supported within the confines of the continent.

References

Brass, W., *et al.* (1968) *The Demography of Tropical Africa.* Princeton U.P., Princeton, N.J.

Coale, A.J., & Demeny, P. (1966) *Regional Model Life Tables and Stable Populations.* Princeton N.J.

Page, H.J. (1970) Infant and child mortality. *African Population Conference, Accra.*

Page, H.J., & Coale, A.J. (1969) Estimates of fertility and child mortality in Africa South of the Sahara. *Seminar on Population Growth and Economic Development, Nairobi.*

United Nations Organisation (1970) *Demographic Year Book.* New York.

Demographic data collection procedures for public health studies

O. Ayeni

Introduction

Demographic data in their various forms are essential to any public health study. Their position in investigative studies is akin to that of bricks in building a house. The various statistics and rates derived from demographic data indicate the state of health of the community. They also provide us with critical measures of the effectiveness of medical care. Records of births and deaths give definite information as to the progress achieved in controlling the population and the extent of disease within that population. The excess of births over deaths, or vice versa, indicates the net change in the population and the rate of this change.

However, for special investigations designed to provide useful information for health planning much more than the primary data is often required. For example the investigator may need to draw attention to the prevalence or incidence of an undesirable condition within the community with a view to instituting a correctional programme. We might like to ascertain the knowledge of, attitude to, and practice within the community of some characteristic of the way of life such as family planning or health education. The objective may be to encourage existing behaviour or to change it. On other occasions the interest might be mainly to find out how successful a correctional programme has been. Occasionally epidemiological surveys are undertaken to throw light on the aetiology and prognosis of a certain disease and the effectiveness of control measures. Of importance also to health planning is the knowledge of the levels of fertility and mortality in the various socio-economic sectors of the population, and the trend of these with time.

The type of demographic data required for each category of investigation enumerated above will vary in nature and sophistication. Some will utilise just the basic population data distributed by age, sex, occupation, socio-economic class, religion, geographic

location, urban-rural stratification etc. But in other studies use will
have to be made of more specialised data on each relevant group
under investigation.

Of paramount importance to any type of investigation is the
quality and quantity of the data used in arriving at the various
conclusions. The quality and quantity of the data in turn depend
very largely on the procedures adopted in collecting the information.
In the developed countries, the conventional sources of the bulk of
data used in public health studies are the censuses and the vital
registration systems. Census returns provide the basic records of
population size, while returns from the vital registration systems are
the sources for births, deaths, marriages etc. In these countries census
systems have been so much developed with regard to the quality and
quantity of information collected, and vital registration systems are
of such accuracy, that supplementary sources of information are
only required for greater depth of study.

But in the developing countries the situation is very different.
Though by 1969 most developing countries had had at least one
count of the entire population, the quality and quantity of the
census data leave much to be desired. Apart from the inaccuracy of
the returns in coverage and data quality, there are other deficiencies
which diminish their usefulness for specific investigations in public
health. For any particular country the total enumerations are few
and far apart. Sufficient personal details are not collected. A
breakdown of population figures into local areas is not always
published in the reports. The census organizers often give limited
attention to uses of the data outside national economic purposes.

For vital registration, the position is much worse. As at 1969,
only about 3% of the population in black Africa was covered by
some kind of vital registration system. In the very few places where
the system exists, the returns are so poor and sketchy that even
approximate estimates made by methods such as those advocated by
Ajit Das Gupta [1958; 1963] are not possible.

Thus, because of the difficulties and the deficiencies of the two
main sources of data in developing countries, special efforts have to
be made to find alternatives. These special efforts consist mainly of
extensive use of sampling procedures and ad hoc survey-type
investigations using a battery of questions specially designed to bring
in additional information, basically on fertility and mortality. Even
in developed countries such special efforts are also popular. They
satisfy the need to supplement information from the two major
sources in more detail, and they are less expensive. In developing
countries most of the investigations in public health are done on an
ad-hoc basis. These special efforts, apart from fitting the two roles
mentioned above, are well suited to these health investigations since
they can be closely integrated with the aims of the studies. Four of

these special techniques will now be examined in relation to their suitability for furnishing good data for use in the different types of public health investigation already described.

Creation of special areas for investigative purposes in community health

The idea of designating special areas to serve as testing grounds for community health studies probably developed from notions only remotely connected with public health in the first instance. A good example in tropical Africa is that of the Ibarapa Project in Nigeria. It is organised jointly by the University of Ibadan Medical School and the Ministry of Health of the Western State of Nigeria. The project was started solely to give the medical students of the University the necessary training in, and an insight into, the practice of medicine in rural areas.

The Ibarapa district is a mainly rural area in Western Nigeria. It had a 1963 population of 130,000. The largest town is Igbo Ora with 30,000 people at that date. In 1964, when the Medical School project commenced, there was only a health centre at Igbo Ora. Like all other areas in Nigeria, there was no system of registering vital events. With the commencement of the project, a programme of collecting vital statistics was instituted with the appointment of six local registrars who make periodic visits to all the houses to record the vital events occurring in them. These statistics are published in bulletins issued annually by the project. A more detailed description of the project with estimates of running costs will be found in Ayeni [1971], Igbo Ora Project, [1971] and Ogunesi [1965].

Public health investigators were quick to realise the various opportunities presented by the facilities of the project. Apart from the availability of a continuous and fairly complete system of registering vital events, there are the local registrars to act as guides and interviewers for special investigations. These opportunities were quickly grasped and by 1971 more than twenty public health inquiries, mostly by members of the Faculty of Medicine of the University, had been carried out.

Such an organizational structure as that of the Ibarapa project is particularly suitable for evaluating health programmes and case-control studies. The area is one of those selected early this year by the World Health Organization to participate in a world-wide study of the control of hypertension. The procedure is also convenient for some KAP (Knowledge, Attitude, Practice) studies, especially on family planning; and also for MCH (Maternal and Child Health) studies. In fact, early in 1973 an MCH programme was at the planning stage in this area. The facilities can also be used to establish levels of fertility, mortality and the prevalence of any condition in the area.

A deficiency inherent in the use of community health areas is that results from the studies conducted in them will necessarily be limited in scope. The ability of the investigator to draw general inferences may be severely restricted simply because the area may not be representative of the rest of the country. Igbo Ora, for instance, was regarded as a typical rural area in 1964. But, because of the attention drawn to the diseases by the reports of the various investigators and the consequent curative and preventive measures adopted, the state of health is now comparable with, if not better than, that found in many urban areas in Nigeria.

Sample vital registration systems

This involves the selection of areas or population units within a country and the establishment of vital registration systems in them. The selection of the areas may be purely purposive, as in Tanzania [Wood, 1970] with their 'ten-house chairmen' system; or based on some fairly strict probability sampling, as in Turkey [Rumford, 1968; Turkish, 1967], Pakistan [Pakistan, 1968; Brass, 1968], and India [Agrawal, 1969]. Each system may or may not have incorporated in it a subsystem of periodic independent checks to improve the accuracy of the data collected.

The general advantage of this procedure is the provision of some vital statistics for a place where none was hitherto available, with the consequences for public health inquiries already listed. In addition, because of the spread of the sample over different localities, epidemiological surveys, prevalence and incidence studies can be organised to fit meaningfully into the sample structure. It is also possible for the investigator to make geographic comparisons of estimates. A further valuable feature is that, with properly selected samples, reasonable estimates can be made for the whole country.

Against these have to be weighed the fact that the control of widely scattered areas may be difficult and lead to reduced accuracy. Again, sampled units may not remain for long representative of the areas for which they were initially selected. Also, a public health investigator has to tailor the design of his study to the existing sample design and this may be inefficient for his purposes. Moreover, because of the heterogeneity of areas, sample sizes have to be large to enable the investigator to make finer comparisons between sub-groups whose relative sizes were not taken into consideration in the original design. A combination of bias in the sample selection and the magnitude of the sampling errors may swamp small but real differences between sub-groups. This makes trend estimation and detection of inter-group differences unreliable.

Single round retrospective sample surveys

The use of sample surveys constitutes one of the earlier attempts to provide vital statistics through substitute means. The history of the method in developing countries is fairly long but its development has been slow. For example, medical sample censuses were periodically conducted in the British Colonies in Africa as far back as 1931. The improvement in the demographic uses of such surveys is, however, quite recent, notably since the exposition of a body of techniques by Brass and others [1970] through which estimates of mortality and fertility can be made from the reproductive and mortality histories of respondents. This has added a new dimension to the importance of sample surveys in providing reliable vital data through simple retrospective questioning.

By means of a one round interviewing process in a carefully selected sample, it is possible to obtain estimates of the population size by the major categories that are of interest to the investigator. The number of those affected by some particular condition, and reporting behaviour or attitudes can also be found. From answers to questions on the proportion of living children to total children born, on the parity of each woman together with the average number of live births per woman in the twelve month period preceeding the interview date, all tabulated by age, reliable estimates respectively of child mortality and fertility can be made. These involve the use of the techniques already mentioned. The system has now been satisfactorily extended to provide estimates of adult mortality from information on the proportions of children whose fathers or mothers are still alive.

The procedure appears particularly suitable for some types of public health investigation since it does not require a drastically different approach from that which would be adopted for medical purposes. It ties into the individual investigator's plan of operation, the only extra requirement being additional questions on the interviewer's schedule. Olusanya [1969] has used the procedure to estimate urban-rural fertility levels and differentials in some parts of Western Nigeria. One round retrospective surveys have been particularly well exploited to estimate levels of fertility and in French-speaking Africa, e.g. in Cameroon [INSEE, 1965], Upper Volta, Ivory Coast and Guinea [Brass, 1968]. Harrington and Pool [1970] have also used it to establish survivorship patterns in Upper Volta and Niger. Most KAP studies in developing countries collect data to which the Brass methods of analysis can be applied, but few of the published reports contain estimates of fertility or mortality, which are so necessary (especially child mortality) in assessing health problems and in interpreting stances taken by the population on topics like family planning.

However, this approach has its own shortcomings. One round of questioning can establish levels with reasonable reliability. Trends over time cannot be determined. Because of this the procedure can not be used without extension in studies which seek to evaluate continuing action. Furthermore, estimates of fertility and mortality derived through the use of the techniques are really averages over a period in the recent past based on the assumption that the factors measured have been constant over that period. Also the power of the estimates to detect inter-group differences depends largely on the relative stability of the groups concerned. Finally, the number of events remembered by the respondents may be inaccurate because of errors due to memory lapse and confusion about the reference period within which they occurred. Although the analysis methods are designed to determine and correct such errors, the adjustments are not always dependable.

Multi-round surveys

These, basically, are extensions of one round retrospective surveys. Essentially, data are collected from the same sample through repeat visits by the registrar or the interviewer. There are variations on this scheme. All subsequent visits may be pure revisits by the same registrar to record events which occurred since the last visit. On other designs, some of the revisits may be independent checks on the accuracy of data collected during previous visits. If independent checking revisits have been made, it is usual to follow up with a matching operation of events on the two lists. The accuracy of the data may be improved by applying thereafter the Chandrasekar-Deming correction technique [1949] to estimate the probable number of events that have actually occurred.

This procedure has all the advantages and overcomes some of the deficiencies of the last one. Reference-period errors are reduced and recall lapses are cut to a minimum if the interval between revisits is not too long. There is a further increase in data accuracy from the matching operation and the use of the Chandrasekar-Deming correction technique.

The scheme can supply reliable demographic data for a wide variety of public health studies provided either that these are designed to fit into the existing sample survey scheme, or that the data collection procedure is incorporated into the design of the study. It can be used efficiently to evaluate health programmes, to establish fertility and mortality levels as in Nigeria [Federal Office, 1966], Senegal [Cantrelle, 1965] and Liberia [Rumford, 1971], and to study trends over time in both fertility and mortality. Cantrelle and Leridon [1971] have applied data thus collected in a specialised study on the effect of breast-feeding on child mortality and fertility in Senegal.

Among the failings of the method are the possible loss of sample units between rounds through immigration, and the difficulty of allowing adequately for emigrants. Also, the matching operation is tedious and subject to errors. Since the number of vital events in a year is small relative to the population at risk, sample sizes have to be large if trends are to be determined with reasonable precision. Such schemes, therefore, tend to be large, demanding in managerial skills and costly.

Conclusion

Useful as some of the results from the special efforts described above appear to be, they are no real substitute for the yields from accurate censuses and vital registration systems. Estimates of mortality derived from the special techniques can not, in general, be broken down by causes nor by groups in any considerable detail. Some of the conditions basic to the estimation techniques may not be true in many developing countries. For example, they depend heavily on the assumption of constant fertility and mortality in the near past. The experience in many developing countries is that mortality has been declining in the last twenty years and there may be signs that fertility is beginning to do the same. Apart from this, there is the constraint that these techniques work well only if the data behave. Unusual fluctuations or errors can cause heavily biased conclusions.

Moreover, all of the special efforts described involve one form of sampling or the other. Many reports of sample surveys pay little or no attention to sampling errors, probably because of the difficulty in estimating them. There is a real possibility that, in many cases, calculation of sampling errors would render some of the conclusions invalid. Secondly, selection of a representative sample requires skill and considerable knowledge of the population to be sampled. In several of the countries of Africa simple estimates, even of population sizes, are in doubt. These, however, should in no way discourage the use of such approaches in public health studies.

In many developing countries, public health investigations involving the use of demographic data have been relatively few. This is no doubt due to lack of vital data from conventional sources. Little use has been made of the various approaches discussed here, partly because the techniques are new and most public health investigators are unaware of them. It is hoped that, henceforth, more use of these procedures will be made in health studies.

References

Agrawal, B.L., (1969), Sample registration in India, *Population Studies* 23 (3)

Ayeni, O. (1971) Guidelines for the establishment of a vital statistics registration system in Nigeria, *Nigeria Medical Journal* 1 (4).

Brass, W., *et al.* (1968) *The Demography of Tropical Africa.* Princeton University Press, Princeton, New Jersey.

Brass, W. (1970) Review of Report of the Pakistan Population Growth Estimation Experiment, *Pop. studies* 24 (3).

Cantrelle, P. (1965) Repeated demographic observation in a rural area in Senegal: method and first results, *World Population Conference Document No B6/V/F/207, Belgrade.*

Cantrelle, P. and Leridon H. (1971) Breast feeding, child mortality and fertility in Senegal, *Pop. Studies* 25 (3).

Chandrasekar, C., and Deming, W.E. (1949) On a method of estimating birth and death rates and the extent of registration, *Journal of American Statistical Association* 44, pp. 101-115.

Gupta, A.D. (1958) Determination of fertility level and trend in defective registration areas, *Bulletin of the International Statistical Institute 30th Session.*

Gupta, A.D. (1963) Estimation of vital rates for developing countries, *Proceedings of the International Population Conference, Ottawa.*

Harrington, J.A., and Pool, D.I. (1970) Patterns of survivorship in Upper Volta and Niger 1969-1970.

Igbo Ora (1971) *Births and Deaths Analysis 1965, 1966, 1967, 1968, 1969, 1970* (Mimeographed).

Federal Office of Statistics, *Nigeria Rural Demographic Sample Survey 1965-1966.* Lagos.

Ogunesi T.O. (1965) The Ibarapa Project. A new look at Ibadan. *Journal of the Nig. Med. Association* 2 (2).

Olusanya P.O. (1969) Rural-urban fertility differentials in Western Nigeria, *Pop. Studies* 23 (3).

Pakistan Institute of Development Economics (1968) *Report of the Population Growth Estimation Experiment: description and some results for 1962 and 1963.* Karachi.

Rumford J. (1971) Factors influencing the casefinding of vital events in the Liberian Fertility Survey. *African Regional Population Conference Accra, Ghana.*

Rumford J.C. *et al.* (1968) The Principles and Preliminary results of the Turkish Demographic Survey, *Public Health Reports* 83 (7).

Sabagh G. and Scott C. (1965) An evaluation of the use of retrospective questionnaires for obtaining vital data: the experience of the Moroccan Sample Survey of 1961-1963, *Proceedings of the World Population Conference, Belgrade.*

INSEE (1965) *The Population of West Cameroon: main findings of the 1964 Demographic Sample Survey,* Paris.

(1967) Vital Statistics from the Turkish Demographic Survey 1965-1966, *Ministry of Health and Social Welfare, Ankara.*

Wood C.H. (1970) Recording of births and deaths in Tanzania: a preliminary report, *The Bulletin of the International Epidemiological Association* 20.

Human population and the disease factor in the development of Nigeria.

H. I. Ajaegbu and Christine E. Mann

Introduction

Nigeria's potential for development is influenced considerably by the numbers and quality of her population. Development planners now realize that human resources constitute the most lasting economic asset, but have not fully appreciated that the quality of the human resource, and its capacity to contribute towards the country's development, is largely dependent on the health of the people. Analyses of manpower problems in Nigeria have rarely considered the effects of disease and ill-health on working efficiency. Moreover, health programmes have been conceived more as a social amenity than as a direct investment aimed at improving the effectiveness of manpower in development.

The relationship between the health of the population and its effectiveness as a labour force is so precarious that it should directly concern manpower planners. Unfortunately, understanding of the ecological situations within which diseases flourish, and of the implications these should have for development planning and health programmes, is incomplete. Medical-geographical studies might contribute to increased appreciation of the interrelations between environment and disease.

Nigeria's human resource

Nigeria has 56-60 million inhabitants, and an annual population growth rate of 2.8-3.0 per cent. The gross reproduction rate is 3.6-3.8, the crude birth rate is 53-57 per thousand (60.2 per thousand in Lagos city in 1960), and the crude death rate is 23-26 per thousand. The expectation of life at birth is estimated to be over 40 years at present, and to be likely to rise to 56 years by 1995 [Okonjo, 1971]. About 43 per cent of the population is aged under 15 years, 52 per cent between 15 and 54 years, and 5 per cent over

55 years. About 54 per cent of Nigeria's population falls within the 'economically active' group, of which males comprise 52 per cent.

Hence, Nigeria has a considerable reservoir of manpower, aged between 0 and 14 years, which, at 15 years, will enter the potential labour force. In addition, increasing life expectancy implies that, in future, even greater numbers can be expected to enter this pool. Thus, numerically, Nigeria's human resources offer a potentially adequate manpower supply.

Manpower quality, however, must also be considered. Such consideration requires study of the health and nutritional levels of individuals and communities, and of associated ecological factors. Regrettably, most manpower planners have focussed greater attention on population numbers, distributions and trends, growth rates, age and sex characteristics, size of the active population, and size and composition of the labour force. More recently, in Nigeria, the content and quality of education and educational programmes has been emphasised, whilst the implications of nutrition, health and disease for manpower development and efficiency in relation to national development have seldom been adequately considered. Nevertheless, the Inter-African Labour Conference in 1953 noted that among the specific factors affecting productivity and labour relations in Africa were 'certain objective influences: nutrition, disease, climate', and included 'diets and efficiency' among the items 'requiring immediate action' in human resource/manpower development [Chukwumah, 1964]. The statement represents an important recognition of the effects of disease and ill-health on working capacity.

It has also been confirmed that 'among the human factors influencing the productivity of the African labour is the will to work, which derives from individual, physical, environmental and social factors' [Chukwumah, 1964, p. 4]. Such a 'will to work' is significantly affected by the debilitating effects of disease.

Prevalence of diseases among Nigeria's population

Disease is widespread, a large proportion of the Nigerian population being affected by one or more pathogens at any one time, and particularly by parasitic infections. Parasites may be harboured in chronic form for many years, with debilitating effects on vitality and working efficiency. Nutritional diseases, either long-term or seasonal, are common, especially among infants, pregnant mothers and the aged [Collis *et al*, 1962a; Bassir, 1965; Hendrickse, 1966; Ajaegbu, 1970].

Generalisation concerning the health and disease situation for the whole of Nigeria is, however, difficult. Considerable differences occur between the predominantly rural population (over 80%) and

Type of disease	No. of cases reported	% of total reported cases
Malaria	438,233	48·7
Dysentery	116,386	12·9
Measles	89,030	9·9
Gonorrhoea	64,920	7·2
Pneumonia	46,934	5·2
Chickenpox	18,815	2·1
Whooping cough	17,880	2·0
Schistosomiasis, vesical & intestinal	16,991	1·9
Filariasis	15,047	1·7
Tuberculosis	14,360	1·6
Syphilis	10,854	1·2
Others (18)	50,550	5·6
Total	900,000	100·0

(*Source*: Federal Office of Statistics, 1967 p. 166)

TABLE 1   *Diseases reported in Nigeria, 1966*

the small proportion who live in the major urban centres; and between, for example, settled nucleated villages, small bush hamlets, and migratory herdsmen. Moreover, some physical environments, including the coastal creeks and lagoons, swamps and infested streams, constitute local health hazards. For many rural communities, distance and travelling costs prevent the effective utilisation of existing medical facilities [Ajaegbu and Ikusemiju, 1970], whilst poor environmental sanitation has created additional disease problems in both urban and rural communities [cf. Okediji and Aboyade, 1967].

Table 1 shows the dominant disease types reported for several hospitals and health centres in Nigeria during 1966. Major causes of

Type of disease	No. of deaths recorded
Pneumonia	892
Gastritis, duodenitis, enteritis & colitis	663
Diseases peculiar to early infancy & immaturity (unspecified)	605
Senility without mention of psychosis, ill-defined and unknown causes	604
Malaria	388
Others classified as infective and parasitic diseases	337
Chronic rheumatic heart disease & other diseases of the heart	221
Birth injuries, postnatal asphyxia & atelactasis	202
Anaemias	200
Measles	181
Hypertension, with or without heart disease	141
Tuberculosis of respiratory system & other forms	118
Vascular lesions affecting central nervous systems	103
Infections of the new born	54
Dysentery	45
Small pox	29
Influenza	7

(*Source*: Federal Office of Statistics, 1967)

TABLE 2   *Major disease types in Lagos, 1966*

death included measles (806 cases), pneumonia (773), cerebrospinal meningitis (524), and smallpox (405). Recent surveys in Lagos (1966) identified over fifty diseases as responsible for mortality in the city. The most important are listed in Table 2.

These figures reflect large scale under-reporting, and indicate the limited and often unrepresentative coverage of official surveys. Problems of data collection and interpretation are increased by the continued reliance on spiritual healing, native doctors, illegal drug sellers, and quack injection dispensers. Many illnesses are never reported to hospitals and dispensaries, and published figures inevitably grossly underestimate actual totals [Ajaegbu and Ikusemiju, 1970].

A number of independent reports provide valuable insight into the real situation. Investigations in the Uboma area of the East Central State [Oluwasanmi, 1966] showed that about 42 per cent of children aged five years and under, and 52 per cent of adults, were infested with malaria, round worm, threadworm or hookworm, whilst 41 per cent of the children registered haemoglobin counts of only 40-60 per cent. In Calabar, surveys by Hinz [1966] revealed hookworm, ascariasis and trichuria infection in 23 per cent, 25 per cent and 15 per cent of the population respectively. In villages of the Western State [Collis et al, 1962a], 52 per cent of those aged between six and fourteen years suffered from malaria, and, of those over 45 years, 84 per cent were T.B. positive, 58 per cent had ascariasis, and 42 per cent hookworm. In Epe town 90 per cent of school children examined had bilharzia [Okpala, 1961], and in Lagos incidences of 25 per cent, 16 per cent and 31 per cent were recorded for hookworm, ascariasis and trichuria [Hinz, 1966].

The extensive range of diseases discovered in Akufo village [Gilles, 1964] typifies the rural situation in most parts of Nigeria. Malaria parasites were found in 65 per cent of the population, 4 per cent had filariasis, 100 per cent amoebiasis, 26 per cent guinea worm, 70 per cent intestinal helminthiasis, 45 per cent trichuris trichura, 21 per cent strongyloides stercoralis and 71 per cent hookworm. In addition, 10 per cent of boys aged between 8 and 14 years had schistosomiasis.

Prothero [1965, p. 101] considered that most mortality before puberty in western Sokoto Province (up to 500 per 1,000 live births) was associated with intense malaria infection. In the Katsina area, leprosy incidence reached 29 per 1,000 [Bechelli et al, 1966], and several other diseases, including 'river blindness' and measles, were also prevalent.

Trypanosomiasis has long been known in Nigeria [Anon, 1961], p. 53-61], and today the tsetse fly has extended into much of the formerly tsetse-free northern strip and eastern highlands. Major foci include the Niger-Benue trough, the Lake Chad basin and the Bauchi plateau. Between 1930 and 1940 sleeping sickness was diagnosed in

Areas	Date of survey	No. of people examined	Infected cases of sleeping sickness identified	% Infected	Overall infection rate %
Plateau Province	1951-1952	1,130,868	7,429		0·2
Plateau Province	1952-1953	1,044,211	6,060		0·23
Bida town (Niger Province)	1954-1955	4,272	21	0·5	—
Jima-Doko district of Bida Emirate	1956	16,451	181	1·1	—
Leve district of Zaria Province	1956	1,833,362	5,911		0·15
Bida area	1957	1,135,764	2,657		0·15
Bauchi area	1958	1,717,713	4,862		0·14
Within known endemic areas of Bauchi, Bida, (a)	1959	1,527,892	4,536		0·14
Plateau, etc. (b)	1959	1,127,912	1,643		0·14
All areas	1949-1959	13,895,030	59,000		0·23

NB.   Benue Province supplied about one third of all the sleeping sickness cases.
(*Source*: Anon: The tsetse problem in N. Nigeria, 1961 pp. 53-81)

TABLE 3   *Incidence of human sleeping sickness, 1951-9*

300,000 of 2,756,343 people examined, and the infection rate estimated at 10.9 per cent. [McLetchie, 1953]. Pentamidine prophylaxis proved successful in the campaign against sleeping sickness between 1946 and 1955, but incidence remained high and reached epidemic proportions in places (Table 3). More recent surveys (Table 4) show continued, but reduced, occurrence; epidemics are rare, but debilitating endemic conditions persist.

Malnutrition and related diseases

Nutritional diseases prevail among both children and adults. Young children are especially vulnerable, and physical and mental damage caused during early childhood may have irreparable ill-effects. Thus, malnutrition poses grave problems for manpower efficiency.

Dietary provision in many areas is frequently inadequate to meet requirements, either on a long-term or a seasonal basis. Nutritional inadequacies are debilitating in themselves, but the synergistic interaction between nutrition and infectious disease renders dietary deficiencies even more serious [W.H.O., 1965]. In both rural and urban areas calorie and protein deficits are basic to Nigeria's nutritional problems, but the actual nature, timing and severity of the diseases are not uniform throughout the country. In the predominantly grain-producing regions north of the Niger and Benue rivers, food supplies, especially among the cattle-herding Fulani, are generally adequate in both calories and protein during the greater part of the year [Bassir, 1965], though a pre-harvest 'hungry

Area	Date of Survey	No. of people examined	Infected cases identified	% Infected	Overall infection rate %
Fika area of Bornu Province	1960	21,905	41		0·18
Gashua area of Bornu Province	1960	7,862	7		0·08
Bauchi Province	1960	135,043	158		0·11
Bauchi-Maiduguri railway extension area	1960	13,331	6		0·10
Adamawa Province	1960	20,963	78		0·37
Bornu Province	1961	48,057	27		0·05
Bauchi Province	1961	268,667	192		0·07
Bauchi-Maiduguri railway extension area	1961	16,740	10		0·03
Adamawa Province	1961	80,338	41		0·05
Bedde Emirate of Bornu Province	1962	32,984	40		0·12
Gujba district of Bornu Province	1962	16,614	—		—
Bauchi Province	1962	162,904	104		0·06
railway extension area	1962	6,610	—		—
Nafada district of Gombe Emirate	1962	21,899	—		—
Adamawa Province	1962	33,903	121		0·35
Gushua town in Bornu Province	1963	13,757	5		0·03
Bauchi Province	1963	291,969	252		0·08
Bauchi Maiduguri railway extension area	1963	11,320	8		0·07
Yamaltu district of Gombe Emirate	1963	10,368	63		0·06
Adamawa Province	1963	44,360	88		0·20
Biu Emirate	1963	69,172	219		0·30
Bauchi Province resurvey	1963	71,244	32		0·04
Adamawa resurvey	1963	25,059	38		0·10

(*Source*: Aitchison and Glover 1970, pp. 46-49).

TABLE 4   *Incidence of human sleeping sickness, 1960-3*

season' from April to June, similar to that in Northern Ghana [Hunter, 1967] may occur in Northern Nigeria.

In the south and east, root crops poor in protein form the staple diet, and animal protein supplies are limited. Population pressure has resulted in reduced crop acreages, overcropping and soil exhaustion, and per capita subsistence production has declined. In areas suitable for commercial crops, such as the cocoa belt, production for export or local industries has reduced food availability, and led to the paradoxical situation in which the richest areas in terms of total crop production and overall rural income support a largely malnourished population, incapable of working at maximum efficiency or achieving maximum crop potential (Table 5).

	Akufo	Igun	Abebeyun	Vodni Jos Plateau	Jos Plateau
Location	cocoa belt	cocoa belt	Marginal cocoa-belt	Agricultural	Cattle herders
Survey date	Nov 1961	Nov 1960	Nov 1960	Oct 1961	Oct 1961
Calories/hd/day	1943	1914	2487	2704	3282
Calory intake as a % of requirement	88	86	116	125	147
Protein intake as a % of total calory intake	7·2	10·6	8·8	10·1	10·6
Protein intake as a % of requirement	49	78	77	103	135

(*Sources*: Gilles, 1965; Dema, 1963; Collis *et al*, 1962b)

TABLE 5   *Calorie and protein intake among selected Nigerian rural communities*

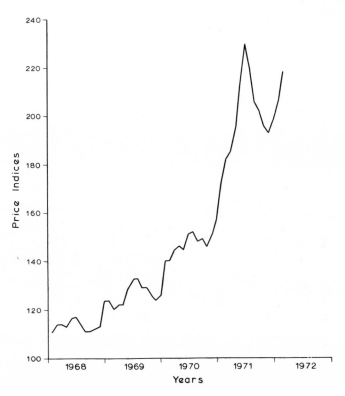

SOURCE :– Federal office of statistics monthly publications on "Retail prices and Consumer price indices for selected urban centres"

FIGURE 1   *Ibadan food prices index, lower income group, 1968-72*

Urban areas present an equally discouraging situation. Hills [1960] concluded that protein malnutrition has become more common in Nigeria in the past thirty years, and suggested that a major factor is that urbanization causes increased reliance on bought foods of low nutritional value, such as the cheapest protein-poor flours, especially of cassava and white maize. Moreover, apart from the recent growth of market gardening and poultry keeping in and around some towns, a large number of urban dwellers have no access to the significant dietary supplements provided by foraging in rural areas [Jelliffe, 1962]. Finally, the higher cash income of the city dweller proves inadequate for his basic requirements and extended family commitments [cf. Hendrickse, 1967], partly because of the high rate of price inflation in recent years (Fig. 1).

Nutritional deficiencies are most pronounced and harmful in pregnant and lactating women, infants and growing children. Janes [1968] has shown that the growth curves of children of the urban poor in Ibadan are far below those of the elite children (Fig. 2); and it seems unlikely that this deficit is recovered later in life. This former group is characteristic of the bulk of Nigerian children, and underfed and undersized infants will perhaps become physically and emotionally handicapped adults, unable to attain full working capacity.

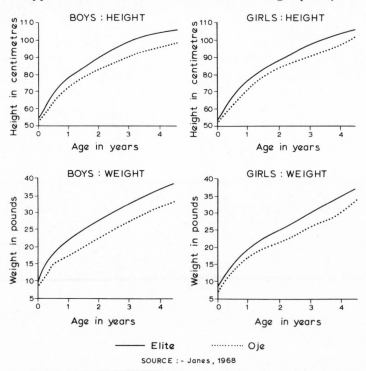

FIGURE 2 *Comparative height and weight curves for Ibadan elite and Oje children, 1962-8*

Furthermore, since poor nutritional status contributes to the high infant mortality rate of between 40 and 50 per cent of live births, it also has adverse effects on potential manpower resources. Malnutrition causing kwashiorkor is widespread in southern Nigeria, and virtually all untreated cases die. Even where treatment is available, between 20 and 45 per cent of patients die [Collis, 1972].

In view of the debilitating effects of malnutrition and disease among all sectors of the population, research into environmental influences on ill-health is urgently needed.

Case studies in Oje, Ibadan and in Ayinde

Investigations into economic and socio-cultural aspects of child nutrition in Oje, one of the poor traditional areas of the old city of Ibadan, and in Ayinde village (about 50 miles from Ibadan), indicated a high correlation between nutritional levels and differences in child growth patterns (heights and weights), and the interaction between nutrition and infection [Mann, 1972].

In Oje, the area surrounding the traditional cloth market, the inhabitants still live in mud-walled, tin-roofed huts in an agglomeration of family compounds. There is no sewage system, and water supply comes from a few common pumps. Mothers interviewed were usually illiterate, and, in a sample of forty-four households, only 45 per cent of the husbands had received any education. Income levels for the household heads seldom rose to £250 per annum. 34 per cent of the men were polygamous, and 58 per cent of the mothers belonged to polygamous families [Lloyd, 1967].

Ayinde village, with a population of just over 200, has no sewage system and water is drawn from a stream half a mile from the village. All sample families lived in mud-walled huts, more than half of which were thatched. Household possessions were minimal, and much fewer than among the Oje group; but the huts were often cleaner and more widely spaced. Only one of twenty-two mothers interviewed had had any education, and 85 per cent of the fathers were illiterate. All the men were food crop farmers, and the women prepared gari for sale at the five-day market held two miles away. Monogamous families were more common than in Oje, 37 per cent of the wives being polygamously married.

The home environment in both areas was unsatisfactory. The number of persons per household ranged from six to forty-four, with 51 per cent of the households having more than two occupants per room. Densities per bedroom were even higher, just 9 per cent of the dwellings having less than two persons, and over 30 per cent more than four. In only one third of the 43 dwelling units visited in Oje was daytime illumination and ventilation considered good. 66 per cent of the households had electricity, although lighting was seldom

Type of illness	No. of cases	% of total cases
Fever	86	47·0
Diarrhoea	53	29·0
Cough and head cold	33	18·0
Measles	5	2·8
Malaria	2	1·1
Tuberculosis	2	1·1
Whooping cough	1	0·5
Tonsilitis	1	0·5
Total	183	100·0

(*Source*: Survey by C.E. Mann 1971-1972.)

TABLE 6   *Cases of illness recorded for 49 children in Oje area Ibadan, between September 1971 and July 1972*

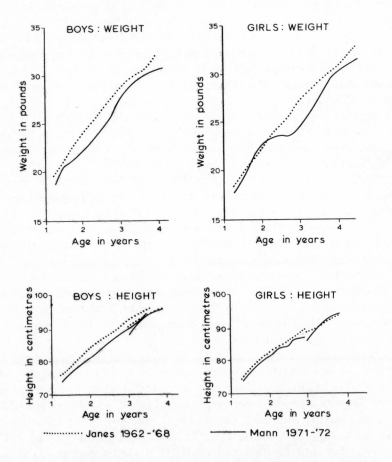

FIGURE 3 *Height and weight measurements of 49 children in Oje area of Ibadan*

of a high standard. No such facilities existed in Ayinde. Of all the families interviewed in Oje, only 60 per cent had bathroom and 51 per cent toilet, facilities, and many of these were shared by several households. The remainder had either no provision, or used a variety of makeshift structures.

The incidence of childhood diseases associated with insanitary, crowded living conditions was found to be high (Table 6), and the situation seemed to be deteriorating. The 1971-1972 height and weight curves for Oje sample children fell below those for Oje infants studied in 1962-1968 [Janes, 1968] (Fig. 3). Their nutritional levels and growth patterns were well below the optimum, but the infant mortality rate had fallen from 55.7 per cent for children born before 1962, to only 11.8 per cent for those born since 1962. The reduced death rate, viewed against the rise in food prices for people whose income levels have increased only marginally, suggests that an increasing number of mouths must be fed on a proportionately lower income. Thus the general nutritional and health levels of these infants might be expected to fall even further.

As Jelliffe [1962] has stressed, the main nutritional problems of early childhood in Africa in the near future are likely to occur in the rapidly growing towns. Many local foods are often not available in the urban centres, or are beyond the means of the urban poor. In Ibadan, though poverty and ignorance appear important causes of nutritional deficiencies, they may be over-shadowed by the impact of culture conflict between traditional and modified 'western' lifestyles. Traditional ideas limiting the intake of nutritious foods, particularly among infants, are retained, whilst harmful 'western' habits are adopted. Social and financial commitments often hinder adequate dietary provision, and the locally restricted range of Nigerian foods, adherence to traditional dishes, and the misplaced advertising of prestige imported commodities add to the problems of child nutrition. Clearly the factors influencing nutrition and growth are complex and, if the growing incidence of malnutrition is to be curbed, a thorough understanding of the ecological aspects of the problem is vital.

A case study at the University of Ibadan

Preliminary study of the University junior and intermediate staff affords an insight into the nature and extent of the effects of the disease on manpower efficiency. 227 workers in three halls of residence were studied. They included porters, gardeners, washermen, messengers, cooks, stewards and similar employees, with salaries of between £200 and £600 per annum.

Authorized 'off-sick' papers were examined. Of the 227 workers, 84 (37 per cent) had one or more off-sick days or light-duty

Year	Month	Total Man-days lost (off-sick)
1971	January	44
	February	82
	March	30
	April	62
	May	81
	June	31
	July	23
	August	80
	September	41
	October	86
	November	93
	December	74
1972	January	53
	February	24
	March	16
	April	68
	May	75
	June	59
		1,022
	Mean Monthly	56·8

TABLE 7   *Frequency of off-sick days among junior and intermediate staff at the University of Ibadan, January 1971-June 1972*

concessions between January 1971 and June 1972. Male workers formed 78.6 per cent of this total, a reflection of the preponderance of men in University employment. A total of 1,022 man-days were lost, and 27 light-duty days were granted to four individuals. Maternity leave was excluded from the investigation.

Reported diseases included jaundice (69 man-days), chest troubles (60), hypertension (20), fractures/dislocations (18), and malaria (13). Other minor ailments were mentioned, but many papers did not specify the illnesses involved.

The mean number of man-days lost by each of the 84 workers was 12.2, the average for females (18 individuals) being 22.6 man-days, and that for males (66) 9.3. The monthly distribution is also significant (Table 7). There was a peak of illness during the early rains in April and May (Fig. 4), and a higher dry-season peak between October and December during the harmattan. Apart from the anomalies explained in Table 7, there was a continuous low from June through September 1971, corresponding to the university vacation, when most workers took their annual leave and when those remaining were underemployed. An average of 56.8 man-days per month was lost during the 18 month survey period, but the actual loss exceeded the mean in 10 months. Deviation from the mean during the month of greatest loss was approximately 64 per cent.

The data thus indicate a high loss in man-days per worker per month, and a seasonality in disease occurrence. Initial results stress the relationship between wet and dry seasons and specific illness, and emphasise the influence of the general environmental situation. Preliminary conclusions must be tentative, but the incidence of ill-health may be regarded as typical of, or more favourable than in, much of Nigeria, since adequate basic amenities and health facilities are provided by the university.

The ecological setting for diseases in Nigeria — preliminary observations

The discussion has pointed to the importance of environmental factors in disease causation. The concern of the medical geographer must be that of identifying the differing ecological conditions under which diseases develop.

Several disease regions, for example the Niger-Benue trough, the Bauchi Plateau, and the southern forest belt, may be isolated, and seasonality in the incidence of some illnesses emphasised. Diffusion or transmission of disease from one area to another may occur, this being related to the distance and degree of interaction between regions, and to the time interval separating contacts. Transmission may be influenced by:

a)   The rural situation, marked by poor environmental sanitation, poverty and ignorance, from which most urban immigrants originate. They bring infections and undesirable attitudes to disease and sanitation into the urban centres.

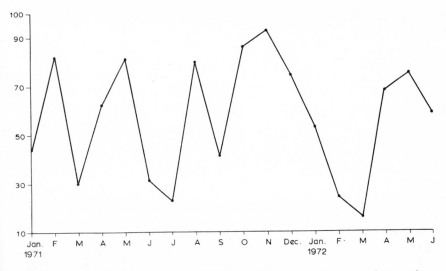

FIGURE 4   *Off-sick days, January 1971-June 1972, among sampled workers at the University of Ibadan*

b)   The existence of pockets or belts of high rural population density, which facilitate the occurrence of epidemics and the transmission of disease.

c)   Migration trends in the country (mainly north-south or rural-urban), which bring diverse populations together and lead to the spread of disease over considerable distances.

d)   Rapid urbanization and the unhealthy urban environment, which today constitute the most vulnerable ecological setting for disease prevalence and spread.

The most significant factor is probably that of widespread poor environmental sanitation among both urban and rural populations. Particularly important are (a) the generally unhealthy physical surroundings; (b) inadequate refuse disposal methods; and (c) unsatisfactory personal hygiene and unhygienic food preparation techniques. Environmental sanitation problems must be fully appreciated before effective programmes for the improvement of the health levels of the Nigerian population can be instituted.

Conclusion

The full economic advantage of Nigeria's large actual and potential manpower resources is not being realized because of disease, and the present labour force is not working to capacity owing to frequent illness and general debility. Problems of malnourishment in the early years of life reduce the expected manpower potential. Thus 'Nigerian manpower cannot contribute fully to development if it is unhealthy . . . . . Improved health and housing leads to the raising of the level of productivity and output in the various sectors of the economy' [Ahimie, 1971, p. 701]. Health levels of the population in general and the labour force in particular cannot be raised until a greater understanding of the ecological aspects of disease is achieved, and until the . problem of environmental sanitation is satisfactorily tackled.

References

Ahimie, P.O. (1971) Health, housing and social welfare (in Nigeria); in: Ayida A.A. & Onitiri, H.M.A. (ed.), *Reconstruction and Development in Nigeria*, NISER, Oxford.

Aitchison, P.J. & P.E. Glover (1970) *The land resources of North East Nigeria, Volume 2: Tsetse and trypanosomiasis*, Land Resource Study, No. 9, Directorate of Overseas Surveys, O.D.A.

Ajaegbu, H.I. (1970) The problems of population growth and urban influences on food supplies and nutrition needs in the rural areas of southern Nigeria, in: Addo, N.O. (ed.), *Implications of population trends for policy measures in West Africa*, Ghana Population Studies, No. 3, pp. 69-78.

Ajaegbu, H.I. and B.F. Ikusemiju (1970) The distance factor in medical geography: examples from studies in Nigeria, *West Afr. Sci. Assoc. Conf. Paper*, Ibadan, 30th March-4th April.

Anon (1961) The tsetse problem in Northern Nigeria, Printed by Patwa News Agency (E.A.) Ltd., Nairobi, Kenya (Preface by P.E. Glover).

Bassir, O. (1965) Problems of human nutrition in Nigeria, *West Afr. Med. J.*, 14, pp. 54-68.

Bechelli, L.M.: V. Martinez Dominguez; and Patwary K.M. (1966) WHO epidemiology random surveys of leprosy in Northern Nigeria (Katsina) Cameroon & Thailand, *Int. J. Lepr.*, 34, 223.

Chukwumah, P.A.L. (1964) 'Developments in the search for Higher Productivity in Africa', Paper presented to seminar on Manpower Problems in Economic Development with special Reference to Nigeria 22nd-23rd March.

Collis, W.R.F. (1972) Some reflections on the teaching of paediatrics in Nigeria, *Overseas Universities Special Issue on Child Health and Paediatrics*, 18 February, 8-9.

Collis, W.R.F.; Dema, I.S. and Lesi, F.E.A. (1962b) Transverse survey of health and nutrition, Pankshin Division, Northern Nigeria, *West Afr. Med. J.*, 11, pp. 131-154.

Collis, W.R.F.; Dema, I.S. and Omololu, A. (1962a), On the ecology of child health and nutrition in Nigeria villages, *Trop. Geog. Med.*, 14, pp. 140-229.

Dema, I.S. (1963) The nutritional assessment of peasant farming in Nigeria, *Proc. Agric. Soc. Nig.*, 2, pp. 4-18.

Federal Office of Statistics, Nigeria (1967) *Annual abstract of statistics*, Lagos, Table 15.6, p. 166.

Ford, J. (1971) *The role of the trypanosomiasis in African ecology: a study of the tsetse fly* O.U.P.

Gilles, H.M. (1964) *Akufo: An environmental study of a Nigerian village community*, Ibadan Univ. Press.

Harbison, F.H. (1967) A system analysis approach to human resource development planning: Nigeria, *South Atlantic Quarterly*, 66, 3, pp. 341-366.

Hendrickse, R.G. (1966) Some observations on the social background to malnutrition in tropical Africa, *Afr. Affairs*, 65, p. 341.

Hendrickse, R.G. (1967) Social and economic factors in the etiology of malnutrition in Nigeria, *Proceedings of the Joint Congress of the Society of Health, Nigeria and the Nutrition Society of Nigeria*, Zaria, pp. 65-68.

Hills, M.A. (1960) Protein malnutrition in the Western Region of Nigeria, Unpublished M.D. thesis, Univ. of Sheffield.

Hinz, E. (1966) Intestinal helminth infection in West Africa (southern Nigeria), *Z. Troponmed. Parasit.*, 17, p. 427.

Hughes, C.C. and J.M. Hunter (1970) Disease and 'development' in Africa, *Soc. Sci. & Med.* 3, pp. 443-493.

Hunter, J.M. (1967) Seasonal hunger in a part of the West African savanna: a survey of body weight in Nangodi, north-east Ghana, *Trans. Inst. Brit. Geog.*, 41, pp. 167-85.

Janes, M.D. (1968) Report on a growth and development study on Yoruba children in Ibadan, Western Nigeria, *Int. Chrn. Centre, Rev et Conf.*, XIV, pp. 104-9.

Jelliffe, D.B. (1962) Urbanization and child nutrition in Africa, *Int. Child Welfare Rev.*, 16, pp. 67-73.

Lloyd, B.B. (1967) Indigenous Ibadan, in Lloyd, P.C., Mabogunje, A.L. and Awe, B. (ed.), *The city of Ibadan*, C.U.P., pp. 69-70.

Mann, C.E. (1972) Economic and socio-cultural influences on child growth patterns and nutrition levels in Western Nigeria, Study in progress for a Ph.D. thesis of the University of Liverpool.

McLetchie, J.L. (1953) Sleeping sickness activities in 1931-1952, Part I: *W. Afr. Med. J.*, 2, pp. 70-78; Part II: pp. 138-150.

Okediji, F.O. and Aboyade, O. (1967) Social and economic aspects of environmental sanitation in Nigeria: a tentative report based on the study of Ibadan, Lagos, Ilora, Idere and Lekki, *Journ. Soc. Health*, 2, 1, pp. 15-25.

Okonjo, C. (1971) Population dynamics and Nigerian development, Paper presented to the *African Population Conference, Accra, Ghana.*

Okpala, I. (1961) Studies in schistosoma haematobium infection in school children in Epe, Western Nigeria, *West Afr. Med. J.*, 10, p. 402.

Oluwasanmi, H.A. (ed.), (1966) *Uboma: a socio-economic and nutritional survey of rural community in Eastern Nigeria*, Occasional paper of the World Land use survey, No. 6, Bude, England.

Prothero, R.M. (1965) *Migrants and Malaria*, Longman, London.

WHO (1965) *Nutrition and infection: Report of a WHO expert committee*, WHO Tech. Rep. Ser. No. 314.

Social, Economic and
Political Aspects

Introduction

L. Katzen

It is part of my brief in writing this introduction to the following four papers on the social, economic and political aspects of the population factor in African Studies, to try and tie these papers together. While there are some points of complementarity between them, their diversity in both theme and approach suggest relatively few links other than their obvious connection with the broad subject of the conference. I will largely confine myself, therefore, to briefly introducing each paper in turn and presenting the main points of criticism and elaboration that emerged in the discussion that followed.

Dr Goody's paper on 'Population, economy and inheritance in Africa' is not so much a presentation of findings as an outline of an ongoing piece of research to test the hypothesis that differences in population growth rates can be partially explained by a society's preference or lack of preference for children of a particular sex, as expressed in actual behaviour rather than just by attitudes; and that these preferences are connected with the economic role of the sexes and the nature of marriage transactions in these societies, these in their turn being linked, if only indirectly, to the prevailing economic system and resources. Preferences can only manifest themselves if there is a limitation on natural fertility or 'stopping rule' when a particular preference has been achieved. But the point at which this rule comes in to effect will be influenced by the economic and demographic conditions that prevail in different societies.

In these respects there are considerable differences between Africa and the major societies of Europe and Asia. In the latter, sons are preferred because of their role in the rural economy. But, because of limited land, there is a counter-balancing influence not to overproduce sons so as to avoid excessive subdivision of the land. When infant mortality is high, several sons will have to be born to ensure the survival of at least one. Although 'stopping rules' may be submerged at first, they will take effect as population conditions change.

In Africa, on the other hand, economic conditions provide no such limitation. There is little land shortage. The technique of hoe farming is such that one person can only cultivate a limited amount, so there is no surplus of labour in relation to food supply. Therefore, as death rates fall and population growth rates rise, there are no 'stopping rules' to limit growth; one can therefore expect high rates of growth to persist in Africa for longer than in places where there is land shortage and a different system of agricultural production. There is also a stronger tendency towards a balanced sex ratio in Africa than in, say, India. Although African men prefer sons, in general they are reconciled to their daughters as they bring them bridewealth on marriage rather than acting as a drain on resources as in dowry societies. In addition they perform a dominant role in the African agricultural system based on the hoe, as compared with their lesser role in the more advanced plough or irrigation systems in Eurasia.

In the discussion that followed, attention was largely focused on problems connected with proving Dr Goody's hypothesis about sex preference and desired family size. Was his sample large enough or representative enough? How do you determine that people want a family of a particular composition and size? Professor Goody explained that there were a number of ways in which the problem could be tackled. One is by attitudinal studies. While this method was not used in his study, there have been a number of important investigations of this kind in Africa which suggest that, while there is a mild preference for males, couples generally desire an approxima- tely balanced sex ratio in their children. In his study, Professor Goody is trying to get evidence for sex preference or lack of it by analysing the distribution of siblings by sex and order of birth, and the delays between births. The length of period between births is the main means of measuring hesitation, which gives an idea of the decision as to whether or not to have more children. He admitted that there were serious statistical problems in doing this kind of work in Africa because of the unreliability and irregularity of census data, the absence of comprehensive marriage records or of continuous registration of births and deaths; instead he is using a genealogical method. He pointed out, however, that similar problems also exist in India, where considerable work has nevertheless been done in this field.

While Goody's study is aimed at increasing our knowledge about the factors determining the population growth rate in Africa, Smith's paper on 'Trends in Population Policy Making in English-Speaking Sub-Saharan Africa' attempts to explain why there is a general lack of official concern over the fact that sub-Saharan Africa has the highest regional birth-rate in the world and a rate of population growth above the average for the developing world. This is reflected, with a few exceptions, in little official interest or support for, and in some cases open hostility to or even proscription of, population control measures.

The paper was criticised largely for its implicit assumption that a slower rate of growth of the population and therefore population control measures were invariably a 'good thing' under all circumstances. While there is no general agreement on this matter, there is a respectable body of economic thought that regards population growth as a positive stimulus to output growth. This may be particularly the case where, as in most of Africa, countries have small populations with a low density. In 1969, 27 independent African countries had populations of 5 millions or less, with an estimated density per square mile of only 20 to 25 for the whole continent— much lower than for other continents. A small, sparse, poor population with a consequent narrow market puts severe limitations on the scope for industrial development based on import substitution. But, more important, it even restricts highly essential development projects such as the provision of water supplies which are only economical in relatively densely populated areas. Attempts to form wider African regional groupings as a way of increasing market size and the scope for industrialisation have, of course, been made, but these have not as yet proved very successful, and the political realities are such that they are unlikely to make much progress in the near future. In defence of the population controllers, it was pointed out that a high population growth rate increases the dependency ratio, thereby increasing the need to devote scarce resources to things with a long-delayed pay-off period such as education, as against more quickly-yielding directly productive activities.

In his paper on 'Employment and the Growth of Towns', Weeks further develops the thesis which he expounded in his paper to the Sussex Conference on Urban Unemployment in Africa [1971]. In that paper he was critical of the view that looked at the employment/ unemployment problem only in terms of slow growing enumerated employment in the high wage 'modern' sector, neglecting the rapidly growing low income 'traditional' urban sector. He rejects the view that regards the latter sector as underemployed, unproductive or uneconomic. The problem as he sees it is not unemployment, but the unequal distribution of income due to the privileged access of the 'modern' sector to power and resources. In this paper he broadens his attack on 'modernisation theory', which views development as a movement away from traditional, indigenous institutions and attitudes, towards a modern, cash-orientated, labour-committed, Western-type capital intensive economy. Applied specifically to the growth of towns in Africa, he argues that the development rôle of what he calls the 'informal' sector in the towns, with its small scale, indigenous-owned enterprises using mainly local capital and other inputs and simple technology, is largely neglected in the literature. This emphasis on the 'formal' sector with its capital intensive, sophisticated technology sustains the view that Africans (or people in any other developing area) are doomed to indefinite poverty unless they are helped by foreign aid, enterprise and experts and unless they adopt the value systems of advanced countries.

In the discussion Weeks was criticised for exaggerating the neglect of the 'informal' sector. Polly Hill and others had done a considerable amount of work on African entrepreneurship, particularly in West Africa. It was suggested that the impact of colonial policy raised interesting empirical rather than ideological questions. Why, for example in Ghana in the early twentieth century, was a class of successful merchant princes eliminated? To what extent was this a consequence of colonial policy or other influences? In defence of his position Weeks maintained that there were ideological interpretations of economic behaviour taking the opposite standpoint to his own in the literature. Berg, for example, had suggested that there was an historical necessity for forced labour to condition Africans to working in the 'modern' sector.

Doubts were also cast on the assertion in the paper that it was contact with Europe via trade and the indigenous response and adaptation to new economic opportunities in the last 150 years, rather than European control, which was the necessary condition for the transformation of the West African economy. It was pointed out that, in the case of Liberia, where there was a long period of external contact but no control, there was little indigenous response to these opportunities. This suggested that more is involved. There was also some uncertainty as to the policy implications of Weeks' thesis. How were resources to be channelled to the 'informal' sector? Was the inflow of foreign resources to be discouraged? Using the case of Nigeria since World War II, Weeks argued that there had been a net outflow of capital in the form of profits, royalties, overpriced imports etc. This was offset by the inflow of technology, but even here there was increasing scepticism as to the applicability and desirability of much of modern foreign technology for developing countries.

Finally, Margaret Peil's paper on 'Social Life in the Burgeoning Suburbs' contains the preliminary results of a study of social life in what might be called the 'informal' housing sector of several large cities in Ghana and Nigeria. The findings in her paper can be said to complement those of Weeks' paper, not only because a large proportion of the residents of these suburbs are occupied in the 'informal' sector—providing various services and other jobs in the suburb itself—but also because of the picture it presents of neglect by the city—the 'formal' sector—of the suburb and the reactions of the inhabitants to their environment. It is in the suburb, in particular, that life in African cities contrasts sharply with that in contemporary European cities. With the state or local authority providing no social or economic security, people have to rely entirely on relatives and friends for their well-being and assistance with their economic problems.

Note

I am indebted to Mr. S. Patel for his help as rapporteur of the discussion in this session.

Reference

Weeks, J. (1971) *An exploration into the nature of the problem of urban imbalance in Africa*, Conference on Urban Unemployment in Africa, Institute of Development Studies, University of Sussex, September. (unpublished).

Employment and the growth of towns

J. Weeks

Interpretations of Urban Economic Development in Africa

In the 1960's the literature on migration in Africa was dominated by a discussion of labour force 'commitment' [Elkan, 1967; Mitchell, 1959; Hutton, 1970; Gugler, 1969], a concept derived from modernisation theory, which in its crudest form identified an ideal-type 'traditional Africa', undergoing an attitudinal and cultural change from 'tribal' life to 'modern' life. In general, 'tribal' life was judged as enervating and change resistant [Kenya, 1955; Gutkind, 1969], and migration served to instil Western values which would remove the 'dead hand' of traditional culture and foster behaviour patterns consistent with economic development. Thus the move to wage employment was seen implicitly, not only to represent a change in economic status and therefore to be analysed in economic terms, but also to play a much more important role of cultural transformation (indeed, even a *civilizing* role). 'The African' was seen as a being conditioned to values and norms essentially different from those of the ruling white colonists. The 'racialist' interpretation of this was that such norms were inherent, congenital; while the 'liberal' position was that such norms and values were subject to change by careful management of 'the African's' social environment. The most important aspects of the new social environment which would 'modernize' attitudes were urbanisation and wage employment [Sahlin, 1972].

A branch of the economic literature on poor countries emerged to deal with the alleged 'traditionality' of African attitudes—the backward-bending supply curve of effort [Berg, 1961; Vatter, 1961; Gutkind, 1968]. It is important to note that much of the literature on 'commitment' and 'circular migration' derived from the experience of East and Central Africa, and was generalized to an entire continent. As we shall see, this is quite important for, in most of East and Central Africa, there was little pre-colonial urbanisation. In addition, it was in East and Central Africa (particularly Kenya,

Zimbabwe, and Zambia) where the competition over resources between blacks and whites was keenest. In a context of competition for resources (in particular land), the entire 'commitment' discussion provided an ethical and ideological justification for dispossessing local populations of their land. For this dispossession forced wage employment upon the subject peoples at a time when the demand for alienated labour was acute among the white farmers, ranchers, mine-owners and government bureaucrats.

Liberal interpretation of this process of forced change of economic livelihood experienced by local peoples was one of historical necessity, tempered with regret for the sometimes unnecessarily harsh means pursued—land seizure, conscript labour, recruitment through tribal leaders and cash head taxes. The orthodox interpretation can be summarized as follows: initially 'African' wants were limited and aspirations restricted, and coercive measures were required to generate a 'positive' response to wage employment opportunities; however, once exposed to such opportunities and the new consumer goods they allowed, 'the African's' attitude changed quickly and coercive policies became unnecessary [Berg, 1965]. This position has come under sharp attack by Miracle and Fetter [1970], who point out that the supply response changed as a consequence of improved conditions of work. It was not the attitude of 'the African' that accounted for the change from labour shortage to labour surplus, but the gradual elimination of inhumane work conditions and the raising of wage rates.

The point is further underlined by conditions in West Africa [Weeks, 1971a]. Here labour migration for cash income long pre-dated colonial rule. In the nineteenth century the availability of slave labour inhibited the development of wage labour, but men still migrated long distances to seek employment as traders, craftsmen, farmers and soldiers. Yet in the 1890's British bureaucrats and businessmen in Lagos complained of a labour shortage and attributed it to 'the African's' cultural or racial characteristics. In fact, as Hopkins has shown [Hopkins, 1966; Weeks, 1972a], the shortage was due to low wages and appalling working conditions. The migrants simply preferred the rural work to that provided by Europeans, and quite rationally. In West Africa the 'labour commitment' problem was never taken seriously at an official level [Weeks, 1971a], and appears rarely in the academic literature on the area. Similarly, 'the transition to the money economy', a process of alleged paramount importance in East and Central Africa, has had little prominence in the literature on West Africa, except marginally in ethnographic studies.

Whether or not the ideal-type conceptualization of tribal societies moving from 'subsistence' to 'cash' economies is useful as an interpretation of colonial rule elsewhere, it certainly is not in West

Africa, where the 'cash' economy (and its resultant division and specialization of labour tasks) long preceded the imposition of any significant degree of European-owned economic activity. This is an important point, and may be relevant to East Africa as well. It implies that, if in some sense West Africa has become 'modernized' (in the sense of behavioural changes in economic dealings) in the last 150 years, it occurred through indigenous *response and adaptation* to the emergence of new economic opportunities, not as a consequence of European business organization taking the lead and indigenous peoples becoming 'modernized' as a consequence of contact with these organisations. In brief, trade transformed the West African economy, not Europeans.

If one believes that it was Western rule of Africa which, by 'opening up' the continent to Western capitalist enterprise, transformed the economic system from one of traditional stagnation to modern dynamism, then it follows that foreign economic control was basically a good thing, despite rather appalling filibustering and robber-baron tactics. Thus one can conclude that the angels of modernisation chose some rather unsavory agents to execute their good works. However, if one believes that there was emerging in many parts of Africa in the 18th and 19th centuries (particularly in Ghana and Nigeria) indigenous responses to the growth of world trade which were innovative, adaptive and dynamic, then the long run favorable impact of European economic control in Africa (as opposed to European trade) is in serious doubt. This latter interpretation implies that European enterprises *replaced* local entrepreneurs within Africa. For example, the amalgamation of European trading firms after World War I in Nigeria, stimulated by the fall in the volume of trade in the 1930's, led to a substantial decline in the role of Nigerians in the import-export commerce [Bauer, 1954; Bowers *et al*, 1947; Colonial Office, 1938; Gavin, 1972]. Further, this analysis implies that the extension of European control over trade and commerce in West Africa did not represent a 'modernizing' process, but the conceptually much more straightforward process of transferring control of lucrative trade from local to foreign hands [cf. Baran, 1961]. If we define indigenous economic activity and behaviour as 'traditional', this implies that European economic domination was a necessary ingredient for economic growth, which pre-judges the role of foreign enterprise.

The relevance of the nature of development to the current situation

The objection might be raised that, whether or not the analysis of the previous section is correct, it is of historical interest only. The conditions of labour shortage of previous decades have given way to labour surplus throughout black Africa. What point is there in resurrecting the issues? The point lies in the fact that the traditional-modern analysis (and its 'transition from subsistence to cash economy'), in which the motive force of economic change is Western economic penetration of African economies, is still social scientific orthodoxy, particularly in the literature in English. The emphasis on 'commitment' and 'transition to the cash economy' represents historically specific applications of the general thesis that economic development only occurs under Western political and economic domination. At present, the specific application of this thesis lies in its analysis of indigenous entrepreneurial development and innovative adaptation. The 1970's analogy of 'labour commitment' is the treatment of the indigenous non-agricultural sector of African economies. Within the traditional-modern political economy analysis this has become defined as a 'traditional' sector—among economists it is a vogue to identify it as the 'traditional urban' sector [Todaro, 1969].

Presented in a context of analyzing unemployment and 'under-employment' [Myrdal, 1968], the new message is the same as the old one—indigenous enterprise, using indigenous techniques, skills and capital, and catering to indigenous demands for goods and services, is 'traditional' and 'backward'. Such enterprise is seen as harbouring unproductive and inefficient labour; the 'urban traditional' sector is inherently unable to survive the 'modernisation' of the economy; and the basis of economic growth must be imported modern techniques, which (unfortunately perhaps) will be foreign-owned. Again, as in the case of coercion into wage employment, such foreign control is regretted by progressive-minded social scientists, but they argue that foreign involvement is a value-free necessity for economic 'modernisation'. This analysis concludes that the choices are clear-cut: foreign involvement and economic development, or exclusion of foreigners and perpetual poverty [Gutkind, 1969]. This argument represents a quite effective flanking attack against those who see Westernisation and foreign domination as the *cause* of underdevelopment. Detrimental effects of foreign investment become irrelevant or ideological, for foreign investment is the *necessary condition* for economic development. The only course of action open to the ruling groups in poor countries, if they want 'progress', is to try to bring in foreign investment on the best terms possible. Any attempt to rely primarily on indigenous sources of economic growth ' . . . is a doctrine designed to achieve a take-off into sustained poverty' [Myrdal, 1968]. It is important to stress that this ideological position maintains that it is not only *Western values and technology* that modernize, but also that *Westerners,* through corporate business organization and colonial rule, are the agents of this modernising process. To put the argument in its crudest form: if Africa had not fallen to European conquest and thus been opened to exploitation by European (and later American and Japanese) business interests, the continent would still be economically and socially in the stone age.

An understanding of this ideological position is a pre-requisite for any intelligent analysis of urbanisation in Africa. Sense cannot be made of the literature on 'unemployment' in Africa without first realising the ideology behind the conceptual categories employed in this literature. To say that African cities are characterized by widespread unemployment and underemployment 'outside the modern sector', is not a description of reality, but a disguised statement that economic development is the consequence of Western economic control.

This ideological statement couched as an empirical description comes out most clearly in the work of Frank, ' . . . the rate of under- and unemployment [in urban areas of Africa] can be inferred by comparing modern sector urban employment with estimates of the labour force . . . ' [Frank, 1971]. 'Modern sector' in this context means *measured* employment, and in Africa this means government and foreign enterprise. Once this point is realised, the absurdity of the approach is revealed: African economies are 'traditional' and 'backward' to the extent that economic activity is African. It is not valid to object on the grounds that over time 'modern' enterprise will move into African hands as entrepreneurial skills are developed [Marris and Somerset, 1971], capital markets emerge, and so on. Experience in Latin America refutes this argument. Not surprisingly, the inflow of foreign investment into Latin America has not generated indigenous entrepreneurship to a degree that it challenges the foreigner for control; the inflow of foreign investment has achieved its obvious goal—a growing degree of control over the local economy [Baer and Maneschi, 1971; Morley and Smith, 1971]. Barring a sweeping programme of nationalisation, which may not achieve the desired end, the inflow of foreign capital leads to foreign control of the economy.

Development and urbanisation

The analysis of the previous two sections allows us to move toward an analytical framework for understanding the growth of cities in Africa. I have sought to cut through the ideological terminology which characterizes most of the literature [but cf. Oshima, 1971] in order to derive useful generalisations. The analysis, arguably like all social scientific theory, incorporates certain value premises and assumptions. The most important assumption, which is probably not subject to verification, is the following: the various African peoples who came into forced contact with Europeans in the last one hundred years were in no significant way less amenable to innovation and alteration of norms and behaviour patterns than the Europeans themselves. Briefly, this means that African workers, traders, farmers, etc, did not need *to be changed,* but were fully capable of changing themselves to new conditions. It is fully recognised that this prejudges many specific steps in the analysis; for example, it follows that no external agent (as opposed to an external stimulus such as trade) was necessary to bring about economic progress. Our analysis implies from the outset that European economic domination was not the consequence of 'modernity' but of power.

With this general framework in mind, we can distinguish at least two significantly different urbanisation situations arising from colonial rule. The first might be called European urban transformation, referring to the situation wherein foreign bureaucracy and enterprise were imposed on a pre-colonial urban area and, by its control, transformed the process of urbanisation; and the second, European urban creation, wherein urban areas grew up in colonial times. Examples of the former would be Lagos, Ibadan and Kano in Nigeria (these being only the most important), Mombasa in Kenya, Zanzibar in Tanzania, and most of the cities in North Africa. Examples of the second would be Jos and Port Harcourt in Nigeria, Nairobi in Kenya, Lusaka in Zambia, and Dar es Salaam in Tanzania. The first type of colonial urbanisation is more characteristic of West and North Africa (though not exclusively so), and the latter of East and Central Africa.

The distinction is important for, in the former case, colonial urbanisation proceeded in a context in which the indigenous labour force possessed a tradition (sometimes centuries old) of urban craftsmanship, commercial expertise, and entrepreneurial skills. In such situations, Africans and Europeans came into direct conflict in trade, particularly in import-export commerce. The failure of indigenous entrepreneurs to dominate the export-import trade and other new economic opportunities was not the consequence of 'traditional' norms and values, but the lack of access to colonial administrative favours and international financing institutions, and the inability to establish links with shipping enterprises. In such a situation, European business enterprise did not 'modernize' the economy, but restricted the commercial fields into which indigenous businessmen could operate. For the craftsmen and traders in urban areas operating for the domestic market, the impact of European economic control was less directly harmful. The importation of certain consumer goods no doubt virtually wiped out some crafts, but others flourished and continue to flourish, catering to the consumption needs of the growing low income population.

Where Europeans created urban areas, the historical process was somewhat different. This case is complicated by the fact that in some areas it was intended that the new cities would be white settlements, and the African was at best tolerated in his own land [see Van Zwanenberg, 1972]. In other cases (Port Harcourt, Dar es Salaam, and Kaduna) it was only intended that Europeans would control the strategic economic activities, and that the towns would be essentially African in population and culture. In the case of European-created urban areas there was obviously no urban craft or commercial tradition in the immediate area and, in East and Central Africa, none among the migrants who came to populate the cities. Thus, in East Africa, Asians filled the economic niches occupied by Africans in West Africa. It is in these areas where no urban tradition existed, with its associated diversity of economic roles, that the growth of indigenous enterprise is most impressive. The example of Nairobi is instructive. At the time of the 1962 census, those engaged in small African-run enterprises were probably not more than a few thousand, yet by 1970, small African enterprises provided employment for almost 40,000 men and women [I.L.O., 197?].

But in both situations a *dual* urban economy has emerged, which can be described in terms of *formal* and *informal* sectors [Hart, 1971; I.L.O., 1972; Weeks, 1972; Remy and Weeks, 1972]. On the one hand, a large-scale, foreign owned sector developed, financed by overseas capital, using imported, adopted technology and drawing on few local inputs other than labour. This sector at first was almost exclusively involved in the import-export trade, but in recent years has increasingly developed along import-substitution lines catering for an elite market [Weeks, 1971b, 1972c]. The sector was never competitive, always relying on state favours for monopoly profits. But with the switch to import-substitution, this has become increasingly the case. Tariffs, quotas, operating licences, and partial state ownership [Cooper, 1970, *inter alia*] have all served to restrict competition. It is a misnomer to identify foreign enterprise as being in the 'private' sector [Stewart, 1971], for this implies that operations occur in the context of impersonal market forces. This, in turn, suggests that, in response to changed economic conditions, economic agents must respond by adjusting economic variables—cutting or raising prices, altering input combinations to achieve minimum unit costs, and so on. Because of their relationship with government, foreign enterprise has other resources in the face of profit squeezing economic change. Enterprises can petition for increased tariffs or decreased quotas on competitive imports, liberalisation of regulations on transfer pricing and profit remittance, and tax reduction through accelerated depreciation allowances, tax 'holidays', and so on. The essence of 'formality' lies in the enterprise's relation to the state. Formal sector capitalist enterprises pursue economic goals by employing political means.

The *informal sector* in urban areas, on the other hand,

comprises operations which are small-scale and indigenously owned, financed from local capital, using largely indigenously developed or *adapted* technology and a high proportion of local inputs. These are *characteristics* which are the consequence of informality, and informality is the consequence of a lack of access to state favours. Markets are unregulated, so competition is keen. The absence of tariff and quota protection precludes the earning of monopoly profits except briefly, when combined with freedom of entry into the market.

The relationship between formal capitalist enterprise and informal enterprise can be seen by reference to an ecological analogy. Formal enterprise expands and becomes predominant in those lines of commerce, finance, transport, and manufacturing when their competitive advantages are strategic. Informal sector enterprise then must adapt itself to the remaining economic 'niches'. But our ecological analogy is not complete because, in an eco-system, an organism comes to dominate a zone or niche as a consequence of natural competitive advantages which are the result of natural selection. In the case of formal capitalist enterprise, competitive advantages are bestowed as a consequence of the power relationships in the economy. Strategic resources are scarce, and formal capitalist enterprise has privileged access to these resources, not because it uses them more efficiently, but because of access to the state, which acts as a 'gatekeeper' [Somerset, 1971]. The most important of these strategic resources are foreign exchange and financial capital. Both can be rationed by the state through the financial system. In economic activities where foreign exchange or financial capital are strategic to successful operation, formal capitalist enterprise reigns supreme.

I have not sought to glorify what has been called the 'informal sector'. It is modernisation theory which has embarked upon glorification, explaining the growth of capital-intensive Western enterprises in terms of some mystic dynamics arising from 'modernity', rather than in terms of the competitive advantages such enterprises have obtained from the state bureaucracies in countries in which they operate.

As should be clear from the foregoing discussion, like modernisation analysis, our sectoral division is based on the 'kingpin' of our analysis. In modernisation theory behavioural patterns and value systems play this role. In our analysis it is *economic power* which determines the role of economic success and pre-eminence, and the institution through which both economic power is secured and expansion of economic control is facilitated is the state. Thus *informal* sector enterprises, once they grow relatively large, seek to achieve *formality*; i.e. they seek to establish a symbiotic relationship with the state.

Conclusion

The analysis of the previous sections allows us to describe concisely the pattern of urbanisation in Africa. Under conditions of foreign economic control, the population of many cities has grown rapidly. Employment has also grown rapidly, and most immigrants find work [Killick, 1966; Nigeria, 1970; Ray, 1966; Clignet, 1969; Kenya, 1968-9]. But because of differential access to resources, a dual economic structure has emerged. High-wage,formal sector employment has grown rapidly. The problem inherent in this type of urban development is not unemployment, nor short-time working [I.L.O., 1972], but the distribution of income. This problem is itself a consequence of differential access to resources.

The traditional-modern analysis misunderstands the nature of employment in the process of urbanisation because it attributes income differences in the urban area to some dichotomy in behaviour patterns among the poor and the rich [Weeks, 1970]. As we have tried to show, pseudo-scientific analysis serves primarily to whitewash the fundamental reality of urbanisation—privileged access to strategic resources.

The traditional-modern analysis is, however, more pernicious than merely diverting attention from fundamental reality. Its ultimate message is that Africans or Asians or Latin Americans cannot develop their own economies. They require Western enterprises, Western experts, and, above all, Western values. This doctrine is profoundly elitist, for its deeper message is that poor people cannot develop themselves, for they lack the values, motivation and Western acquisitiveness—they are 'traditional'. They must be developed from above through development 'plans'.

I have sought to argue that the traditional-modern dichotomy is analytically impotent, that what it seeks to explain it does so poorly, and that the same phenomena can be explained in a much more straight-forward way—in terms of access to resources.

References

Baer, W. and Maneschi, A. (1971) 'Import Substitution, Stagnation, and Structural Change: An Interpretation of the Brazilian Case', *Journal of Developing Areas* (January).

Baran, P. (1961) *The Political Economy of Growth* (New York: Monthly Review Press).

Bauer, P.T. (1954) *West African Trade* (London: Routledge and Kegan Paul).

Berg, E.J. (1961) 'Backward Sloping Labor Supply Functions in Dual Economies—the African Case', *The Quarterly Journal of Economics* LXXV.

Berg, E.J. (1965) 'The Development of a Labor Force in Subsaharan Africa', *Economic Development and Cultural Change* 12, 4 (July).

Bowers, P.A. *et al.* (1947) *Mining Commerce and Finance in Nigeria* (London: Faber and Faber).

Clignet, R. (1969) 'Preliminary Notes on a Study of Unemployment in Modern African Urban Centres', *Manpower and Unemployment Research in Africa* 2, 1 (April).

Colonial Office (1938) *Cocoa Marketing Commission Report* (London: H.M.S.O.).

Cooper, C. (1970) *The Mechanisms for Transfer of Technology from Advanced to Developing Countries*, MS., Science Policy Research Unit, University of Sussex (November).

Elkan, W. (1967) 'Circular Migration and the Growth of Towns in East Africa', *International Labour Review* (December).

Frank, C.R., jr. (1971) 'The Problem of Urban Unemployment in Africa, in R.G. Ridker and H. Lubell (eds.) *Employment and Unemployment Problems in the Near East and South Asia* (Delhi: Vikas Publications)

Gavin, R. (1972) 'A History of Economic Development in Nigeria', MS.

Gugler, J. (1969) 'The Impact of Labour Migration on Society and Economy in Sub-Saharan Africa', *African Social Research* 6 (December).

Gutkind, P.C.W. (1968) 'African Responses to Wage Employment', *International Labour Review* 97, 2 (February)

Gutkind, P.C.W. (1969) 'Traditional Urbanisation, Modernity and Unemployment in Africa: the Roots of Instability', *Canadian Journal of African Studies* 3, 2 (Spring).

Hart, K. (1971) 'Informal Income Opportunities and the Structure of Employment in Ghana', paper presented to the *Conference on Urban Unemployment in Africa, September, (Institute for Development Studies, Brighton)*.

Hopkins, A.G. (1966) 'The Lagos Strike of 1897: an exploration in Nigerian labour history', *Past and Present* XXXV.

Hutton, Caroline (1970) 'The Causes of Labour Migration', in J. Gugler, (ed.) *Urbanisation in Sub-Saharan Africa* (Kampala).

I.L.O. (1972) *Employment, Incomes and Equality: A Strategy for Increasing Productive Employment in Kenya* (Geneva: ILO).

I.L.O. (1973) *Employment, Incomes and Equality: A Programme for Increasing Productive Employment in Kenya* (Geneva: ILO, forthcoming) Vol. 2.

Kenya (1955) Colony and Protectorate of Kenya, *Report of the Committee on African Wages* (Nairobi, 1955), pp. 11-12.

Kenya (1968-69) *Urban Household Survey, Nairobi, Mombasa and Kisumu* (unpublished)

Killick, T. (1966) 'Labour: A General Survey', in Walter Birmingham, *et al* (eds.) *A Study of Contemporary Ghana* (London: George Allen and Unwin).

Miracle, M., and Fetter, B. (1970) 'Backward-sloping Labor-supply Functions and African Economic Behavior', *Economic Development and Cultural Changes* 18, 2 (January).

Mitchell, J.C. (1959) 'The Causes of Labour Migration', *Inter-African Labour Institute Bulletin* VI, 1.

Morley, S. and Smith, G. (1971) 'Import Substitution and Foreign Investments in Brazil', *Oxford Economic Papers* (March).

Marris, P., and Somerset, A. (1971) *African Businessmen: A Study of Entrepreneurship and Development in Kenya* (London: Routledge and Kegan Paul.)

Myrdal, G. (1968) *Asian Drama* (New York: Pantheon).

Nigeria (1970) *Second National Development Plan, 1970-74* (Lagos).

Oshima, H.T. (1971) 'Labor-Force Explosion and the Labor-intensive Sector in Asian Growth', *Economic Development and Cultural Change* 19, 2 (January).

Ray, R. (1966) *Labour Force Survey of Tanzania,* mimeo (Dar es Salaam).

Remy, D. and Weeks, J. (1972) *Employment and Inequality in a Non-Industrial City* (forthcoming).

Sahlin, M. (1972) *Stone Age Economics* (Chicago: Aldine-Atherton).

Somerset, A. (1971) 'Education Aspirations of Fourth Form Pupils in Kenya', paper presented to the *Conference on Urban Unemployment in Africa, Institute for Development Studies (Brighton),* September.

Stewart, F. (1971) For more on this see 'Appropriate Intermediate or Inferior Economics (Review Article)', *Journal of Development Studies* 7, 3 (April).

Todaro, M.P. (1969) 'A Model of Labour Migrant and Urban Unemployment in Less Developed Countries', *American Economic Review* LIX, 1 (March).

Van Zwanenberg, R. (1972) Paper presented to a *Seminar at the Institute for Development Studies (Nairobi),* April.

Vatter, H.G. (1961) 'On the Folklore of the Backward-sloping Supply Curve', *Industrial and Labor Relations Review* XIV.

Weeks, J. (1970) 'Uncertainty, Risk, and Wealth and Income Distribution in Peasant Agriculture', *Journal of Development Studies* VII, 1.

Weeks, J. (1971a) 'Wage Policy and the Colonial Legacy—A Comparative Study', *The Journal of Modern African Studies* 9, 3, pp. 361-387.

Weeks, J. (1971b) 'Does Employment Matter?', *Manpower and Unemployment Research in Africa* 4, 1 (April).

Weeks, J. (1972a) 'Impact of Economic and Institutional Forces on Urban Real Wages in Nigeria', *Nigerian Journal of Economic and Social Studies.* (forthcoming).

Weeks, J. (1972b) *Factors Determining the Growth of Output and Employment in the Labour Intensive Sector in Poor Countries,* MS.

Weeks, J. (1972c) 'Employment, Growth and Foreign Domination in Underdeveloped Countries', *The Review of Radical Political Economics* IV, 1 (Spring).

Trends in population policy making in English-speaking sub-Saharan Africa

T. E. Smith

Introduction

Although sub-Saharan Africa has the highest regional birth rate in the world and has a rate of population growth rather higher than the average for the less developed countries, there has been a relative lack of concern in the region with rapid population growth as a factor impeding development. This paper starts by describing a selection of views on population growth in the English-speaking countries of the region in the 1960's, and then attempts to gauge the extent to which the governments of these countries are moving towards decisions to make real attempts to control the natural rate of growth of population through fertility reduction.

On Human Rights Day, December 10, 1966, U Thant, then the Secretary-General of the United Nations, issued a Declaration on Population signed by the heads of state of twelve countries. This Declaration recognised that family planning was in the vital interest of both the nation and the family, and stated that the opportunity to decide the number and spacing of children was a basic human right. A year later the Declaration was signed by eighteen additional heads of state. Of the entire group of thirty signatories, only four were African heads of state, and three of these four were North African—President Nasser of Egypt, President Bourguiba of Tunisia, and King Hassan of Morocco. The solitary head of state from sub-Saharan Africa was General Ankrah, who in December 1967 was Chairman of the National Liberation Council of Ghana.

Population programmes: reasons for African reluctance.

Why, it must be asked, was Tropical Africa so poorly represented among the signatories of this Declaration? And why is it that, even in 1972, African governments are so hesitant about developing national family planning programmes when in Asia all the independent

157

countries of the Commonwealth have such programmes, as do Jamaica, Trinidad and Barbados in the Caribbean? A number of factors must be taken into consideration in trying to find the answers to these questions.

In the first place, there can be no doubt that the opinion has been and still is widely held in Tropical Africa that the region is underpopulated and needs a larger population quickly. To take a few examples of this attitude, the Tanzania Minister for Economic Affairs and Development Planning, commenting in 1968 on census results which showed that the population of the country had increased by over one-third between 1957 and 1967, stated that Tanzania was underpopulated and had room for millions more, though his Government had not set an 'ideal optimum number'. In neighbouring Kenya, the Royal Commission which did its work in the mid nineteen-fifties had discounted concern about the rate of population growth, arguing that East Africa was sparsely populated and that a growing population was a pre-requisite to the full use of the area's resources. Fifteen years later, despite the fact that Kenya had by that time an official family planning programme, the Minister of Health was asked by an MP whether he would ban the use of contraceptives in view of the fact that Kenya was under-populated and that large tracts of land were uninhabited [Daily Nation, 1970]. And in 1967 Oginga Odinga had argued his opposition to family planning for Kenya, stating that the Government should encourage people to have as many children as possible in order to increase the proportion of black people in the world's population. On the other side of the continent, former President Nkrumah of Ghana supported the belief, widely held at the time, that socialist economies could benefit from rapid population growth, and he pressed the 1965 Population Advisory Committee to accept the desirability of reaching a figure of 20 million for the population of Ghana as rapidly as possible [Caldwell, personal communication].

A further factor militating against the acceptance of population policies dependent in part on the development of family planning programmes has been the important role which Roman Catholic politicians and leaders of public opinion have played (and continue to play) in the countries of Tropical Africa. In the French-speaking countries of sub-Saharan Africa, the legislation passed in France in 1920 forbidding the dissemination of contraceptive propaganda effectively prevented the formation of family planning associations in the former French colonies, and, although new and more permissive legislation was approved in France in 1969, the old law still remains on the statute books of many of the African Francophone countries. In the English-speaking countries of the region, the Catholic Church's opposition to family planning does not carry quite the same weight, but it was noticeable that such an outstanding politician as Tom

Mboya was clearly affected by the publication of *Humanae Vitae* and took the view after its release that Kenya's rapid rate of population growth was not a source of alarm to the Government, in contrast to his earlier stress on the economic arguments for initiating a national family planning programme.

Even when politicians, civil servants and other members of the establishment accept in principle the thesis that a large excess of births over deaths, with a consequently high natural rate of growth of population, does give rise to difficult social and economic problems, whatever the density of population on the ground, there is frequently an understandable unwillingness to initiate the kind of population policy which might ultimately help to provide solutions. Except in urban areas, few Africans are convinced of the desirability of small families, and politicians are concerned with the opinions of those who can make or break them, whatever may be the route to political power. Decisions to attempt to control immigration can pay immediate political dividends—not so decisions to attempt to control fertility. There is a time-lag of a good many years between the start of a reduction in the birth rate and a let-up in the difficulties involved in rapid population growth. For instance, the rate of growth of the labour force is not immediately affected by changes in the birth rate.

It is not only in Africa that politicians have been indecisive about tackling the problems of rapid population growth, even when coupled with high population density. Ceylon and Mauritius can be cited as examples of countries within the Commonwealth where such indecision has been marked until very recently. Only a few outstanding politicians in less developed countries have been willing to assert consistent leadership in the field of population policy in the last decade or two.

Population programmes: acceptance in Africa

As in other continents, it has been the voluntary family planning associations which have demonstrated that there *is* a demand among local people for the information and their materials which enable them to control the size of their families. By 1971 most of the English-speaking countries of tropical Africa had such associations, including Gambia, Ghana, Kenya, Liberia, Nigeria, Sierre Leone, Tanzania, Uganda, and Zambia. Tropical African countries without any such associations, apart from the former French colonies, included Malawi and, within Tanzania, Zanzibar, and in each the governments in power totally reject the desirability of any form of birth control. In Malawi, President Banda has publicly expressed opposition to population control, and the government does not allow dissemination of family planning advice or propaganda by public or private agencies. In Zanzibar, the local Government banned all contraceptives in March 1967 and, according to the *Daily Telegraph* of 20 January 1970, 'anyone found guilty of performing an abortion will face the death penalty'. In African conditions, the scale of operation of a voluntary family planning association cannot be such as to provide services to more than a very small percentage of the population, and government intervention is required if there is to be any intention of trying to provide a family planning programme on something approaching a nation-wide basis.

Where national family planning programmes have been initiated in tropical Africa, the decisions have been taken by the planners on economic grounds. In Kenya, the Government in 1965 commissioned the Population Council to produce a report for its guidance before a decision in principle was reached. The report, *Family Planning in Kenya*, was published in 1967, and Tom Mboya persuaded the Government to accept its main recommendations although, since then, the national family planning programme has nearly foundered on at least one occasion. The existence of the programme does not appear, as yet, to have led to slower population increase, and services are at present provided for the most part by teams led by expatriates working in Kenya under the auspices of the International Planned Parenthood Federation and other donor organisations.

In 1969 Ghana became the second Tropical African country to start a family planning programme, the report *Population Planning for National Prosperity and Parenthood: Ghana Population Policy* having recommended restrictions on immigration and reduced internal migration from rural to urban areas, as well as a planned reduction in the birth rate. The Ghana programme appears to have received more full-hearted backing from the administration than the Kenya programme, but has not yet developed the large-scale support among the general population which is needed if fertility is to be reduced significantly. Nigeria decided in 1970 to develop national or state family planning programmes within the period covered by the Second National Development Plan [Nigeria, 1970], but this appears still to be a statement of intent rather than an accomplished fact. Other governments in sub-Saharan Africa to provide financial and other forms of assistance for family planning for black Africans include Rhodesia and South Africa, but there the motive for such government support is more a wish to prevent the proportion of whites in the population falling than the developmental considerations which motivated the creation of such programmes elsewhere [Caldwell, 1970].

Role of population programmes in Africa

It seems reasonable to postulate that a growing number of Tropical

African countries will develop family planning programmes in the current decade. Botswana, for instance, is moving in this direction. Mainland Tanzania is now providing facilities in some of its government clinics. Many international organisations, including the Economic Commission for Africa, the United Nations Fund for Population Activities, and the World Bank are beginning to stress the need for such programmes. Nevertheless, it is difficult to conceive of any sub-Saharan African programme developing both the mass capability and the mass appeal to have much effect on the fertility rate in the next few years. The few really successful national family planning programmes in Asia spend more money and employ more medical and para-medical personnel per head of population than is feasible in any African country, and political and religious opposition to such programmes in Asia has now been largely overcome. In the meantime, there is still plenty of scope for mortality decline in tropical Africa and, therefore, a likelihood of an even more rapid rate of growth of population than the continent is experiencing at present. Africa therefore stands in contrast to Asian and Latin American regions of the developing world for, in respect of the latter, there is reason to believe that the peak rate of growth of population has been reached, or has even been passed.

National family planning programmes form, of course, merely one of several types of population policy. Virtually all African governments now restrict immigration, and even eject immigrants of several years' standing, to the detriment of relations with their international neighbours. Many African governments favour, in principle, the diminution of the volume of internal migration to the towns, though only the East African Anglophone countries and the Francophone countries appear to have taken practical steps to control residence in urban areas. The trends and prospects for levels of urbanisation and the proportion of the population living in urban areas are, however, important, not merely from a distributional point of view, but also because the urban population in English-speaking countries is certain to be more highly motivated to restrict family size and will have contraceptive services more readily available than people in the rural areas. Hence, the higher the future level of urbanisation, the lower the anticipated rate of population growth, high though this rate is certain to be for several decades.

Public health programmes can also be regarded as a form of population policy, in so far as the more money that is spent on public health (efficiency and other factors being ignored) the lower the death rate is likely to be. Most African Governments do, in fact, spend a relatively high proportion of their budgets on public health, but in absolute terms the expenditure per capita is very low. For this reason, and also because of the difficult organisational problems involved in providing medical and health services in the rural areas of developing countries with poor communications, the reduction in the death rates in tropical Africa may prove to be less spectacularly rapid than has been the case in the more prosperous developing countries of Asia and Latin America in the last two or three decades. Nevertheless, death rates in Africa seem likely to fall gradually, whereas birth rates cannot be expected to be reduced by more than a point or two in the next few years. The inevitable conclusion is that, even if a much larger number of African governments accept the need for national family planning programmes during the current decade, the population of tropical Africa will grow very rapidly for a good many years to come—almost certainly for the remainder of the century.

References

Caldwell, J.C. (1970) 'The Demographer and Political Intervention to Change Population Growth Rates', paper presented to *Population Council Conference*, October 1970.

Daily Nation, May 19, 1970. References provided by Mr David Radel of the East-West Communication Institute, Hawaii.

Federal Republic of Nigeria. *Second National Development Plan, 1970-1974*, pp. 77-78.

Population, economy and inheritance in Africa

J. R. Goody

Introduction

The *Guardian* of June 3, 1972, carried a report of the trial of Mr. Gurdial Singh Sahota who was sentenced to imprisonment for obtaining money by deception, having sold a herbal medicine reputed to make pregnant women give birth to boys. So sure was he of the success of his product that he offered to pay the Judge's return fare to India so that he could see how successful the medicine was.

The demand for products of this kind reflects a widely reported preference for male children. Gini's seminal study, *Il Sesso del Punto di Vista Statistico (Sex from a Statistical Point of View),* begins with the words 'Health and male children is the salutation with which the wedding party takes its leave of the young couple, who go out to meet new trials in life' [1908:3]. Williamson [1965] summarizes reports on similar attitudes in different parts of the world.

Population and the preferred sex of children

The population growth rate is directly affected by the question of the choice of sex of children. If a society displays a tendency, weak or strong, to prefer say two males or two females, then the average family size will inevitably be greater than if those parents remained content with whatever two children the lottery of birth prescribed for them. There will be a greater number of children, too, than if a balance is the aim, in that (assuming an equal ratio of men and women) there are twice as many chances of getting a combination of one male and one female as of getting two males or two females.

Preferences for a particular combination obviously have a much wider significance than a purely numerical one. They have significance for the organisation of labour; they have social and psychological importance for those sexes that are favoured and for those

163

that are disfavoured; they may positively or negatively affect the chances for survival of one sex or another.

We can test for the presence of a preference for a particular sex in a number of ways, of which the most obvious is by the questionnaire or interview. However, the method is less simple than at first appears since in many societies preference will vary (i) as between men and women, (ii) with the age of the respondent, and (iii) with the existing holding of offspring. Taking these factors into account, there are also clear differences between 'ideal' (or, better, 'stated') preferences and achieved family size. For example, the discrepancy is very marked in Puerto Rico, where widespread acceptance of a small family ideal is associated both with high fertility and also with favourable attitudes towards birth control [Hill *et al.* 1959:2]. Similar situations exist in Africa. Cauldwell reports that members of the Ghanaian elite recommend smaller families to others than they have themselves [1968:27, 83, 89]. Partly for this reason, the research in which I am currently engaged is not primarily concerned with 'attitudes'. In any case, the cross-cultural information on these has recently been summarized by Nancy E. Williamson [1968], who included sub-Saharan Africa among the areas displaying a 'moderate' preference for sons.

Instead, we have tried to collect evidence for preferences or aversions by analyzing the distribution of uterine siblings by sex and order of birth. If preferences are to manifest themselves in the birth of children, then they can only do so when a limitation on natural fertility exists, i.e. where one finds a 'stopping rule', a tendency to stop having children after some combinations rather than others.

This enquiry was not simply designed to elicit information on the possible existence of such rules, but was based on a hypothesis about the nature of African societies. Much of the literature about attitudes to family composition in societies throughout the world has claimed·that a strong preference is expressed for males, especially in North Africa and India. Not only are attitudinal preferences strong, but there is some evidence from India that this preference for males also manifests itself in the composition of sibling groups [1]. The strong preference for males is associated with the male contribution to the rural labour force. In most societies in Asia and Europe, it is a son who is going to take over responsibility for running the household as well as for running the farm itself. It is he who will provide for the parents in old age, as the daughter is likely to marry out and thus not be available to give such support [2]. In many African societies, however, it is women who do much of the farming. It has been argued that, because of their role in hoe agriculture, they are especially valuable to men, who attempt to accumulate them in polygynous marriage. However this may be, by farming and trading, women make a considerable contribution to the livelihood of the family in traditional societies, and hence it would be interesting to see whether the same preference for males emerged from a study of sibling groups in Africa, despite the different form of the division of labour.

Of course the preference for sons is not only connected with economic problems. The worship of ancestors is largely carried out by and for men, and therefore it is important to have a male offspring (or a nephew) in order that one may be worshipped after death. At LoDagaa and Tallensi funerals, men are treated very differently depending on whether they have sons to survive them [Goody 1962; Fortes 1949]. Does this differ in matrilineal societies where it could be argued that, to provide for the continuity of the lineage, a sister is more important than a son? We are trying to test this hypothesis by collecting data from matrilineal and patrilineal societies in order to see whether there is any tendency for different combinations of uterine siblings to be associated with these two types of society [3].

As I have noted, the evidence for the translation of attitude preference into action, as reflected in the actual constitution of sibling groups, is related to a restriction upon natural fertility. That is to say, unless there is a tendency to stop after certain combinations, the result will be a random distribution of siblings, if we assume that the sex of successive siblings is independently determined. The main hypothesis to be tested is related to differences in the economy as between Africa on the one hand and the major societies of Europe and Asia on the other. In the latter societies, where sons are preferred, there is clearly a danger of the over-production of heirs. Given a limited amount of land at the disposal of the family, the production of more than one son means the search for an alternative occupation or the subdivision of the holding [4]. Consequently the preference for sons is likely to be counter-balanced by the pressure to avoid too many. Under conditions of high infant mortality, the definition of too many sons is difficult to determine. It has been estimated that, where mortality is high, a couple may have to have 4-5 live-born sons to ensure that even one will survive to adult life [5].

While this is true under conditions of high infant mortality, the existence of 'stopping rules', however submerged they may be under earlier conditions, should result in an adjustment being made to improved mortality rates. That is, the actual demographic change is anticipated by the pre-existing situation.

Preference and predisposing factors in the African situation

In Africa no such predisposing factor was present. By and large, there was no shortage of land: under the prevailing conditions of hoe farming, men could only cultivate a limited amount. Population densities were not high: in most areas there was sufficient open land into which new members of the society could move. Consequently there was no such thing as the overproduction of heirs. When the medical services and the ending of local famines helped to reduce mortality rates, making for much higher population growth rates, no submerged stopping rules came into play to limit the pace of expansion [6]. Hence one might expect higher rates of population growth in Africa than in those parts of the world where there was a different system of land tenure and of agricultural production.

The global figures appear to be consistent with this argument. The rates of growth in Africa are faster than in other parts of the world. With the continuing prevalence of hoe agriculture, land is still available for food farming. A man has no need to stop having children because of a shortage of primary productive sources. I am not concerned here with the obvious effects of such high rates of population growth on the economies of underdeveloped countries, nor with the fact that high child dependency ratios make it difficult to secure any kind of social and economic advance. In Ghana, imports of baby food are likely to go up while exports of cocoa remain the same, at least until those same children reach late adolescence and enter the labour pool. Even then it seems optimistic to suppose that a significant proportion of this increase in the total pool is going to find its way into the production of export crops. Furthermore, a greater and greater proportion of the national income is likely to be eaten up in maintaining the growing population, and this fact alone is likely to lead to a fall in the standard of living, and difficulties for those governments that permit it to happen.

If the rate of the demographic change (and this is the question at issue) is affected by the existence of submerged stopping rules, then clearly it is important to discover whether or not these exist in Africa by looking at more detailed data than overall rates of growth. For this reason we are examining the constitution of uterine sibling groups to see whether we can locate any such tendencies. Empirically this is a difficult problem. In the first place, it is always difficult to prove a negative hypothesis—and our hypothesis is that the results from Africa will show a random distribution. Secondly, we need a large amount of data. We have already collected 4,000 sibling groups from Ghana and are collecting another 4,000. But we would hope for similar data from other parts of the continent. Thirdly, and more importantly, there are certain difficulties in adapting models of decision-making to account for data, even from those societies in which we earlier supposed stopping rules had some effect. This is perhaps a temporary problem but it is a difficult one to solve. Meanwhile we are looking at various measures such as the sex ratios of the last and penultimate siblings in order to see if we can discover any significant differences between these and the overall sex ratio.

The data we are analyzing consists of fertility histories collected from women. Difficulties arise in studying the decision-making process in polygynous families, but, it is possible to break down the women's histories by the paternity of the children. The difficulty is one that also arises where divorce is frequent. It should be remarked, however, that any effect that expressed preferences for number or sex have on patterns of fertility generally, must be manifested in the constitution of uterine sibling groups, which can consequently be taken as the critical unit for study.

There are two ways of analyzing a woman's fertility history. In the first place, we can study the completed family with regard to the order and sex of children. In the second place, we can analyse the 'existential family', the family as it exists at a point in time or dynamically over successive points, specifically to see whether, in the event of a death, a male is more likely to be replaced than a female. To make any such assessment, there needs to be a prior pause in natural fertility for a number of years (say three). If such a gap is followed by a birth, we can test to see whether the sex ratio of such births differs from the cases where no stopping occurs.

What other approaches can we use in dealing with this problem? The negative side of the preference for men found in European and Asian societies is likely to be an aversion to girls. This aversion may be expressed in various ways. Firstly, girls might be more frequent victims of infanticide than boys. Secondly, there is the question of a possible sex difference in infant and child mortality due to differential care in infancy. There is no way of collecting figures on infanticide but, when we look at the question from a qualitative point of view, we find relatively little evidence from Africa, except in some cases of adulterine children and malformed births. We do not find any of the sex differentials in the disposal of children that was so marked a feature of certain Indian groups in the 19th century. Looking at the cross-cultural material on infanticide, which has been summarised in Devereux's book on abortion [1955], we find some evidence of a difference in the frequency of infanticide as between Africa and Eurasia. For the practice was by no means confined to Asia. In Disraeli's novel, *Sybil* [1845], there occurs the statement: 'Infanticide is practised as extensively and as legally in England as it is on the banks of the Ganges' [cf. Langer, 1972; Tod, 1829]. We have no evidence that European infanticide displayed a sex bias, but it seems to have been much more widespread than in Africa.

With regard to the differential care of infants, it should be possible to make some more precise measurements. Does infant mortality vary with sex? In India there are clear indications that male children receive better treatment. Even if we disregard the evidence of the astonishingly high masculinity reported (retrospectively) for first births, the mortality of male children is lower than that for girls, which is certainly a rare occurence [May and Heer 1963: 200]. In Africa, on the other hand, the trend runs the other way, at least in the age specific death rates by sex for francophone countries reported by Etienne van de Walle [W. Brass *et al* 1968: 75-78]. The mortality for males is regularly higher than for girls up to the age of 10. In this connection I would like to mention the remarks contained in an unpublished paper by W. Brass. 'Observations for some populations, e.g. Guinea, indicate an excess male mortality very much in conformity with the experience of European countries; but in others, e.g. Upper Volta, there is no evidence of any differential. There is no sign, however, of the higher female child death rate experienced in some of the poorer Asiatic communities, presumably because of the neglect of what is regarded as the less important sex.'

Bridewealth and dowry

The immediate reason for these differences in revealed preferences is, perhaps, connected with the nature of marriage transactions. In African societies, a daughter is an asset. She brings in bridewealth which can be used for a variety of purposes. It is in dowry societies (and dowry is not found in Africa except where Islamic law obtains) that women tend to be seen as a burden. From the parental point of view, a daughter is a drag on the family fortunes because, in order to maintain her status and thus to enable her to make a good marriage, she has to receive a substantial portion of the available funds. This may consist of land, as in Ceylon, Greece and other parts of the Mediterranean world; or it may consist primarily of movables, as in North India and in northern Europe. But in both cases the woman takes her 'portion' from the family funds. She takes property out rather than bringing wealth in. Hence, while men in Africa may prefer sons in a general way (the preferences of women are less frequently consulted), they are likely to be reconciled to the birth of daughters because bridewealth will enable the sons to get married. And it may well be that the institution of bridewealth has saved the females from the gory fate of some of their northern counterparts.

The existence of bridewealth and dowry is indirectly linked to the different economic systems of Africa and Eurasia. African agriculture was primarily based on the hoe, with women playing a dominant role. The dowry systems of Europe and Asia were associated with more advanced systems of agriculture linked to the plough or to irrigation; where there was considerable differential economic status in the village and at more inclusive levels. Consequently, it mattered who one's daughter married, and it was important to maintain her position in the differentiated society in which she found herself. This could be done by settling upon her a certain part of the family funds. Thus, the marriage system which led to the preservation of women's status was also that which increased the preference for males in the sibling group. In Africa, on the other hand, I would expect little preference to reveal itself in the constitution of groups of uterine siblings. This, at any rate, is the hypothesis I am trying to test in the present project.

Acknowledgements

The data from Ghana is being collected and analysed by Dr. N. Addo of ISSER, Legon, and the author. Thanks are due to Graham Harrison, and to Dr. Pat Altham and Geoffrey Rendel of the Statistical Laboratory, Cambridge, for the statistical analysis and other help.

Notes

[1]   Halder and Bhattacharya concluded that a larger proportion of couples with two female children (FF) had a third child within three years of the second child's birth than did the couples having other sex-combinations of the first two children (MM, MF, FM). They add that these results might be indicative of the common desire to have a male child and of the prevalence of some form of family limitation practice among couples with one or more male children [1970: 406].

[2]   For a discussion of the reasons for the preferences for males, see May and Heer [1968: 200].

[3]   For combinations of the first two children, the Indian data shows a definite excess of MF couples, especially in the traditional areas. However, when the figures are broken down regionally, the excess tends to be smaller for states like Kerala and Manipur where the female child carries a higher value (Halder and Bhattacharya 1970: 411-12). Kerala is, of course, renowned for its matrilineal institutions.

[4]   The hypothesis here bears a certain resemblance to Yasuba's attempt to relate the decline in fertility in America to the decrease in availability of 'easily available land' (Potter 1965: 677). We have not taken into account the families with daughters as heirs.

[5]   For a discussion of this point for Africa see Gumbi and Hall [1968]; on India, see Heer and Smith [1968], May [n.d.]; and for the introduction of 'dynamic programming' to ascertain optimal strategies, see O'Hara [n.d.] who shows that, by hesitation (or delay), the rate of natural increase at the important intermediate mortality levels can be substantially reduced.

[6]   Such limitation does not, of course, have to take the form of mechanical or chemical means. Avoidance of intercourse and coitus interuptus are available to all societies. It is relevant to note that the Khanna Study, carried out in the Punjab, found that Euopean contraceptive techniques, even after intensive instruction in their use, had less effect in population control than indigenous practices (Wyon and Gordon 1972).

References

Brass, W. *et al.* (1968) *The Demography of Tropical Africa,* Princeton University Press.

Cauldwell, J.C. (1968) *Population Growth and Family Change in Africa*, Australian National University Press.

Devereux, G. (1955) *A Study of Abortion in Primitive Societies*, New York.

Gini, C. (1908) *Il Sesso del Punto di Vista Statistico*, Milan.

Goody, J.R. (1962) *Death Property and the Ancestors*, London.

Gumbi, M.A., and Hall, S.A. (1968) Attitudes of rural workers in the tropics to family planning, *The Lancet*, 508-509.

Halder, A.K., and Bhattacharya, N. (1970) Fertility and sex-sequence of children of Indian couples, *Recherches économiques de Louvain*, 4: pp. 405-15.

Heer, D.M., and Smith, D.O. (1968) Mortality level, desired family size and population increase, *Demography*, 5: pp. 104-12.

Hill, R. Styles, J. N., and Back, K.W. (1959) *The Family and Population Control* Chappel Hill.

Langer, W.L. (1972) Checks on population growth: 1750-1850, *Scientific American*, 226, pp. 92-99.

May, D.A. and Heer, D.M. (1968) Son survivorship, motivation and family size in India: a computer simulation, *Population Studies*, 22: pp. 199-210.

May, D.M., n.d. *Reduced fertility in India and its causes*, Manuscript.

O'Hara, D.J., n.d. *Mortality risks, sequential decisions on births and population growth*, Manuscript.

Potter, J. (1965) The growth of population in America,700-1860. In Glass, D.V. and Eversley, D.E.C. (Eds.) *Population in History*, London.

Tod, J. (1829) *Annals and Antiquities of Rafosthan*.

Williamson, N.E. (1968) *Preference for sons around the world.* Manuscript Harvard School of Public Health.

Wyon, J., and Gordon, J.E. (1972) *The Khanna Study*, Harvard University Press.

Social life in the burgeoning suburbs

Margaret Peil

Introduction

Population studies are essentially concerned with masses of people—the migrant streams leaving home in search of work, the hundreds of thousands who reside in a particular city, the numbers who survive to a given age. This paper is concerned with individuals, specifically those who find themselves in the rapidly expanding slums on the outskirts of so many African towns. What sort of social life do these individuals establish to fill their time outside the hours of working and sleeping? How aware are they of the heterogeneity of their neighbourhood and what is their political response to the conditions in which they find themselves?

The studies on which this paper is based combined a census to establish the size and demographic composition of the population with an attitude survey to investigate the meaning of life for these new urban residents. Surveys were conducted in four suburbs which have shown very rapid growth (see Table 1). The first studied was Madina, near Legon in Ghana, which had grown from a few hundred to nearly 2000 in the previous six years. Ashaiman, near Tema, grew from 2624 residents in 1960 to about 30,000 in 1970. Kukuri and Makera, contiguous villages south of Kaduna which are almost surrounded by textile mills, had between them less than 10,000 people in 1963 and about 30,000 in 1972. Ajegunle, on the outskirts of Lagos, has the largest population of the four. With the growth of Apapa, less than a mile away, it rapidly became a refuge for low income workers. Ajegunle and Olodi, the two main sections, had 12,951 people in 1952. They averaged 17.9% annual growth between 1952 and 1963 [Sada 1970: 42]. Together with Amukoko, across a swamp but part of the same urban complex, there are now about 145,000 people in what is collectively known as Ajegunle. These four towns are used to present a general picture of the effects of size, age, marital status, nationality, heterogeneity, and other factors on the

171

	Madina	Ashaiman	Kukuri	Ajegunle
Year of Study	1965	1970	1972	1972
Total population (estimate)	1970	30,000	30,000	145,000
House censuses	271	95	96	120
Persons per house	7·3	15·8	18·1	20·9
Persons per household	3·3	2·5	2·8	3·8
Persons per room	b	2·1	2·3	3·0
Adult sex ratio[a]	129	164	213	163
% under age 15	40·7	30·1	29·9[c]	37·7

[a]Aged 15+
[b]Not available. 25% of houses had over 2·4 persons per room.
[c]Wives under age 15 count as adults

TABLE 1   *Populations of the four suburbs*

social life of the residents. It must be emphasised that this is a preliminary paper, since much of the data have not yet been subjected to
systematic analysis.

In many western countries, young migrants move into the city
centre and married couples move out to the suburbs to rear their
children. In the West African case, the central cities are often
overcrowded with established residents, and new migrants can more
easily find rooms in the suburbs. Hence, the demographic patterns in
suburbs differ both from the central cities and form the Western
stereotype. West African suburbs tend to house the poor manual
workers, the single and young married migrants. Housing may not be
as crowded as in the cities, both because there is still room to build
new houses and because people who can afford the higher rents in
town or have relatives there who can accommodate them prefer
living closer to jobs and amenities. Transport from the suburbs is
relatively expensive and amenities are often lacking. Ajegunle still has
no public water supply; Ashaiman has only recently been supplied
with electricity and a middle school.

Activities

The main activity of people of all ages is sitting and talking. This
costs nothing and passes the time pleasantly. It may be combined
with a game of Ludo, cards, draughts or owere; with watching a
tailor, carpenter or barber at work; with hair plaiting or cooking; but
often the group (two to four people is most common) just chat and
watch the passing scene.

Suburban life can be completely anonymous if one desires, and
there are a few people who find that this suits them very well. A
single man may spend his free time sleeping in his room. People in
poor health or doing heavy labour may find such a regime necessary.
Other isolates tend to be unwilling, long-distance migrants who care

nothing for city life. For many others, social life begins and ends with their household. Married men often prefer the company of wife and child; many men can be seen on their verandahs after work playing with the baby. Landlords with large households also find that they have plenty of company without leaving the house.

Women have more opportunity than men to associate with others in the house, but they appear to be no more likely than men to have good friends among their co-tenants, perhaps because of the friction which inevitably occurs in such crowded conditions. Getting to know the neighbours appears to be more a matter of personality than of sex. Preliminary evidence indicates that single people have only a slightly wider circle of friends and acquaintances than the married, but that married people see less of their friends than the single. The latter are more likely than the married to socialize by eating out. Men and women who are married but not living with their spouse or who are divorced or widowed seem to have the smallest social networks [Peil 1972].

Those who want a more active social life find relatively few alternatives within their suburb. There is often one cinema featuring mainly Indian films. Prostitutes may be centred in one area or live all over the town. The fairly high sex ratio ensures them business, though domestic arrangements can be established fairly easily by men who want a longer-term relationship. There are a large number of 'hotels' where one can drink palm wine or local spirits or, if one is more affluent, beer or stronger drinks [see Aduamah 1972]. These bars are usually small and cater for a regular clientele. They are crowded at the weekend following payday; business is much slower at other times, and some only survive by extending liberal credit. A large number of residents claim that they never drink, but those who do are often regulars, drinking with friends several times a week. Pools offices are also very common in Nigeria, and compete with the bars for the workers' spare cash. Some of the regulars use the offices as a social centre.

Associational membership provides social opportunities for some residents, but not as many as the proliferation of studies of voluntary associations might lead one to believe. A majority of Ashaiman residents belong to no formal association at all. Membership in ethnic or hometown improvement associations is somewhat more common in Nigeria, but many do not belong and, in any case, membership only involves attending meetings once a month or less—hardly a sustaining social outlet, though the bond provides security in time of need. For those who choose to participate, church activities can be far more time consuming. Members of spiritualist sects may have prayer meetings every evening. Others attend choir practices and/or youth activities or mothers' groups. Attendance at church services on Sunday mornings is a social as well as religious affair, involving a large section of the population. Mosques provide similar social centres for Muslems.

Another form of organized activity is sports. Football teams may be based on home areas, parts of the suburb, churches, or factories. Games may be advertised in advance and attended by large crowds, or spontaneous affairs involving a group of friends. Volleyball and ping pong are even less formal than football, since fewer players are needed. Except for the balls, the equipment is often homemade. Sports provide opportunities for young men to make friends and settle into the community. Married men generally feel that they have no time for participation, but they may be team supporters.

Housing

As a suburb grows, speculators are attracted and land values rise. As a result, new houses are larger than the earlier ones, and houses in the larger suburbs are often owned by absentee landlords. Many of the new houses being built in Ajegunle have three stories of twelve rooms each. Since residents can seldom afford more than a single room, large houses accommodate many households. The largest house in Ashaiman had fifty two people in twenty six households. There is seldom any relationship between members of different households, though resident landlords sometimes favour families of their own background, and occasionally men from the same village share a house. Generally, there is considerable ethnic, religious and occupational mixing in the larger houses. Casual observers are often completely unaware of this mixing, which is unlike the housing pattern of nineteenth century immigrants to many American cities, and certainly not what one would expect in Nigerian cities, given the prevailing animosity between various ethnic groups.

Heterogeneous housing may be a potential source of friction, an opportunity for getting to know other peoples, or a reason for not making close friends among one's co-tenants. In a study made in Tema [Peil 1968], it was found that most people reported getting on well with their co-tenants, but the proportion who said this decreased with the heterogeneity of the residents of the house. However, cultural differences between residents are more often minor than major. Where there are many long-distance migrants, they tend to live in certain parts of the town or on certain streets. These are not *zongos* in the usual sense, since there is no formal demarcation and there is always a mixture of people within houses as well as in the area. Ibos and Yorubas live on Taiwo Street in Ajegunle, which is known as a 'Hausa street'; the Frafra chief's house in Ashaiman is surrounded by houses where Frafras live, but southern Ghanaians and other northerners also live in these houses.

Getting to know other people is a good way of cutting down prejudice against them. People in Ashaiman who had lived and/or worked with aliens were more favourable to them than those who had not had this experience. Nigerians who had never migrated from their hometown (Abeokuta) were more likely than migrants to want to have nothing to do with members of other ethnic groups, and more prejudice was shown among migrants toward peoples they had never contacted than toward peoples they knew.

However, contact may be limited even when people live in the same house because of language differences. In Ashaiman and Madina, most people know enough English for it to serve as a *lingua franca*; in Kukuri, Hausa serves this purpose. But in Ajegunle, language poses a very serious problem. Many people have not had enough schooling to use English, and it is a matter of pride not to learn another group's language. Midwestern Ibos even claim to be unable to converse with an Ibo from the other side of the Niger. This means that a southerner living in a house where the rest of the tenants are Hausa can have no verbal contact with them, a situation which increases the chances of misunderstanding and conflict.

While some tenants stay for many years in the first room they rent, others move from one house to another—the roof leaks, the landlord wants to raise the rent, the co-tenants are too noisy, they need more space or want to live in the same house as a relative or friend, etc. In many houses, all or most of the tenants have moved in within the past year. This continual shifting makes it difficult to establish solid relationships with co-tenants. Even though they may see a great deal of each other while they live in the same house, the relationship is usually broken when one member moves out. Relatively few respondents mention co-tenants among their close friends; only rarely does someone have a close friend with whom he previously shared a yard.

Generally, the larger the house, the greater the chance of heterogeneity among the tenants and also the greater the likelihood of impersonality in co-tenant relations. In a house with only three or four households, one can easily be introduced on arrival and get to know people in a short period of time. A house of twenty households becomes more like a European block of flats; contacts with co-tenants are casual and unimportant to the participants. This is particularly true if there is no resident landlord or caretaker.

A factor which increases socialization is the lack of water supply. Households which have their own supply have notably less contact with co-tenants or neighbours than members of households who must draw their water from a well in the yard or a standpipe down the street. Communal water may result in frustrating shortages and frequent controversy, but it is almost guaranteed to help the newcomer get to know the neighbours.

Political awareness

Suburbanites have abundant evidence of lack of government interest in their town. Comparisons between it and the nearby city are easy to make, since many of them work in the city, and such comparisons are always to the suburb's disadvantage. Their attitude towards the situation is affected by the size of the suburb, their intention to settle there indefinitely, the local political situation and the availability of local leadership. The variables are not necessarily independent, but will be discussed separately.

In small suburbs, such as Madina in 1965, a chief can use his influence to organize communal labour and people may have a sense of belonging which can be mobilized for community improvement. As the town grows, it becomes 'nobody's home'. There is a tendency to get on with one's own life and ignore the situation as much as possible. This tendency is increased where residents plan only a short stay (up to two or three years, as is often the case in Kukuri) or are able to maintain close ties with home. The attitude is 'Let the government do it. Why should I contribute anything to this place?' This attitude is strengthened by alienation from the government, either because of military rule or because of widespread corruption and injustice among politicians. Nigeria seems to have considerably more alienation than Ghana, as well as less tradition of self-help, which makes people very reluctant to do anything to improve their environment.

Perhaps the most important variable is local leadership. This may be in the form of chiefs or headmen, religious leaders, teachers at the local school, or anyone else with ability and interest in this direction. The first Ashaiman Development Committee was led by a nurse who ran a private clinic. When this group was disbanded by the government and replaced by a commitee of PP supporters, a parallel committee developed, consisting of representatives of various churches and ethnic groups. This successfully lobbied the City Council for improvements as well as organizing 'clean up days' under the aegis of various churches. While only a small number of people was actively concerned with improving Ashaiman, there was a notable change of attitude among quite a few residents from, 'It is not my town; I don't care' to 'I'm fairly settled here; this town needs amenities and something ought to be done about getting them.' The government action which resulted should encourage people in other suburbs.

Ajegunle is an example of a suburb whose development is hampered by out-of-date administrative arrangements. It is part of Awori-Ajeromi District Council, which officially caters for a rural population. This relieves the city of Lagos of any responsibility beyond Boundary Road. Some of the older residents remember a somewhat more responsive elected local goverment before the war, but they are generally cynical about any government action on their behalf at present. In addition, quite a few are genuinely fearful of any action which might be evidence of leadership aspirations, feeling that the regime does not look kindly on such activities. The result, extreme passivity and alienation, increases the hostility and suspicion which easily develops among strangers with competing interests and no cross-cutting ties. People feel free to ignore the neighbours and throw their rubbish into the street. Absentee landlords have been similarly unconcerned, but there is some evidence that the landlords may eventually form a pressure group to lobby for government action. The ethnic heterogeneity of this suburb also works against the development of community consciousness. People seem to get on well enough with people they know, but they tend to be very suspicious of anyone they do not know personally.

Summary and conclusion

At this stage of the project, one can only state hypotheses which seem to be supported rather than report findings with conviction:-
  (i) Although there are some people who migrate because they want more contacts than are available at home, the majority of migrants seem to have a relatively small circle of friends and to have much the same sort of social life (except for traditional rituals) as they would have had at home.
 (ii) Young migrants who make up a large share of the population are more likely than older, married people to have the time and money for social activities. Hence, the suburbs support innumerable drinking bars and pools offices and some cinemas and football teams. However, because the migrants prefer associating with small networks of close friends, most recreational time is spent in casual activities—card games and just chatting or walking about the town. The preference for small groups leads to the proliferation of churches, some of which take up all of their followers' spare time.
(iii) The larger the suburb, the less feeling of belonging seems to exist. But size of house is probably more important than size of town in its effect on a man's relationships with his neighbours. Large houses encourage privatization and impersonality, whereas small houses encourage neighbourliness.
 (iv) The preference for primary groups inhibits the development of political consciousness among suburban residents, and allows the government to provide less than adequate services without local repercussions. This situation may change as more educated and affluent people are forced to live in these suburbs because of severe housing shortages in the central cities.

Many of these preliminary findings may seem familiar to those acquainted with conditions among industrial migrants in nineteenth century England. On the surface, here are certainly many similarities, and the space limitations of this paper do not allow extensive treatment of the differences. But it should be pointed out that differences certainly exist, due to several factors in the twentieth century West African context. The most important of these is that migrants are free to return home at any time, and quite a few of them do go home after relatively short (and not necessarily unsuccessful) stays in town. Secondly, the climate makes it possible for people to spend much of their time out of doors, which certainly increases the opportunities for interacting with one's neighbours. Thirdly, widespread primary education makes some contribution to broadening people's social and political outlook as well as their occupational opportunities, and gives children a different role in the society. The influence of these and other factors on urban social life will be discussed elsewhere.

Acknowledgements

Research in Ashaiman was supported by a grant from Birmingham University Centre of West African Studies and an affiliation with I.S.S.E.R., University of Ghana. Research in Kukuri and Ajegunle was supported by a grant from the U.K. Social Science Research Council.

References

Aduamah, Y. (1972) 'Akpeteshie in uniform', *West Africa*, No. 2878, pp. 1052-3.

Peil, M. (1968) 'Reactions to estate housing: a survey of Tema', *Ghana Journal of Sociology*, IV: 1-18.

Peil, M. (1972) 'Men's lib? The effect of marriage on the social life of men in Ashaiman', paper presented at the *Second Interdisciplinary Family Research Seminar, Institute of African Studies, University of Ghana*.

Sada, P.O. (1970) 'The rural urban fringe of Lagos: growth and planning problems', *Nigeria Magazine*, no. 104, pp. 40-5.

Environmental Aspects

Relations with the environment

R. P. Moss and K. Swindell

Preamble

The study of population in relation to environment is a broad field of interest. Climatic, nutritional and disease relationships have been discussed in Section III, in the context of their physiological effects on the individual and their numerical effects on populations. Thus the present Section concentrates upon the ability of the environment, both local and general, to provide the resources needed for the operation and development of the local community as a social, cultural and economic system; that is, upon its 'resource' relationships with its environment. These are of two kinds:-
1. *ecological and agricultural*—the materials provided by living, biological systems, and the socio-economic implications of those systems. These are expressed in the agricultural, animal husbandry and forestry activities of the communities;
2. *non-agricultural*—mineral exploitation and energy production, and their implications, expressed primarily in activities such as household and community crafts and small-scale industries, and more rarely in modern industrial development.

Related to the former is the relatively new problem of the conservation of natural ecosystems and their significance to tourism, and to the latter the increasing problems, social, cultural and economic, posed by the accelerating development of modern industrial complexes in Africa.

Populations and environmental resources

Thus this Section is concerned with the interactions between population size, technological level, cultural character, social organisation and economic constraints on the one hand, with the ability of the environment to provide the necessities for the maintenance and development of these community characteristics, on the other.

The four papers in this Section explore facets of these relationships. M.J. Mortimore and Polly Hill deal with tensions, problems and movements implicit in densely-settled peri-urban and rural-urban situations, the former focusing on the zone of tension between town and country and the latter on the adaptions of particular communities to increasing land shortage. In both studies the available resources are largely restricted to the area occupied by the groups investigated. W.B. Morgan introduces the wider issue of the introduction of resources from outside, and the extent to which even basic food requirements are obtained through inter-regional and inter-national trade. Bawden, Brunt and Murdoch, starting from a static resource model, outline a widely-used method of appraising agricultural and silvicultural resource potential, as a basis for future development.

The papers in this Section are mainly concerned with agricultural and food resources, so, although the social and labour aspects of urbanization and industrialization are referred to in Section IV, the industrial situation needs to be considered, in this introduction, in more detail than other aspects.

Non-agricultural resources—mining and its implications

Mining in Africa is usually highly organised, with massive capital inputs related to localized areas of mineral occurrence, and is an important or dominant element in the money economy of several African countries. Before the colonial era, however, there was a widespread use of mineral resources, including lateritic iron ore, gold and salt, which entered into local and regional trade. Currently there is a limited amount of indigenous mining, the most notable examples being associated with diamonds in Sierra Leone.

The large scale development of mineral resources thus hinges less on the demands of African countries than on the markets and resource bases of the advanced industrial economies. For example, the widespread search for iron ore by Western European nations and North American interests was a function of their increased demand for iron ore together with declining reserves in their home areas, and has led to large mining ventures in Mauritania and Liberia. Nigerian oil development fits into a similar pattern of exploitation.

Capital-intensive mining ventures in Africa are frequently linked to world markets controlled or influenced by a limited number of producers, and internal consumption of the mineral produced is negligible because of the limited market demand in most African countries—a function of the large number of small nation-states, almost all of which are characterised by their low per capita purchasing power. The viability of heavy industry, and especially iron and steel plants, is questionable while this situation obtains.

Economic co-operation amongst countries might seem a solution, but the political problems involved are considerable.

Industrial processing of mineral and agricultural materials is poorly represented in Africa, the notable exceptions being the Republic of South Africa, Rhodesia and, to a lesser extent, Zaïre. Generally, manufacturing shows a high degree of market orientation with a strong locational emphasis on capital cities and ports. This, in turn, may have an important influence on the movement of populations from lower order town and rural areas, although the number of actual job opportunities may be limited. Manufacturing is commonly designed to process export commodities (for example, the preparation of groundnut oil and the reduction of copper ore), local materials for local markets (furniture, cigarettes), and imported raw materials for local markets (beer, wheat, flour and petroleum). Both mining and manufacturing rely on the importing of capital and skill, and sometimes of raw materials. There are some who see serious limitations to industrial ventures which are highly capitalized and labour saving, and most industrial operations apart from mining have shown little promise of providing large numbers of job opportunities.

Africa's position with respect to mineral energy resources is characterized by localized but significant deposits of coal and petroleum, and there is widespread abundance of potential water power which is scarcely tapped. Africa has some forty per cent of the world's potential water power, but only about one per cent has been utilized so far. Where there has been water resource management, either for power or for irrigation, this has been attempted through large-scale multipurpose enterprises such as the Volta, Nile, Kainji, Congo and Orange River schemes. In tropical Africa integrated development projects based on large man-made lakes have been fostered by the concept of the growth pole, but there are reservations about the effective diffusion of consequent benefits over the regional or national areas which surround them.

The impact of mineral extraction activities has been primarily to increase population movements, and to create cultural, social and economic tensions in the communities close to the location of the resources being exploited. This is exacerbated by the fact that the stimulus to development has rarely been indigenous and local community needs, but rather the demands of technologically advanced communities remote from the location of the resource. The advanced community has thus generally provided the expertise and skilled personnel needed for large-scale extraction.

Mining, industry and population problems

These observations concerning mineral resource relationships have important implications for the study of populations and the problems of planning development, especially since the labour factor is one of the keys to the problem of economic growth.

The impact of mining, industry and plantation farming is usually seen in the appearance of enclaves or tracts of industrial and agricultural development often sharply demarcated from the surrounding countryside. A less obvious but especially important phenomenon associated with colonial and post-colonial economic development has been the emergence of systems of migrant labour. Migrations were not uncommon in pre-colonial times, but new agriculture and industry have altered the volume and changed the orientation of movements; temporary labour migration is widespread and persistent, taking the form of seasonal, periodic, or circulatory movements involving several million people each year. The most important flows of workers are associated with the development of mineral resources and cash cropping systems, where labour inputs are drawn from wide areas; other important flows reflect the search for employment in urban areas.

Within West Africa the most important seasonal and periodic movements are into the groundnut areas of Senegambia and northern Nigeria, and into the cocoa and coffee growing areas of Ghana and Ivory Coast; thus patterns of movement are predominantly from the drier and more hazardous environments of the interior, towards more economically diversified areas. It is estimated that about one million people move each year from their homelands looking for seasonal or periodic employment. Mining areas in Liberia, Mauritania, Sierra Leone and Ghana are subsidiary zones of periodic and semi-permanent migration. The migrants are chiefly men and youths, but there are considerable numbers of men who have womenfolk with them. Migration in West Africa is voluntary, there is minimal labour recruitment and contracting, and indigenous social organizations are well-developed for the reception of those working away from home.

Southern Africa exhibits a more formalized and structured system of labour migration with recruitment agencies abroad, and contracted workers housed in labour compounds separated into ethnic groups. Despite recent efforts at controlling border movements, the South African economy is still heavily dependent on foreign migrants working in mines and towns and on farms. The neighbouring countries of Lesotho, Botswana, Swaziland, Malawi and even Zambia, are important sources, and the economies of these countries are to some extent dependent on the backflow of cash and goods, together with the commission received by the governments on labour recruitment. Within South Africa, the separation of the ethnic groups and the establishment of homelands and reserves perpetuates short term, seasonal, or semi-permanent internal migration, and it is estimated that between fifty and seventy per cent of the males of working age in the Bantustans are away from home in white areas.

Labour migration is thus well established throughout Africa, but whether, from an economic standpoint, it is a system to be commended is often disputed. There is the view that it is little more than a low level equilibrium trap, which perpetuates low wages and inhibits the growth of the economy of the source areas by removing the most active members of the society. On the other hand, there are those who believe that the system represents an efficient adaptation to the prevailing economic circumstances, and achieves an equilibrium situation between areas of labour deficit and surplus related to the uneven spread of natural resources. Either of these contentions may be true for particular cases, but their respective operation is related to the volume of migrants to and from given areas, to the 'duration' of migration, and to a whole spectrum of economic and environmental situations, functioning at different scales.

Biological resources

The mineral and energy resource-use patterns and their implications are thus complicated, but biological resource relationships present a different kind of complexity. In the first place there is an *interaction,* a reciprocity of relationship, between the human and the non-human elements in the pattern, rather than a non-reciprocal, use-by-extraction linkage. There is thus the possibility of undesirable ecological consequences arising remotely and inadvertently through lack of understanding or mismanagement of the biological systems involved, as well as the localized environmental damage associated with mining and urban development. Soil erosion, disease in man, livestock and crops, deterioration in fallow types, or encroachment of vigorous but useless or harmful species all fall into this inadvertent category, and in some situations acute environmental problems have arisen in this way.

Indigenous population-environment systems are, however, often relatively stable, and the popular notion of 'primitive' tropical cultivators relentlessly 'slashing and burning' their way indiscriminately through tropical forests and savannas to the detriment of the available biological resources needs to be considerably modified or, preferably, completely abandoned. Imbalance increases as indigenous local economies and social systems begin to break down, as new technologies become generally available, and as international commercial motives and stimuli replace the value systems of pre-European societies. However, even this effect can be considerably overemphasised, since the systems display considerable resilience and powers of adaptation under such stresses.

Thus the idea of an 'environmental resource' attains real meaning only in the context of a particular 'use system', with more or less unique social, cultural and economic characteristics, and a definite technology of exploitation or utilisation. And the resource relationship is different according to whether the environmental requirement is susceptible, at least partially, to the use of a static resource model (as in the case of minerals), or whether it can only be understood in terms of dynamic constructs (as in biological resources).

Resource assessment

Mineral and energy resource potential may be readily surveyed using a wide variety of techniques, including the geobotanical [Cole, 1973]. Even here, available technology is a major criterion, for it determines what crustal materials are needed and what forms of those materials are capable of reduction and refinement to the form in which they are required. Furthermore, the predicted profit from the materials to be mined or extracted determines the amount of money which can be reasonably invested in prospecting. Thus, even in this context, there must be a relationship to a requirement by a community and to the economics of the exploitation of the resource.

In the biological resource field, the situation is much more complex. The resource material is not a substance in a stable state in a particular location, but the product of a dynamic system operating according to its own laws of supply and demand, relating to energy, water and nutrient elements. To a greater or lesser degree, the operation of these systems is controlled or influenced by human activity and decision, the human agents themselves being part of the systems of exchange and transfer, when these are viewed on a broader scale than that of the actual productive systems. Thus the generally-used methods of land resource assessment have real limitations, since they are almost all based on a static view of resources; this was particularly reflected in the discussion of the final paper in ths section. In effect, they measure and map characteristics which· relate, to some degree, to the idea of a particular kind of resource, but do not evaluate the resource itself. They provide information which needs to be taken into account in assessing the resource relationship; they do not measure or map the resources themselves. These environmental resources can only be measured and understood in the context of a social, cultural, economic and technical frame of reference. Nonetheless, land resource surveys provide useful and essential data, and the methods available are the nearest approximation so far to evaluating the role of environmental factors in relation to the populations occupying the areas so studied. Much more work is needed in this field.

Conclusion

This Section explores some of the complex and intricate relationships between populations, considered as social, cultural and economic entities, and the resource factors in their environments. It thus complements the environmental relationships dealt with in Section III. It is neither an exhaustive treatment of one aspect, nor a general survey of all, but pinpoints some of the important problems of evaluating and studying the relationships, both in the present situation, and in relation to the planning of future development.

References

Cole, M.M. (1973) Geobotanical and biogeochemical investigations in the sclerophyllous woodland and shrub associations of the eastern goldfields area of Western Australia, with particular reference to the role of *Hybanthus floribundlus* (Lindl.) F. Muell, as a nickel indicator and accumulator plant. *J. appl. Ecol.* 10, pp. 269-320.

Peri-urban pressures

M. J. Mortimore

The peri-urban fringe is the zone of spatial contact between town and country, urban tract (or built up area) and rural environs, a city and its region, umland, hinterland, or tributary area. The concept presupposes some change, more or less abrupt, in the nature of the culture and the cultural landscape. But the process of urbanization is such that the rural environment is being progressively transformed economically, socially and physically, and the pace of such trans-formation is normally greater, the closer we approach the city, owing to the friction of distance. Such a gradation from centre to periphery, in so far as it springs from an unequal distribution of economic growth, is central to problems of regional planning. Some polarisation is implicit in the process of urbanization, wherever an ordered relationship may be discerned between a city and its region [Richardson 1969, p 418], and underlies several conceptual models of rural-urban relationships. However, the concept of the 'growth pole' itself has been given a specifically industrial connotation in Western European regional economics [Boudeville, 1966, p 11], and its interpretative value in African conditions remains to be estab-lished.

In discussing urbanization in Africa, and especially in West Africa, a distinction must be made between towns which originated as a result of foreign or colonial activity and those which were indigenous to the culture concerned, variously identified as pre-European [Mabogunje, 1968], pre-colonial, pre-industrial [Sjoberg, 1960], 'traditional', indigenous, or primary orthogenetic (as distinct from secondary heterogenetic) [Berry, 1962]. In northern Nigeria, which will be drawn on for examples in the present discussion, the abrupt beginning of colonial rule in 1902-3 facilitates the use of this distinction between what I propose to term *precolonial* and *modern* urbanization. The same basic distinction was made by Southall in 1961 between what he called 'type A' and 'type B' towns in Africa, namely old established towns and new ones [Southall, 1961, pp.

6-13; Krapf-Askari, 1969, pp. 15-19]. Although he characterized type A towns as slowly growing, which is not always or even normally so, he drew attention to a contrast between the continuity in rural-urban relations and the importance of subsistence agriculture in type A towns, and the discontinuity and absence of an agricultural sector in those of type B. The distinction is thus not confined to the characteristics of the towns themselves but includes the nature of the relationships which exist between town and country, and helps to determine the pressures which may be observed in the peri-urban fringe.

Kano

Kano was founded in the ninth or tenth century A.D. by an immigrant Hausa community, who found settlements of a pre-

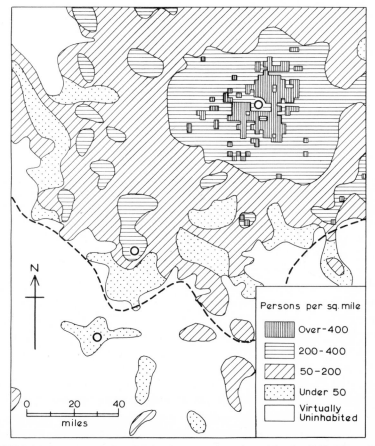

FIGURE 1   *Rural population density in part of northern Nigeria, 1952. Kano, Zaria and Kaduna are shown. (Source: R.M. Prothero,* Northern Region Nigeria 1:1,000,000 Population Density, *Directorate of Overseas Surveys, 1959).*

sumably rural character already established on the site. By the early twelfth century, Kano had a wall of four miles circumference [Palmer, 1928]. As the capital of a Hausa state and, after 1804, of a Fulani-ruled emirate, it grew as the primate city of a hierarchy extending, via intermediate settlement forms, down to separate farming compounds. During the nineteenth century it was one of the most important trading centres in West Africa. In 1911 it became the terminus of the Lagos railway, and then began to attract a large immigrant population, who were settled by the colonial administration in African, Levantine and European reservations outside the walled city. From World War II it began to attract manufacturing industry, and in 1967 it became the capital of one of the twelve states of the Federation. Its present population is over 400,000, of whom at least one-third live inside the walled city.

Kano city is the centre of a remarkable concentration of population, which contained 2.4 million inhabitants in 1962, within a mean radius of 32 miles, at densities at the outskirts in excess of 350 per square mile and rising towards the centre (Fig. 1). Although perhaps ten per cent live in small towns containing 3,000 or more inhabitants, this population maintains itself primarily by annual cultivation of the grain crops, guinea corn and millet, and the legumes, groundnuts and cowpeas.

In any agricultural economy with a large subsistence sector there is likely to be a relationship between rural population density and mean intensity of land use. Thus, in the close-settled zone around Kano, increasing intensity of land use may be observed with increasing density of population, and it is considered that a similar relationship accompanied the progressive building up of population densities in times past, although land use data is inadequate. During the present century some of the central districts have increased in density from less than 400 to 6-800 per square mile, while the area with more than 350 per square mile has doubled or trebled in size. Such population dynamics raise the value of agricultural land, compelling the abandonment of fallowing, and justifying inputs of manure at more than 1½ tons per acre in central areas. By such means 85 per cent of the surface area is kept under annual or perennial cultivation, in order to produce the staple food requirements and cash crops for sale.

In Kano, three sets of peri-urban pressures can be identified. These are: competition for land, competition for markets, and competition for non-agricultural ('off-farm') employment.

The first of these is facilitated by a system of land tenure which, predominantly influenced by Muslim Maliki law, recognizes individual tenure and allows the sale and purchase of farmland. This is the chief means of enlarging holdings as the family grows in size and wealth over the years, and such enlargement is followed by subdivision among the male heirs on the death of the father, whereupon the cycle recommences unless the heirs decide to stay together. Demand for land on the open market is forcing its price up steadily, and it has increased in value ten or twenty times in as many years.

In parallel with this development, a long term trend may be detected toward the fragmentation of holdings under customary divisible inheritance. In one village the number of plots increased by 42 per cent between 1932 and 1964, although the average size of holding was more stable, diminishing by less than 11 per cent [Mortimore, 1967].

This situation is aggravated by the fact that Kano city has a substantial farming population, who use the innermost part of the peri-urban fringe for this purpose and who compete in the land market with the villagers. Although farming may be low in status as a full-time profession, it is attractive as a sideline to urban dwellers and to rich property owners interested in land both as a speculation and as a productive investment, and who work it by means of hired labour or share-cropping. Such purchases are growing in number and give cause for concern, for the poor man endowed with inadequate land and capital, and at the mercy of a variable climate, is in no position to refuse to sell his birthright.

The pressure for agricultural land is greatest in irrigated vegetable growing areas (*fadama* lands in depressions or perennial river valleys). A direct result of urban proximity, for vegetables require continuous access to markets throughout the harvest period, this fully commercial operation is most active in the dry season, and is usually complementary to the upland farming of the wet season. Despite land values four times higher than average, such areas are not free from erosion by building development, although their extent is relatively stable and every drop of available water is used, if possible, to enlarge them.

The requirements of a rapidly expanding city for land for urban development clearly run counter to the needs of agriculture. The Northern Nigeria Land Tenure Law of 1962 gives landholders under customary tenure little security, for revocation of their rights may take place if land is required by government (which, under the Land and Native Rights Proclamation of 1910, assumed ultimate owner-ship of all land in Northern Nigeria), or for occupation by persons or bodies, or for mining and extraction of building materials [Northern Nigeria, 1962]. This stems from the assumption that customary rights are usufructuary, and puts government in the position, in effect, of exercising powers of compulsory purchase on behalf of private developers. Consistently with the same assumption, compen-sation is only paid in respect of 'unexhausted improvements' (including crops) and the inconvenience caused by disturbance, a

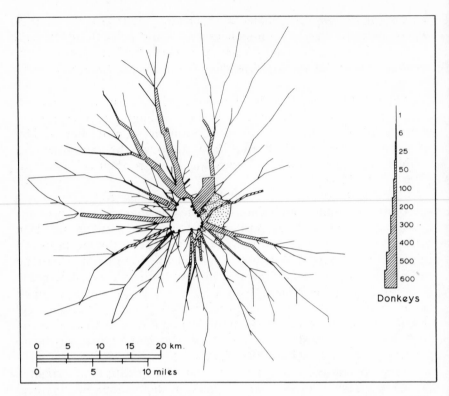

1
6
25
50
100
200
300
400
500
600

Donkeys

0   5   10   15   20 km.

0   5   10 miles

FIGURE 2   *Incoming donkey traffic to the walled city of Kano on one 'day' in the dry season, 1969. (Counts were taken at each gate in turn on normal days and the results summed to give the pattern for one 'day'). The modern township is shown stippled.*

difficult matter to measure since alternative land is only available, if at all, at high cost. Although the rates of compensation may, on occasion, exceed the market price for agricultural land sold voluntarily, they bear no relation to its development value. There is no register of individual titles to land under customary tenure, although such a register, compiled for taxation purposes, was discontinued as recently as 1956 [McBride, 1938]. Thus land may be obtained by speculators in anticipation of urban development and not even the full compensation reaches the dispossessed farmer.

Competition for markets results from a retreat from subsistence, a long-standing rural process most marked at the city gates, both metaphorically and literally. The cash requirements of every family range upwards, in accordance with individual expectations, from an inescapable minimum sufficient to pay taxes. Before 1903 taxes were paid in produce, but soon afterwards coinage was introduced and cash payment insisted on. The chief result was the growing of groundnuts. Production in Kano State for the world market grew from a quarter of a million to half a million tons during the 1960s, and production per family increases towards the centre of the close-settled zone. Now Kano city receives the bulk of its food supplies from far afield, and, except for those grown by city-dwelling farmers, staple foods do not figure large in the movement of commodities in the peri-urban fringe [Mortimore, 1973]. Vegetables and some minor foods, such as the produce of farm trees, assume greater significance.

The most important commodities in short-distance rural-urban trade are, in fact, not agricultural produce but manure and firewood, whose exchange helps supply two basic needs of country and town respectively. The volume of this trade diminishes rapidly with distance from the city, and its symmetrical pattern displays the enduring nature of the precolonial relationship (Fig. 2). Market influences are stronger in the peri-urban fringe than anywhere else in the hinterland.

Competition for non-agricultural employment can be interpreted as an attempt to escape the effects of a growing land shortage. It may take the form either of activities carried on at home or of urban employment. In 1964 the second of these was found to be unimportant in three villages 5-10 miles north of the city, while every family had some local non-agricultural source of income, such as selling firewood or hand weaving, which is a local speciality, and for some families these sources provided a large proportion of total income [Mortimore and Wilson, 1965]. In more recent years, however, wage employment in the booming industrial sector of the city has been taken up on a large scale by workers resident in more than 90 villages around and prepared to travel daily [Lubeck: personal commn.]. Since there is not enough of such employment to go around the urban population, its ability to relieve pressure on rural land, although significant, is limited. The population of the two innermost districts alone exceeds 100,000.

The final alternative available is emigration, to other rural areas or towns. Although Kano farmers are to be found widely in the northern states of Nigeria, the number migrating from the peri-urban fringe to rural areas is considered to be small. Farther away it may be larger. Migration to towns, including even to Kano, has also been relatively unimportant, but commuting, although a convenient substitute at the present time, may become less attractive than urban residence as village ties weaken.

It may be said, therefore, that in providing a market, a centre of employment and a source of manure inputs, Kano city helps maintain the high rural densities around. In doing this it prolongs a precolonial role, which was strengthened and perhaps provoked then by its importance as a political centre in attracting migrants to settle under the shadow of its rulers. Its rapid growth at the present time accentuates an already acute shortage of rural land; however, it is also increasing the power of its market and wage sector to generate income. The peri-urban fringe may still be less at risk than those parts of the close-settled zone less able to benefit from a symbiotic relationship with the city.

Kaduna

Kaduna was founded in 1917, in an area inhabited by scattered Gwari farming communities, as the new capital of the Protectorate of Northern Nigeria. Its population grew initially by immigration from southern parts of Nigeria, and later from Hausaland, and its growth accelerated with the increasing political autonomy of Northern Nigeria during the 1950s, assisted by a vigorous programme to attract industry and commerce. It is now the capital of North Central State.

Today Kaduna remains a strangers' town, with only 0.9 per cent of its inhabitants of Gwari origin [Lock, et al, 1967]. Apart from the large city of Zaria (which is more akin to Kano), its hinterland rarely exceeds 50 persons per square mile, and there are virtually no other towns within 50 miles. Land use is extensive, with only small areas of annual cultivation, but 40 per cent is estimated to be regularly farmed, including fallow [Lock, et al, 1967]

The pressures noticed in Kano are weakly developed or lacking in Kaduna's peri-urban fringe. Competition for land is only beginning to make itself felt, and results not from rural demographic pressure, or the requirements of city-dwelling farmers, but from the demands of urban development. Such demands can, at present, be satisfied within the provisions of the Land Tenure Law and the communal system of land tenure customary to the Gwari with much less difficulty than in Kano. The value of undeveloped land, on which little information is to hand, is low, since vacant land is available and displaced farmers can find more elsewhere. Vacant land, however, facilitates squatting on the city outskirts. Government and its agencies, especially the army, occupy or reserve huge areas of land.

Like Kano, Kaduna receives most of its food supplies from far afield [Lock, et al, 1967]. But, whereas the agricultural surplus in Kano is limited by a shortage of land, in Kaduna it is limited by a shortage of people, given the prevailing technology based on the hoe. The high cost of supplying towns in low density areas has been argued as a constraint on urban development [Boserup, 1965, p. 71]. Only rapid technological change in agriculture can overcome this, and there is some evidence that it may be the urban capitalist elite who will undertake this rather than the existing farmers. Local trade is similarly weakly developed in other commodities, although firewood is brought to Kaduna daily on the shoulders of Gwari women.

Little information is available on the importance of, or trends in, non-agricultural employment in the rural environs of Kaduna, and it must be presumed to be limited in the same way by the distance-cost implications of the sparse distribution of the population.

The population factor

Figure 3 expresses the differences between Kano and Kaduna in terms of population density profiles. That for Kano is the more recent and accurate, but the relationship between the population factor and the types of peri-urban pressures that have been discussed is clear nevertheless. The Kaduna hinterland is characterized by an irregular low profile with occasional peaks but no

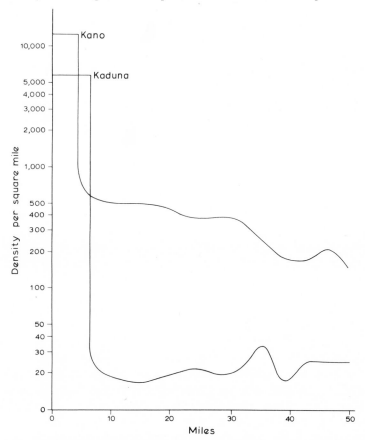

FIGURE 3   *Population density profiles for Kano and Kaduna. Each profile is the mean of 16 radial profiles from the centre to a distance of 50 miles. The densities indicated for the centre of each town are the mean densities within the built-up area of Kano and the Kaduna Capital Territory. The distortion caused by Zaria (42 miles) has been eliminated from the Kaduna profile. (Sources: M.J. Mortimore,* Population distribution in Kano Province, 1962 *(map), Occasional Paper no. 2, Department of Geography, Ahmadu Bello University, 1965; R.M. Prothero, op.cit.).*

general trend; that of Kano displays a constant gradient from the town boundary to a mean radius of about 32 miles, where the gradient steepens at around 350 per square mile. The Kano profile thus bespeaks a long established and basically continuous rural-urban relationship in social, economic and political terms, and the Kaduna profile a non-relationship symptomatic of the recent foundation of an alien urban tradition. In Kano, precolonial centralisation of political power, which had important demographic implications, was essential for the emergence of a primate city. But it was the very marginality of Kaduna with respect to existing centres of power and population that, in the logic of the colonial policy of indirect rule, determined its selection as the capital of Northern Nigeria.

Kaduna, like Kano, now functions as a growth pole with a relatively massive volume of public and private investment in infrastructure and manufacturing industry. There can be little doubt that peri-urban pressures create fewer immediate problems for the administrator in a Kaduna-type situation. In terms of urban and regional planning it offers cheap land, but a weak integration between city and hinterland which is expensive to rectify. In a Third World context of low incomes per capita, there are economies to be gained from the spatial concentration of population, especially when distributed as symmetrically as around Kano. Development in Kano-type situations must be based on intensification of the use of land resources (large irrigation projects are presently being planned); in Kaduna-type hinterlands, more productive use of human resources is needed. In the Kano situation, the development of smaller towns offers a means of reducing the growth of the metropolis and the pressures accompanying it; in the Kaduna situation, such a policy is more debatable.

Other situations

In seeking applications for these conclusions in a wider African context, composite or intermediate situations must be recognised which result from different combinations of our three basic variables, age, rate of growth and population density in the hinterland. To the *precolonial* and *modern* types represented by Kano and Kaduna, at least three others may be added. There are still examples available of *frustrated precolonial* towns which, ignored by modern developments, stand still or decline demographically, thus bringing about no significant changes in peri-urban pressures. This situation may occur in a region as highly urbanized as Yorubaland and, to a lesser extent, in Hausaland. Indeed, the Yoruba habit of maintaining an urban home while working on distant farms is encouraged by modern transport developments so that pressure on the land close to the town may conceivably diminish. The population density profile is a misleading indicator of Yoruba rural-urban relations.

A second possibility is the *modern* town founded in a *high density* area lacking any precolonial urban tradition and centralised political institutions (e.g. Enugu). The density profile might be expected to show a plateau lacking a dominant trend, and the pressures generated by urban expansion to be much more acute than in the *modern low density* (Kaduna) situation.

A third variant is the *modern coastal* metropolis which, owing to its greater size or age or both, may be expected to have proceeded farther than Kaduna in overwhelming or integrating with its peri-urban fringe. However, it is of some interest that the rural hinterland of Lagos is reported to be still partly unoccupied, and the advantage of proximity to its markets ineffectively utilised, on account of low expectations among the rural population [Ajaegbu, 1969].

Peri-urban pressures must be expected to vary widely among individual cities, although the degree of diversity in newly-urbanised countries in Africa may be less than in Nigeria. The purpose of this discussion has been to identify the key variables and to show the importance among these of the population factor in helping determine the nature of these pressures.

References

Ajaegbu, H.I. (1969) Population and local resource development in the Lagos State of Nigeria, *Nig. Geog. Journ.*, 12, pp. 37-52.

Berry, B.J.L. (1962) Urban growth and the economic development of Ashanti. in F.R. Pitts (ed.), *Urban Systems and Economic Development*, University of Oregon, pp. 53-64.

Boserup, E. (1965) *The Conditions of Agricultural Growth.*

Boudeville, J. (1966) *Problems of Regional Economic Planning.*

Krapf-Askari, E. (1969) *Yoruba Towns and Cities.*

Lock, Max and partners (1967) *Kaduna 1917-1967-2017.* Faber, London.

Mabogunje, A.L. (1968) *Urbanisation in Nigeria.*

McBride, D.F.H. (1938) Land survey in the Kano Emirate, Northern Provinces, Nigeria, *Journ. Roy. Afr. Soc.*, 37, pp. 75-91.

Mortimore M.J. (1967) Land and population pressure in the Kano close-settled zone, Northern Nigeria, *Advancement of Science*, 23 (118), pp. 677-686.

Mortimore, M.J. (1974) Some aspects of rural-urban relations in Kano, Nigeria, in P. Vennetier (ed.), *La Croissance Urbaine en Afrique Noire et à Madagascar.*

Mortimore, M.J., and Wilson, J. (1965) *Land and People in the Kano Close-settled Zone*, Occasional Paper No. 1, Department of Geography, Ahmadu Bello University.

Northern Nigeria, No. 25 of 1962, caps. 34, 35.

Palmer, H.R. (trans.), (1928) The Kano Chronicle, in *Sudanese Memoirs*, Lagos 3, pp. 97-132.

Richardson, H.W. (1969) *Regional Economics.*

Sjoberg, G. (1960) *The Pre-industrial City Past and Present.*

Southall, A.W. (ed.), (1961) *Social Change in Modern Africa.*

Some socio-economic consequences of the high population density in rural areas near Kano City

Polly Hill (M. E. Humphreys)

Introduction [1]

The most notable characteristic of farming in the Kano Close Settled Zone (KCSZ) is not that the permanent cultivation of manured farmland is the normal practice—for it is likely that the bulk of basic food crops in rural Hausaland has long been grown on such land [2]—but that there is no uncultivated (bush) land which may be freely appropriated by men wishing to expand their scale of farming. (There is, of course, some uncultivated, though cultivable, land, e.g. land which the owner has failed to cultivate owing to poverty or illness, or land from which thatching grass (*cibci*) is cropped.) As those in the KCSZ are no exception to the general rule that Hausa farmers are usually disinclined to cultivate farms more than 3 or 4 miles from their houses (and as, in any case, it would be necessary to travel (say) 30 miles from Dorayi to find any substantial area of bush), the supply of land is absolutely limited.

Therefore a farmer who requires more land has to acquire it either by purchase (pledging is not common), or by 'borrowing' (*aro*). If, in connection with the question of land purchase, there be any who continue to doubt whether farmland is indeed privately owned in Nigerian Hausaland, let them note that the Kano State government compensates the private farmers themselves when their land is requisitioned: in Dorayi, farmers are currently receiving £60 an acre (the rate being somewhat lower further from the city) for farmland requisitioned for road construction.

A man who wishes to acquire permanent rights over additional farmland is obliged to buy it from another farmer—farm-buying is an ancient and common practice. However, farm prices have risen steeply in the past 15 years (or so), sometimes being well in excess of £60 an acre, an astonishingly high price in the West African rural context; in Batagarawa prices were commonly only £3 to £2 per acre—though sometimes higher. Buying is thus altogether beyond the

198

means of poorer farmers, who are obliged to borrow land—many richer farmers do likewise. In Batagarawa nearly all land-borrowers are relatives or close friends of the lenders. But in Dorayi this is not so and, somewhat surprisingly, *aro* land is an essential safety valve, comparable to bush land, which enables many poorer men to rely mainly on farming for their livelihood. It is because *aro* land is so casually allocated, usually for a single season only (the borrower being entirely devoid of longer-term rights), that it is here denoted as 'borrowed', not rented, land. Unless a farmer is altogether distrusted, he can usually borrow plots at 'rents' which have never risen *pari passu* with the value of land. A large speculative element is often involved in land-buying.

Population density

Dorayi has, according to our census, a population of about 3,500. It is an old farming area where there was probably little bush in 1900, though there was then far more grazing. With the aid of a recent aerial photograph we mapped all the farms (plots) in an area of some 3 square miles, ascertaining the name of each farm-owner. (The work was made possible by the existence of henna (*lalle*) farm-boundaries, which are very clear on aerial photographs; in the areas of the KCSZ where henna is not used, most boundaries are invisible.) Considering that a fair proportion of the Dorayi farmland is owned by non-resident farmers, the effective population density is even higher than the 1,200 per square mile indicated by these figures—this density being higher than any hitherto recorded in the KCSZ [3]. There are two main types of non-resident farmer: first, 'rich men' (usually traders, or professional or business men) from the city who have bought farmland, usually fairly recently and at high prices, much of this land being near (or accessible from) a road; second, men who formerly lived in Dorayi but who migrated to the city, retaining their land.

Until two consecutive reliable population censuses have been conducted (as none has been so far—at least in this locality), there is no possibility of judging whether the Dorayi population is increasing or not—and such figures alone would be of limited value owing to the ever increasing proportion of land owned by rich non-residents. Land-ownership by rich non-residents is nothing new; in the last quarter of the 19th century, as presumably much earlier, there were many farm-slaves in Dorayi, working on farmland owned both by resident farmers and by rich city men. Not only because such slavery persisted until the mid nineteen-twenties, memories of it are very vivid and, with the help of elderly informants, accurate information was obtained as to which houses are of free and slave descent (through the male line) respectively—a few houses being 'mixed'.

Although many men of slave descent remain in the area, they or (more usually) their forebears having acquired land [4], it is certain that the great proportion of ex-slaves (and more particularly of slaves' sons) migrated. Therefore, it should not be too lightly presumed that present population densities are greater than they were in (say) 1900—though certainly, as all elderly informants are agreed, the number of (free) farmers has increased and there are many more very small farm plots.

Migration

One of the most fascinating of all questions is that of migration. How far does outward migration relieve population pressure? Fortunately, some general 'rules' have already emerged from the detailed study of migration from Dorayi, and from another Kumbotso area further south.

1)   Nowadays sons very seldom migrate (whether to Kano city or elsewhere) during their father's lifetime; if they do so, this is rather due to 'trouble in the family' than to extreme poverty. Only 23 married sons with living fathers are recorded as having migrated from Dorayi with its total resident population of 717 married men.

2)   The father's death somewhat increases the sons' propensity to migrate, partly because they then lack any moral obligation to remain to support their father, but also because they become free to sell their share of the inherited farmland—though those who migrate to the city may retain their farms.

3)   Dorayi is within easy cycling distance of the centre of the city and younger men, in particular, prefer to commute there daily, rather than to migrate; however, most commuting occurs in the dry season (*rani*) only, there being only about 47 married men who receive regular wages for work in the city during the farming season. Such men, who are known locally as 'labourers', are always distinguished from those, such as traders, who have no employer and do not receive wages.

4)   Men never migrate in the capacity of farmers in search of new farming land—all those cases (and they are very few) of migration to rural areas involve personal connections with the receiving area: men joining maternal relatives or wive's parents.

5)   About half of all migration from Dorayi is to Kano city, most of it occurring after the father's death; few other cities, in northern Nigeria or elsewhere, exert any strong pull.

6)   A common form of migration is 'vanishing'—one of the idiomatic expressions for which is *ya tafi uwa duniya* ('he joined mother-world'), the man himself being *dan duniya* (son of the world). For this and other reasons, relatives feel much shame about migration, and reliable information can only be

obtained from third-party informants on whom we entirely relied.
7) Virtually no unmarried men migrate or commute.
8) Most migration, except in a few cases to Kano city, is permanent; there is no tendency, as in many regions of West Africa, for migrants to return home for retirement.
9) There is little dry-season migration (*cin rani*) but, as already mentioned, a fair amount of dry-season commuting to Kano.

Considering the circumstances, the incidence of male migration seems strikingly low. (The incidence of female migration to neighbouring rural areas, on marriage, is very high, but is balanced by equivalent immigration.) Statistics relating to nearly a thousand Dorayi married men, both alive and dead [5], which were collected as part of the procedure of compiling genealogies for each house, showed that only about 17% of them were known to have migrated; on a number of heroic assumptions, such a proportion might correspond to an incidence of migration of married men *per year* of no more than 2%.

Scarce factors

The supply of farm-labour is abundant—and many young men seek work as daily farm-labourers outside Dorayi. So men 'fail to migrate' although there is a vast over-supply of farm-labour in relation to the fixed supply of land.

Apart from land, another important scarce resource which limits the production of crops is organic manure. But this scarcity, like that of land, does not limit everybody. A rich farmer can obtain all the manure he requires from Kano city; if he lacks sufficient donkeys or family labour to fetch the manure he requires, he can pay someone else to do it for him. (As readers of M.J. Mortimore's publications will know, this manure basically consists of compound sweepings from the city, which have been enriched by the droppings of sheep and goats; sooner or later, the municipal authorities are bound to exert some control over the keeping of small livestock in the city, so that the quality of the manure will ultimately fall.) Lorry loads of garbage, containing far too many 'tin pans' which will permanently pollute the country-side, may be bought from the Kano municipality. The sheep, goats and donkeys owned by Dorayi farmers and their wives provide much manure. And pit-latrine manure (extracted from house-latrines which have been sealed for a period) has been used (and bought and sold) for generations. There is, nowadays, only one herd of cattle in Dorayi, and this is wholly owned by a city man; there are not even any plough-oxen (or ploughs).

Dependence on farming

Although it is impossible to assess the extent to which Dorayi is dependent on farming for its livelihood, several apposite points may be made.

1) All resident men, save the severely poverty-stricken, aspire to produce much of the grain (guinea corn and millet) which provides their basic subsistence; but many fail to achieve this.

2) It would seem that Dorayi, considered as an 'island economy', 'exports' no grain, farmers with surpluses selling grain to people in neighbouring houses. On the other hand, Dorayi certainly 'imports' considerable quantities of grain, mainly bought at a few rural markets outside daily 'donkey radius', little of it coming from more than, say, fifty miles away.

3) The main 'export crop' is groundnuts which (again) all men aspire to produce; but, interestingly, no groundnuts are sold to licensed buying agents for export outside Nigeria, virtually all supplies being made into groundnut oil by local women, mainly for sale in Kano city, where it is head-loaded by girls, all wives being in full Muslim seclusion. (The women invariably buy the nuts required, whether from their husbands or from others.)

Dependence on Kano city

Despite Dorayi's closeness to economic dependence on the city, the area is, in a real sense, a community of farmers and their dependants—being quite different from an urban community and not a suburb. Only a very small number of the wives of Dorayi men are from the city. No men with any modern educational qualifications (not even primary school) live in Dorayi, and no more than about 2 or 3 Dorayi boys have ever proceeded to higher education.

As already noted, Dorayi is greatly dependent on the city for its manure supplies. It also sells much farm produce there, including groundnut oil, onions (grown in a section of the area only, on farms irrigated from wells), henna (dried leaves and powder) and vegetables (both 'African' and 'European'). Firewood is also an important 'export'—informants say the area is much better wooded than formerly, although there are no baobab. Finally, a large income is derived from selling very simple craft goods, made from crop residues, which are too bulky in relation to value to be worth transporting further than the city. The 'cornstalk bed' (a mat) is the prime example of such goods. It is even said that there are those who derive their whole living from making and selling these crude objects. Poor men who own no donkey eke out a living by head-loading fodder, thatching grass, etc. to the city.

Hardly any income is derived from selling 'traditional style' craft goods in the city, apart from some blacksmiths' wares. Weaving, for example, is almost a dead craft, being pursued by a very small number of women only. Nigerian industrialisation and cheap imports have greatly reduced the rural income from skilled craftwork.

Apart from those 47 (or so) men who commute daily to the city throughout the year (the so-called 'labourers'), there are about 22 men who are city traders (but all of whom are also farmers), about 19 men who go to the city with their donkeys to transport earth for building, and about 19 other men with a variety of occupations in the city. Therefore, about 17% of the 717 married men have non-farming occupations located in the city.

General standard of living

In Dorayi, as in Batagarawa, there is such a great degree of economic inequality that notions of the average standard of living are dangerous rather than useful. Whether or not there is a general sense in which 'rural standards' are declining compared with 'urban standards', it must be remembered that urban standards are very variable also. Even if general social amenities, such as cinemas, piped water, markets and tarred roads are regarded as enhancing the 'standard of living' of city dwellers, it is not obvious that city workers generally enjoy better or more sanitary conditions than those in the country-side, where there are pit-latrines in every house, wells in most houses, where house compounds are much larger and heat much less extreme. Certainly until very recently money wages in the city rose much faster than the price (to the farmers) of groundnuts, but house rents have risen so sharply as to cancel out much of the gain. (Houses are never sold or rented in Dorayi.) Although there are none in Dorayi whose 'income' remotely compares with that of a rich business man in the city (the only motor vehicle owned in Dorayi is one moped), yet there are many in Dorayi who enjoy higher standards and more security, than a great proportion of those in the city.

Average areas of farmland per head in Dorayi are less than half an acre, compared with one acre of manured farmland (bush farms excluded) in Batagarawa where land is plentiful. Although Batagarawa is less than self-sufficient in grain, a higher proportion of grain requirements is grown there than in Dorayi.

Given that the supply of land is fixed and that labour is plentiful, and assuming that neither of these conditions alters within the next few decades, then supplies of manure are the crucial factor determining the quantity (as distinct from the value) of agricultural output. It is for agronomists to determine whether the richer farmers would do better to invest in chemical fertilisers (as they scarcely do in Dorayi at present) rather than in vast tonnages [6] of manurial sweepings from the city. Certainly, anything that could be done to increase the population of sheep and goats [7] would be most beneficial, both because of the manurial value of their droppings and because the community eats so little beef.

Variations in living standards

Preliminary analysis suggests that the proportion of farmers who are judged by their peers [Hill, 1972, for method of assessment] as being 'relatively rich' (*mai arziki*) is about the same in Dorayi as in Batagarawa—perhaps about one-tenth of the population. These are the men who are insulated from the consequences of crop failure by the possession of capital of (say) £50 or more. (Actual capital values could not be estimated, but this is the kind of sum which, in the opinion of informants, qualified a man to be regarded as *mai arziki*.) Their farm holdings (a holding consisting of a number of separate plots) are considerably smaller in Dorayi than in Batagarawa. While the analysis of the statistics relating to farm acreages is not yet complete, it is certain that the proportion of farmers with holdings of over 10 acres is far lower than in Batagarawa.

It seems that about one quarter of all the men in each of the two localities should be considered to be severely impoverished.

The following summary of factors affecting the standard of living of *individual* Dorayi farmers (as distinct from standards generally) is incomplete, preliminary and tentative—a mere list of headlines.

1) *Most richer farmers become rich through farming*
    Informants are often jocular when asked how others became rich: 'Through God and farming' or 'Through God and onions' are common responses. While there is strong emphasis on the element of luck (*arziki*), those who work hard are highly praised by others—it's simply untrue (as is so commonly asserted) that the community sets no store by (has no moral attitude towards) efficiency and effort. Having accumulated capital through farming (and by storing produce for a price rise), a farmer whose affairs are developing satisfactorily may then consolidate his position by becoming a trader—but the number of substantial traders, e.g. grain traders, is quite small.

2) *Many rich farmers earn little from non-farming occupations*
    This is in striking contrast to Batagarawa, where there is a relationship, which is lacking in Dorayi, between a man's scale of farming and his type of non-farming occupation (*sana'a*). The sole *sana'a* of many richer men (if it can be denoted such) is that of fetching manure from the city: asked why they do this

humble work themselves, rather than paying someone else to do it, or relying on their sons, they suggest that there are few alternative occupations in the dry season, and that they get a better quality of manure by going themselves.

3) *Most richer men are middle-aged or old*
Of the 72 married men in Dorayi who were classified as 'rich' (*mai arziki*), only 5 were under about thirty-five years, and 43 were over about fifty years. Whereas nearly a quarter of all older men were rich, only about 6% of all younger men were so classified. In Dorayi most married men continue working with their fathers until they die, or retire from farming, and they do little or no farming for themselves. With the exception of those who happened to inherit large acreages from their rich fathers when they were young (most of whom have few brothers and sisters with whom the inheritance is shared), few men get rich with any speed. But any enterprising, hard-working, middle-aged man, a man with luck on his side, might (in the recent past) have become rich. (This may not be so in future, now that farm-prices have risen.) One of the richest Dorayi farmers is the elderly son of a slave, who inherited no farmland and has no sons.

4) *The severely poverty-stricken are of all ages*
There appears to be little variation in the incidence of extreme poverty by age-group. However, the position of the youngest men is not entirely clear as 14% of them are 'labourers' (a higher proportion than for any other age-group), whose relative standard of living cannot be assessed. (As many as 24% work, in *gandu*, on their fathers' farms.)

5) *Sons (with living fathers) have poor economic opportunities*
Owing to land scarcity, few Dorayi farmers give farmland (*gayauna*) to their married sons, nearly all of whom work on their fathers' farms only. Accordingly, few such men prosper as independent farmers—this standing in great contrast to Batagarawa, where several sons are among the largest farmers. Even when the father retires and divides his farmland, only the sons of rich farmers stand any chance of becoming rich themselves: of the total of 98 sons of retired fathers, 11 only were classified as rich, of whom 8 had rich fathers.

6) *Landlessness is a common condition*
Owing to the possibilities of land-borrowing (*aro*), landlessness is not necessarily associated with extreme poverty. The condition is nothing new, many present-day farmers having inherited negligible acreages from their fathers or grandfathers who had often sold their farmland. It does not directly result from land

purchase by rich city men, who are usually uninterested in the small plots typically owned by small farmers.

7) *Many younger married men get a larger income from farm-labouring than from farming*
Many of the richer local farmers employ farm-labourers, and non-resident farmers provide much welcome employment. As a general rule, farm-labouring is not at the expense of 'own-farming', but rather assists its finance.

Speculative conclusion

The most interesting conclusion is the very small extent to which the extreme pressure of population on farming land in Dorayi is relieved by migration, there being no migration for farming (to less densely populated areas) and a very low incidence of migration of sons (with living fathers). Sons feel obliged to assist their fathers with their farming, even though they are seldom rewarded with a farm-plot for their own use. In Batagarawa nearly all those who migrate for farming are younger middle-aged men with working sons, who are rich enough to afford the heavy expenses of migration; in Dorayi, on the other hand, men fail to flourish while in *gandu*, so that there are not so many who are both young enough and rich enough to migrate as farmers.

No one starves in Dorayi, mainly because of the possibility of borrowing land (*aro*), and it may be that the proportion of men who are greatly impoverished is no higher than in Batagarawa. But few of those under fifty enjoy a relatively high standard of living. As farm prices continue to rise, the tendency for farmland to be concentrated mainly in the hands of the sons of (deceased) rich farmers, especially those with few brothers, will be likely to increase—though it does not follow that rich farmers will own a rising proportion of all the farmland.

Notes

[1]   This paper is based on largely unanalysed field material collected during nearly a year's fieldwork among Hausa farmers in the closely settled zone around Kano city, which ended in July 1972, so that ideas rather than conclusions are presented. The project was financed by the Social Science Research Council. Much material on the rural Hausa generally, as well as a detailed analysis of socio-economic life in Batagarawa (a village in northern Katsina where land is not scarce) are provided in my *Rural Hausa* [Cambridge, 1972]. (The Hausa are probably the largest ethnic group in sub-Saharan Africa, there being more than 10 million of them in Nigeria; most Hausa live in the countryside.)
Most, though by no means all, of my intensive fieldwork in the Kano Close Settled Zone (KCSZ) was done in a locality in Kumbotso District which lies some ½ to 2½ miles south of the city wall; it is made up of 5

contiguous 'Hamlet Areas' which are in 4 'Village Areas' (Ciranci, Dorayi Karama, Gwazaye and Ja'en), being here referred to as 'Dorayi' for short. The entire population of Dorayi, as of most of the vast area (some 5,000 square miles) of the KCSZ, lives in dispersed houses surrounded by farmland, there being no villages, markets, central mosques or other 'central places' anywhere near Dorayi and only one walled town (*gari*) in Kumbotso District with its estimated population of over 60,000. Permanent cultivation of manured farmland has been the normal agronomic system for at least a century.

[2]   This extraordinary fact, which makes rural Hausaland a unique agronomic region in West Africa, is only just beginning to be recorded in the literature.

[3]   We repeated our census several times, each successive enumeration showing a higher figure. One particular difficulty in Dorayi (which is not of general application in rural Hausaland) is the existence of very large (Muslim) houses, inhabited by up to 100 people; for this, and other reasons, there is certain to be considerable under-enumeration in official censuses in Dorayi.

[4]   There is never any question of those of slave descent renting their land from the descendants of the slave-owner.

[5]   Dead men were included both to increase the size of the sample and because it is not necessarily known whether migrants are still alive.

[6]   It is likely that at least 2 tons per acre of compound sweepings are required to maintain fertility [Hill, 1972, p. 288], and rich farmers often apply more. If an average of only 1 ton per acre of Kano sweepings is applied to Dorayi farmland (estimated at 1,600 acres), and if the average donkey carries 100 lb. of this bulky load, nearly 36,000 donkey-journeys annually would be necessitated—or 50 journeys per married man.

[7]   These extremely useful animals do not deplete human food supplies, as is so commonly assumed, but are confined within house-compounds during the farming season, and are not released until all crop residues of any value have been stored or stacked.

References

Hill, Polly (1972) *Rural Hausa: A Village and a Setting*, Cambridge.

Mortimore, M.J. (1967) 'Land and Population Pressure in the Kano Close-Settled Zone, Northern Nigeria', *The Advancement of Science*, April, pp. 677-86.

Mortimore, M.J., and Wilson, J. (1965) *Land and People in the Kano Close-Settled Zone*, Ahmadu Bello University, Zaria.

Food imports and nutrition problems in West Africa

W. B. Morgan

Nutrition research in West Africa is able to make use of a number of unevenly distributed case studies, but lacks data for anything better than guess-work generalizations with regard to the major nutrition problems of any one country or of the region as a whole. The lack of adequate agricultural census information makes it impossible to estimate productivity satisfactorily and quite impossible to compare any two years or to establish whether production is keeping pace with population increase. Perhaps the greatest of all the problems of underdevelopment is the difficulty in finding finance for the survey work essential to establish what the problems are. In the circumstances, additional approaches to the problems of nutrition through related data can be useful. Such an approach may be provided by the study of food imports, for, despite certain problems of error and interpretation, import data provide more carefully checked information than estimates of crop and livestock production. This paper seeks to develop work published in 1963 and 1969 and reported to Section E of the British Association in 1962 and the Deutsche Afrika Gesellschaft Conference in 1963.

On the whole, international trade has received rather less attention than it deserves from those interested in the problems of population and food supply. They have tended rather to stress the role of certain weaknesses in agricultural technique which appear basic to current world food production problems. This has been a pity, particularly in West Africa where food imports into certain countries are remarkably high, and where there is a great deal of regional differentiation in quantity and kind, providing a commentary on the food situations of the countries concerned. Moreover, the food trade has been the subject of a great deal of general comment, particularly from politicians who have seen it as evidence of economic weakness, as a consumer of scarce overseas earnings, or as a part of a chronic trade deficit problem. Few West African governments have failed to regard food imports as undesirable or have failed to encourage investment in home food production in order to reduce or eliminate such imports and save overseas earnings. Despite these efforts food imports have persisted as major features of West Africa's trading patterns—and not just in recent decades. They are much more than the product of some short-lived interest in luxury foreign food, and they are not just the result of the considerable purchasing power of an expatriate community. The roots of the food import problem, if it is a problem, are in West Africa's colonial history and in the foundations of its overseas trade. The growth of such imports has been the product of the evolution of West Africa's trade and of her agricultural systems, and of the changing food preferences and purchasing power of large sections of West Africa's population.

The measurement of food imports

For the analysis of food imports, 1969 data are the latest available for all the major West African countries (excepting Equatorial Guinea, Cameroon and Cape Verde Islands) [sources: FAO, UNO]. The list excludes a few minor items, including some cooking fats, included elsewhere in the trade lists, and it lumps together certain items which should be separated for kilocalorie conversion. However, in all cases these items make contributions so small that their omission in some cases or their crude estimation in others make for only minor errors which hardly affect the final result. (Some of the basic data are estimates as not all the countries concerned have published up-to-date trade figures.) The food imports total is net, i.e. allowance is made for re-exports, especially important in the case of both Senegal and the Ivory Coast. The livestock trade (especially important in the case of Ghana) was omitted, as the food value of livestock imported was thought to be subject to too many errors of estimate. To put all data on a common basis, the kilocalorie was used as the standard energy unit. The calculation of all food available and of the proportionate contribution of food imports would have been preferred. In practice, food production estimates were found to be too unreliable. Instead, food needs were estimated and the total food imports calculated as a proportion of food needs. Professor Stamp's Standard Nutrition Unit (SNU) of a million kilocalories allows a consumption for one year at 2500 kilocalories a day plus approximately 10% for wastage in handling and preparation [Stamp, 1958]. This unit is very convenient as it permits us to assume that each person needs one SNU per year, and allows us to express food imports in SNU as a simple proportion of population, giving a measure of food need.

It is a crude form of analysis, ignoring protein values and vitamin content, and it almost certainly overestimates food requirements in West Africa, thus making our calculations of the food import contri-

	'Needs' at 2500 kilocal./day + allowance for wastage (SNU)			'Needs' at 2000 kilocal./day + allowance for wastage
	1969	1960	1956	1969
Senegal	30·7	32·1	35·2	38·3
Gambia	24·6	18·6	13·6	30·8
Ivory Coast	13·3	7·8	6·5	16·7
Liberia	13·2	10·9	4·7	16·5
Portuguese Guinea	12·0	1·0	0·9	15·1
Dahomey	10·2	2·8	2·3	12·8
Sierra Leone	10·0	9·6	10·3	12·5
Ghana	8·0	11·3	8·2	10·0
Mauritania	5·1	0·8	2·7	6·4
Togo	4·6	2·0	1·9	5·8
Guinea	4·1	5·5	3·1	5·1
Upper Volta	2·0	0·5	0·3	2·5
Mali	1·4	0·5	0·7	1·7
Niger	1·3	1·0	0·6	1·6
Nigeria	1·3	2·0	1·3	1·6
West Africa	4·0	4·9	3·7	5·0

(excluding C. Verde Is. and Equatorial Guinea)

N.B.   Bearing in mind the probable differences between the results of this calculation and the 'real' needs, no actual ordering of the countries concerned is implied, either in this table or in Tables 2 or 3, although the very large differences between some of the countries will, it is hoped, reflect something of the actual situation.

TABLE 1   *Percentage of food 'needs' satisfied by imports*

bution extremely conservative. Crude estimates of food consumption in West Africa [FAO, 1970] indicate a range in kilocalories per day from 1980 in Mauritania to 2430 in the Ivory Coast. If we adopt 2000 kilocalories per day as a likely approximate minimum, and again allow 10% for wastage, then we can estimate the range of food need satisfied by imports (Table 1). The figures are remarkably high for countries which, with the exception of Liberia, Sierra Leone and Mauritania, are dependent for their overseas earnings mainly on agricultural, chiefly food, exports; and even in Liberia, Sierra Leone and Mauritania, agriculture still plays a major role in the economies, if one allows for production for internal markets and for its importance as an employer of labour. In Senegal and Gambia the figures are astonishingly high, being approximately one third and one quarter of food need respectively.

In Figure 1 the geographical distribution is shown based on the SNU calculation. The proportion of the food imports is shown by the shaded sector in each circle. It can be seen that all the major importers were coastal and, in fact, were all major exporters. In this connection it is important to note the frequently observed close relationship between earnings from export produce and expenditure on food. Heavy demand for foodstuffs following high cocoa prices in Ghana led to high food prices, which were frequently pushed up by dealers in anticipation [Seers and Ross, 1952; Poleman, 1961]. In

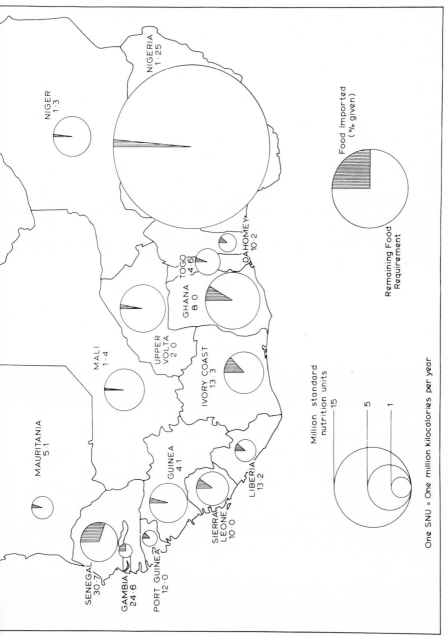

FIGURE 1   *Food requirements and imports in West Africa, 1969*

this situation there was a willingness to buy more expensive canned and prepared foods. However, it can be seen from Figure 2 that the relationship between value of exports and proportion of food need satisfied by imports is weak. Several other factors are operating for which the geographical separation of the extreme cases—(i) Senegal and Gambia, (ii) Liberia and the Ivory Coast, (iii) Mauritania—and the approximate linear grouping of the remainder, provides a clue. In Senegal and Gambia export production is almost wholly dependent on groundnuts, a crop of comparatively poor return for the labour expended and using most of the labour available. In Liberia and the Ivory Coast the export commodities are minerals and tree crops which, together with Liberia's earnings from shipping registration, provide higher returns for the labour expended; and in both countries there is a considerable food production for subsistence and the local market. Mauritania has only reached its high level of exports value per capita in recent years, and this is derived mainly from iron ore mining whereas some 90% of the population is estimated to be dependent on agriculture.

The chief food importers in 1969 can be divided into two major groups:

i) Senegal and Gambia, highly dependent on food imports and with groundnuts accounting for over 70% and 90% of export earnings respectively.

ii) Ivory Coast, Liberia, Portuguese Guinea, Dahomey, Sierra Leone and Ghana, with lower proportions of food requirements met by imports and, apart from the importance of minerals in Liberia and Sierra Leone, and groundnuts in Portuguese Guinea, with export economies more dependent on such perennials as oil palm, cocoa, coffee and rubber.

The distribution is important, not only because of difference in return to labour expended, but because perennial export cropping can be linked to annual food cropping for local markets (a) by the use of food crops such as cocoyams and bananas as shade plants in the young stages of perennial crop establishment; and (b) by the frequent establishment by perennial crop farmers of nearby food farms using their own labour part of the time, since the periodic demands of the various crops differ, and hired labour for the remainder. Perennial crop land, however, cannot easily be converted back to annual food crops. The investment is so heavy for the small-holder that he will continue to maintain his perennial crop holding even when prices are very low. Groundnuts, on the other hand, normally form an integral part of cropping systems which include food crops but in which groundnuts, because of their profitability, have tended to take an enormous share of the small-holdings—some two thirds of the area of individual holdings in

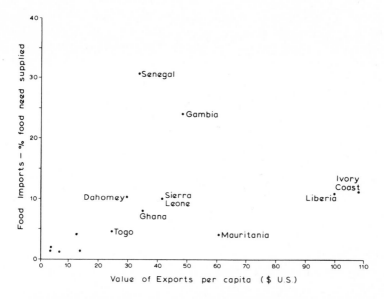

FIGURE 2   *Value of exports per capita in relation to food imports*

the Senegal groundnut belt. They directly compete with food crops for land more effectively than do the perennial crops in their most suitable regions. However, in periods of falling prices, the situation can change quite quickly, and food crops can, in a following season, replace groundnuts. The more dependent countries are therefore also in the more flexible situation. The middle rank countries for food imports contain large numbers of tree crop farmers very reluctant to change their cropping patterns. The lowest rank comprises three inland countries where food imports are very dear; Nigeria and Guinea, which both have a large proportion of their populations well inland; Mauritania, in which the level of food imports is still rising; and Togo, the smallest West African state, with only moderate export earnings and possibly with a high unrecorded level of food movement across its borders.

The persistence of high levels of food imports into West Africa has been a major post-war feature of its economies. Comparison with the author's earlier findings for 1956 and 1960 (Table 1) illustrates this, and graphs (Figure 3) of the trends for the three leading food imports confirm it, although, in making the comparison, one should note that 1960 and 1969 tended to have lower levels of imports than the expected trend, being at the nadirs of a series of fluctuations for at least two of the three major imports. Allowance has to be made for high and varying margins of error in the population censuses, in addition to errors in the estimation of food imports. Probably there has been little or no change in West Africa as a whole in the proportionate importance of imported foodstuffs, but dependence on food imports has become more widespread. In 1956 only six countries satisfied more than 4% of their food needs by imports. By 1960 the number of countries above the 4% level was seven and by 1969 it was eleven. Not much can be said about trends by countries except that they appear fairly consistent, especially in Senegal (some reduction due to success with the home-grown foods policy), Sierra Leone, Ghana, Guinea and the four countries with minor food imports. Portuguese Guinea's recent big increase in food imports, mainly of rice, may reflect internal difficulties due to civil war, but the Gambia had an increase in the import of sugar and also in rice despite considerable efforts to produce more home-grown grain. Dahomey is in considerable economic difficulties, and the Ivory Coast and Liberia appear to be developing economies even more dependent on overseas trading.

Kinds of food imported

85% of the food imported in 1969 consisted of sugar, flour and grain (Table 2), all staple foodstuffs, chiefly consisting of carbohydrates, intended to satisfy basic needs. They are imported, either because home production is simply inadequate, or because they are cheaper in certain West African markets and competition is allowed, or because a local taste has developed for a foreign staple unsuited for production in the West African country concerned. The import of high protein foodstuffs which might have been thought essential is quite low. Fish, meat, eggs and dairy produce, for example, totalled 7.7% of food imports, just as they did in 1956, although dairy produce has shown an increase, apparently at the expense of meat and fish now supplied more from home production and catches, and from the livestock trade. Levels of import of such produce were highest in the high per capita income countries with considerable overseas trade and poor productivity of animal produce: Ivory Coast 11.4%; and Ghana 15.2% (excluding live animals). Estimates of the

	1969	1960	1956
Sugar	29·3	31·1	32·3
Wheat	31·1	28·7	26·1
Rice	26·8	25·5	25·6
Meat	0·6	1·3	1·5
Dairy produce (milk, butter, cheese)	5·3	2·4	2·2
Margarine	0·9	0·0	0·0
Fish	1·8	3·3	4·0
Potatoes	0·4	0·3	0·5
Onions	0·2	0·2	0·2
Maize and Sorghum	2·6	4·9	3·4
Fruit	0·2	0·1	0·3
Biscuits, bread & cakes	n.a.	0·6	1·0
Wine and beer	0·6	1·6	2·9

TABLE 2   *Food imports into West Africa: percentage contribution of each foodstuff to the total (SNU basis)*

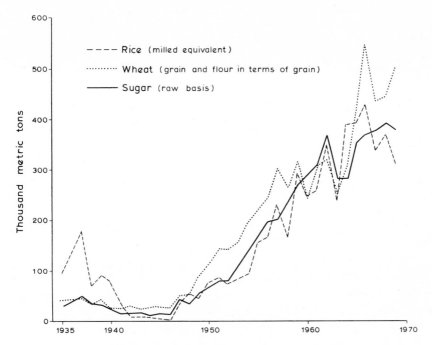

FIGURE 3   *Imports of wheat, sugar and rice into West Africa (totals for 15 countries)*

percentage contribution of these foodstuffs to the diet in 1969 were 4.5 and 3.4 respectively, compared with Senegal's 9.8, Mali's 8.3 and Mauritania's startling 27.7. Animal protein deficiency in West Africa appears to be mainly a problem not of poor but of wet countries. Except in the Ivory Coast, where wine imports still provide 2.9% of the imported food in SNU, the import of alcoholic drinks is now very small, as West African countries depend much more on the products of their own breweries and distilleries.

Figure 3 is useful in that it shows, not only the change from the pre-war situation when, of the three major imported foodstuffs, only rice attained any great quantity, but it also shows the remarkably steep rise in food imports as post-war trading developed, and the greater fluctuation of wheat and rice imports when compared with sugar. This fluctuation in basic foods, as opposed to a food of a 'luxury' character, may reflect the tendency for the quantities imported to be affected by the size of home production in rice and in alternative foodstuffs to wheat flour; although there are several other factors including, for example, variation in purchasing power. Imports of grain have also resulted from crop failure due to drought.

Wheat and, especially, flour, have now overtaken sugar as the largest imported foodstuff in energy terms (Table 2 and Figure 3), owing undoubtedly to the rapid spread in popularity throughout urban West Africa of bread. The innovation of mechanized bakeries

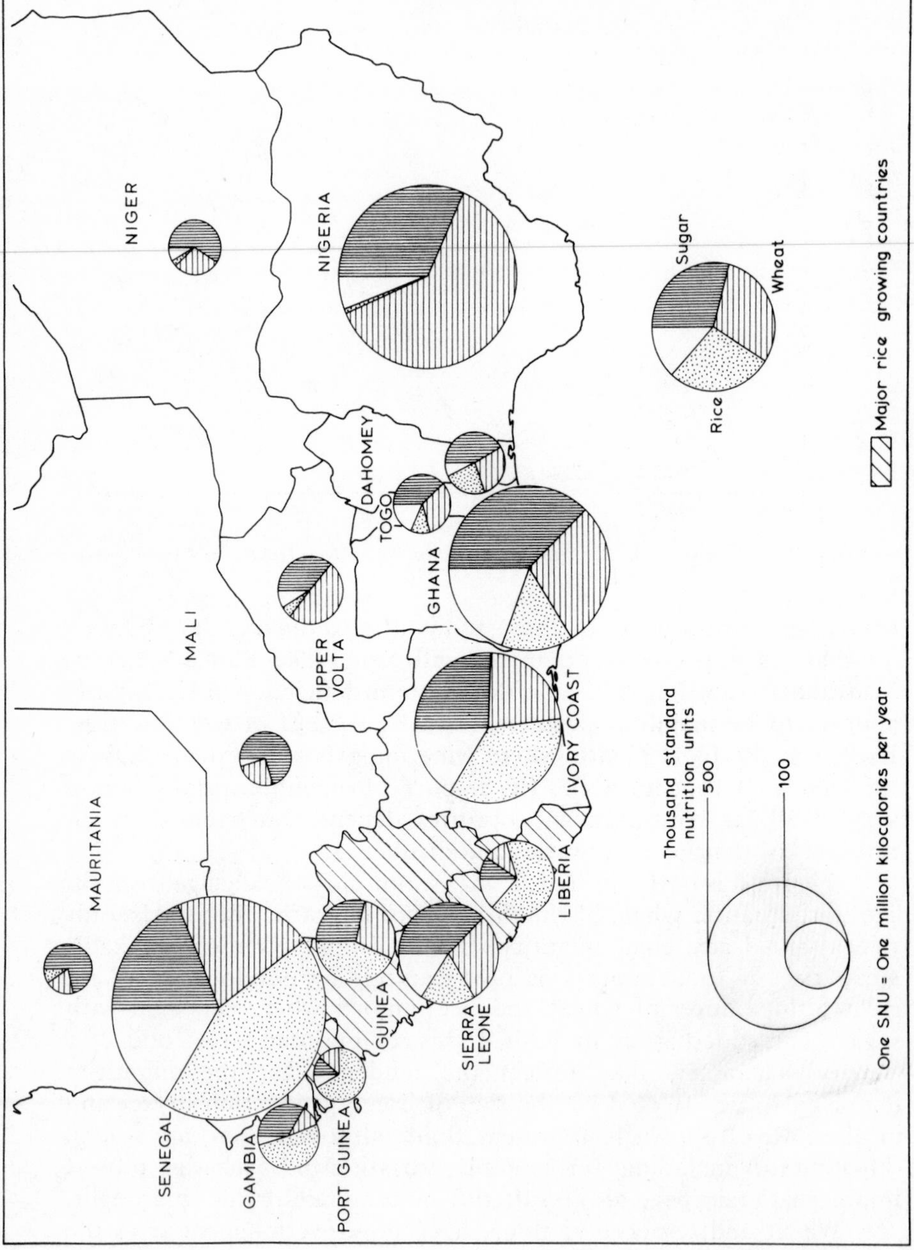

FIGURE 4. Kinds of food imported into West Africa, 1960

needing to expand their markets by widespread deliveries has encouraged the extension of bread consumption into surrounding rural areas [Kilby, 1965; Poleman, 1961; Johnston 1958, 242-249, 1959, a and b]. Wheat and flour provided the highest percentages of total food imports (Figure 4) in Nigeria 62.4, Upper Volta 49.9 (a recent development, possibly encouraged by the return of migrants with bread-eating habits from the Ivory Coast and Ghana), Togo 33.3, Niger 29.9, Sierra Leone 29.4, Ghana 28.8, Guinea 28.5, and Dahomey 28.1. Most of the wheat for the Anglophone countries comes from the United States and Canada, since the flour from North American spring wheat is preferred for the popular light loaf. In the Francophone territories, the softer French flour is mainly used. Except in the extreme north, where it is mainly grown by irrigation, wheat cannot be grown satisfactorily in West Africa. Apart from Guinea, the countries with a high proportion of wheat imports are all in the eastern half of West Africa—although, in the west, Senegal has 21.0 and the second largest total in SNU due to its very high overall level of food imports. Generally in West Africa, the choice of staple foodstuffs available permits substitution of one for another at different seasons and in different circumstances, e.g. working in the fields, meals at home, food in the market places. Differences in urban growth may account for some of this distinction between east and west. Johnston has discussed the evidence for a relationship between high proportions of urban population and high levels of bread consumption in Africa [Johnston 1959 a]. It is, however, hard, in the West African case, to resist the conclusion that this might also be related to the distribution of yams in the east and rice in the west as traditional staples. For the former, the common alternative is cassava flour which, although popular because of its cheapness and ease of cultivation, has not always proved attractive to palates able to afford other foodstuffs. Bread and rice are suitable alternatives, and, of the two, bread with its great convenience has spread more widely, although rice is increasing in popularity. In the south-western portion of West Africa, rice has proved extremely attractive to all levels of income. In these south-western countries and their immediate neighbours, wheat flour is also imported, but even larger quantities of rice have been imported due to their competitive effectiveness compared with the home product; or, in the case of Senegal, as a preferred alternative staple to traditional sorghum and millet, which were reduced to the status of supplementary crops by the early 1950s (Thompson and Adloff 1958, 310). Figure 4 shows the distribution.

Countries with the highest percentages of food imports of rice are Portuguese Guinea 68.8, Liberia 65.8, Gambia 51.2, Senegal 45.3, Guinea 42.6, and Ivory Coast 35.8. In Senegal, the proportionate importance of rice as a food import has increased since

1956, while that of wheat and sugar has decreased. Hitherto, rice has had the advantage of comparative cheapness within the trading system of the former French Union and earlier French Empire. The foundation of the traffic in rice goes back to the import of cheap broken rice from Saigon to Gambia and Senegal at least by the 1880s. This import grew remarkably in volume from the 1930s (Figure 3), when the availability of Indochinese rice in the trading posts of the groundnut districts became a major attraction in addition to cloth, hardware and other goods, to migrant labour—the 'strange farmers' of the Gambia and the 'navétanes' and 'baragnini' of Senegal. The war in Indochina severely reduced imports from that source by 1956, and rice was imported instead from Brazil, the United States and Egypt. Sierra Leone has also developed a rice import, today chiefly from Egypt. In the 1930s the rice traffic grew mainly in response to a rising urban demand which existing hill rice production was unable to satisfy. In the Ivory Coast and Liberia, rice imports have been mainly a post-1950 phenomenon. In Liberia rice was imported under the 'Point-Four' programme and is still almost entirely from the United States, mainly to the towns and the large rubber plantations. In the Ivory Coast the main rice growing areas were distant from the commercial crop and urban areas of rising demand and oriented mainly to local subsistence. The grain was imported, today chiefly from Italy. Apart from Senegal and the Gambia, the major rice importers are also the major rice producers. Some of them, for example the Casamance region of southern Senegal, have even exported small quantities of rice in the past. Most of the West African rice consists of upland varieties. Swamp rices are grown, chiefly in the estuarine polders of the southwestern rias, in Guinea, Portuguese Guinea, Casamance and, more recently, in Sierra Leone. Productivity has been low, both on upland farms and in the polders, and there has been some evidence of declining production in the latter due to poor returns and the attraction of more remunerative alternative occupations [Paulme, 1957]. However, new polders and fresh water swamp rice schemes have been, and are still being, created, mainly in schemes organized by West African government agencies.

The considerable import of refined sugar is due to the development of a taste for a foodstuff which the existing pattern of sugar production, in very small and widely scattered quantities of cane only, could not satisfy. Sugar refineries would have required concentrations of cane production close at hand and, although that could have been developed even at an early stage of agricultural expansion, it would have needed considerable organization. Sugar became at first something of a luxury food, chiefly for higher income groups in the towns. As a proportion of food imports, it attains its highest percentages amongst the minor food importers: Mauritania

71.0, Mali 70.3, and Niger 58.6. Evidently it can better withstand the costs of overland transport than can rice or wheat flour. Levels over 30% are also reached in Dahomey 41.3, Togo 38.0, Ghana 37.6, Sierra Leone 37.0, Upper Volta 36.3, Gambid 33.6, and Nigeria 31.6. Senegal's 18.2 is, however, a large total in SNU—the third largest in West Africa. Apart from Sierra Leone and Gambia, there is a pronounced eastward trend in the pattern of sugar imports. It is somewhat similar to the pattern of wheat imports. Increased tea and coffee drinking account for some of the rise in sugar consumption. Generally demand has grown more rapidly in the tea-drinking Anglophone countries, which account for a large part of the eastward trend and the two western exceptions. Dahomey, Togo and Upper Volta are all moderate food importers and have well developed home food production which helps to keep down the demand for foreign grain, especially in the inland districts. Sugar therefore looks proportionately more important amongst them, as it does in Nigeria, where increasing demand for rice has been met almost entirely by home production. Whilst some of West Africa's sugar import is from tropical countries such as Madagascar, a large part of it is beet sugar from subsidised production in E.E.C. countries and from Eastern Europe and the U.S.S.R. Even the United Kingdom, a sugar importer, exports some sugar to West Africa.

The most important of the minor food import items were dairy produce, a developing trade especially in condensed and homo-genized milk, fresh, canned and dried fish, preserved and canned meat, and wine and beer. In addition, there is a considerable trade in livestock between the West African countries. For this, unfor-tunately, it is virtually impossible to estimate SNU, although we know from work elsewhere that the major importers are Nigeria, Ghana, Senegal and the Ivory Coast.

Causes of the food imports

Many of the 'causes' have already been suggested. The influence of a European minority which for a time governed most of these countries and controlled their trade; a rising urbanism with new ways of living and new standards, often preferring convenience food; a 'backwash' effect from the towns to the rural areas which has been particularly strong wherever export crops have been cultivated, i.e. where farmers have thoroughly engaged in the commercial economy; the transfer of labour from food farming to export cropping and industry, leading to shortages in domestic food production [Oluwasanmi 1960]; new social attitudes which have attached snob values to imported goods; the apparent failure of local peasant or commercial smallholding agriculture to supply the rapidly growing demand; limitations of accessibility which often meant that the rising urbanism of the big ports could be more cheaply supplied from overseas than from sources in their own countries; and physical limitations within West Africa which certainly worked against wheat and which, in the northern countries, occurred in the form of droughts and floods, notably in 1966, 1968 and 1973. An additional factor in the northern lands of West Africa may have been the existence of a long dry season causing excessive dependence on a limited range of stored foods. The hunger season, especially in these northern areas, may have played a role in encouraging some food imports, although this is doubtful as the people worst affected were mostly the poorer, less commercialized farmers.

The evidence for the phenomenon has been the subject of some debate [Miracle, 1961]. These reasons certainly help to explain the growth in demand for imported canned and preserved foods, wine and beer, and wheat flour. They only partially explain the rising imports of rice and sugar, both of which can be produced in West Africa itself. To some extent one can understand the early stages in the introduction of these commodities. They were ready polished or refined, they came comparatively cheaply to the ports and were easily available to townspeople, whereas dealers were unwilling to invest money in plant to treat West African rice or cane, when considerable risks were involved and profits could be made so much more easily from the import traffic. Nor could governments have been anxious to promote an internal traffic when they raised revenues mainly from imports and exports. The rice import is the most remarkable in that, apart from Senegal with its limited productive possibilities for the crop, the greater part of the import is directed to the main producing countries and, although in the 1920s and 1930s the imported refined rice was more attractive to consumers, in all these countries the apparatus for milling and refining has been introduced since and a perfectly acceptable home product can be made available.

In Southern Nigeria commercial rice production has proved extremely successful, increasing rapidly in area in the 1950s in Abeokuta in the southwest and in Abakaliki in the southeast. It has been able to supply virtually all the rising demand from the towns. The low capital requirement, rising prices of grain and availability of hired labour have been important factors in its success since the initial impetus of import restrictions between 1939 and 1945. However, it should be noted that, during the critical early period of its expansion in the early 1950s, it was in no way protected from foreign competition, and that one of its chief markets was the urban population of Lagos to which rice from Abakaliki had to travel considerable distances.

Almost certainly differences in the price of rice and in the availability of labour have been critical factors in the differences in the development of rice cultivation between Nigeria and western West Africa. In Sierra Leone, Guinea, Gambia and Senegal hired labour has been available for food cropping in only a very few areas. Mostly spare labour, seasonal or permanent, has been drained into alternative enterprises—groundnut cultivation in Senegal and Gambia, and mining in Guinea and Sierra Leone. With regard to price differentials, Nigerian cultivators have had the advantage of a rapidly rising market in urban areas with rice possessing a snob value above the modern staple, cassava.

In western West Africa rice has either long been, or has since become, the staple. In Francophone territories preferential pricing arrangements within the French trading system existed until 1966 and, in the case of Senegal, created a situation in which it was normally more profitable to grow groundnuts and buy imported rice than to grow food-crops, which were planted mainly as an insurance against groundnut failure, to gain some local dietary variety or to improve the seasonal spread of labour-use. From 1954 onwards the price of both imported and locally grown rice has been controlled in order to keep down the cost of living. This cheap rice policy rendered the crop unattractive to farmers until 1966 and the ending of the preferential pricing system, which was followed by the withdrawal of the French subsidy in 1968. A mounting trade deficit, increased dependence on rice produced by expensive schemes within Senegal, and worsening sale prices for groundnuts, combined with heavy reduction in groundnut production due to the droughts of 1966 and 1968, have encouraged large numbers of peasants, supported by their religious leaders, to abandon groundnut cultivation for food crops. Thus increased home food production has taken labour out of export crop production with a consequent drop in export earnings, although this was slightly cushioned by rising world prices. What became known as the 'malaise paysan' reached a peak of opposition to production and trade policy when the marabouts refused to give the traditional blessing to the groundnut crop. Additional objections were to delays in payment to producers and to the Government intensification programme.

Purchases of sugar were similarly governed by trading agreements within the French system whereby, in recent years, Senegal paid above world market prices for sugar from Madagascar. In 1969 Senegal refused to abide any longer by the Afro-Malagasy Joint Organization (OCAM) Sugar Agreement and has turned instead to a programme of home sugar production. In Sierra Leone in the 1950s Government buyers purchased rice from growers in the new mechanized rice production schemes at prices above those in the local market. Thus production in excess of local market and subsistence requirements was financed by a form of subsidy (Jack, 1958). Rice imports were also controlled because they were

	Cost of food and livestock imports (million U.S. $)	Cost per capita (U.S. $)	% import costs
Senegal	64·4	17·02	31·7
Nigeria	58·4	0·90	8·4
Ghana	54·1	6·29	15·6
Ivory Coast	38·9	9·27	11·8
Sierra Leone	18·4	7·32	16·5
Liberia	14·6	12·62	12·7

TABLE 3   *Cost of food imported by some West African countries, 1969*

considerably cheaper in most years than local rice at Freetown. Labour has only been attracted to the new schemes in small quantities. It prefers work in the diamond diggings or in the growing towns. In addition labour shortage in agriculture, and especially in food farming, in Sierra Leone, as elsewhere in West Africa has undoubtedly been made worse by social pressures, and education for children. Sierra Leone is not a densely populated territory and, in the country as a whole, there is little pressure on land resources of the kind seen in southeastern Nigeria. The Government Agricultural Department fears overcultivation and soil erosion in the upland rice areas, and the policy of relieving pressure there by developing swamplands goes back at least until the early 1930s. Rice production in Sierra Leone has steadily increased, both in the uplands and the swamps, despite numerous difficulties. The problem is that it has always lagged behind demand by a quantity varying between a very small amount and nearly one quarter of the requirement, and this has had to be made up by imports. In 1969, for example, production was estimated at 390,000 tons of paddy (equivalent to 254,000 tons milled, a figure which has been reached as a result of a steady growth from 150,000 tons milled equivalent in the late 1950s) whilst imports of refined rice in the last 10 years have varied between 600 and nearly 40,000 tons.

Government policies

Some comment on the policies of West African governments with regard to food imports has been offered already. Opposition to food imports sprang, in part, from a basic lack of understanding of the economic forces which made certain home produced foods dearer than their foreign competitors, or of the changes in taste and habit which made new foods attractive. Mostly, however, it came from a desire to save overseas earnings and to avoid the risks of market dependence and the problems of transport which, in some African countries, have even led to opposition to interregional trade in foodstuffs [Johnston 1958, 249-253]. Supporters of Myrdal will no doubt call to mind the argument that, in the less developed countries, international trade has tended to breed inequality [Myrdal 1970, 275]. Fears of this kind, whatever may have been their justification, have undoubtedly encouraged attempts at food self-sufficiency and may extend eventually to attempts at the home production of other commodities. The bill for imported foods in several of the West African countries was considerable. The largest in 1969 were as shown in Table 3. Some small total importers have high per capita expenditures on imported foods, notably (U.S.$) Togo 14.63, Gambia 11.51 and Mauritania 10.23. Clearly some of the West African countries could save considerable overseas earnings if a policy of import substitution were possible. Moreover, bearing in mind their inability to influence world market prices, it could be argued that they are dangerously dependent on overseas food resources, and running considerable risks with economies dependent on fluctuating world prices. In some cases, however, fluctuations in home production due to the vagaries of weather could be as great or greater.

Interest in what were called 'the great natural rice swamps' of Senegal goes back at least to the observations of Baron Roger in 1824 [Papy 1951]. However, import substitution policies in Senegal have involved heavy expenditures, mostly of foreign capital, on rice and sugar schemes, especially at Richard-Toll. Thus a policy designed to decrease dependence on overseas markets has only been bought at the expense of dependence on overseas capital.

In the Ivory Coast there has been emphasis on agricultural diversification since 1960, partly in order to increase the production of food crops. So far, however, more success has been achieved with increasing export crop production, although work has begun on a production complex intended to make the Ivory Coast self-sufficient in sugar.

In Liberia the government aims at ultimate self-sufficiency in rice, and has been conducting swamp rice experiments under the guidance of experts from Taiwan for some years.

In Mali lavish expenditure on the Office du Niger scheme, begun before the war, continues, but has failed not only to make Mali a major exporter of cotton and rice, but has even failed to prevent an estimated decline in food production and the need to import over 20,000 tons of rice in the 1969-70 season.

In Gambia and Sierra Leone the swamp rice schemes policy to reduce dependence on imported rice is now nearly 40 years old. In both countries still, rice imports rise, so further expenditure on such schemes is contemplated. Rice schemes under experts from Taiwan existed also in Upper Volta, and under experts from mainland China in Guinea. In Nigeria sugar production at Bacita is expanding to supply nearly half of Nigeria's requirements, but has to be protected against overseas competition. After failure with the State Farms and mechanization, Ghana hopes to develop irrigated rice production, chiefly in the Accra and Ho-Keta plains and in the North. All these schemes in West Africa are expensive, especially the rice schemes. The expense will be justified if, in the long term, it can lead to viable production in large quantities. Pessimism on this point has been expressed, notably by the eminent botanist Chevalier [1951].

The dilemma facing all the governments concerned is that the low level of productivity and the slow pace of innovation have led to deficiencies in two of the major factors of production: capital and labour. It is true that labour can be found for new manufacturing industries, that there is considerable urban unemployment and that the average hours per week worked in peasant or in small-holder agriculture are low [Clark and Haswell 1964]. Nevertheless, new forms of agricultural practice have to offer very big rewards to attract farmers away from established practice. Export crops have in the past offered sufficiently high inducements, but food crops today offer big rewards only in a few cases—noticeably in Southern Ivory Coast, Ghana and Nigeria, all of which are remarkable for their urban growth rate and their ability to attract seasonal labour from considerable distances.

Generally the problem is that low labour inputs in farming are caused, in large part, by seasonal bottlenecks in demand [de Wilde 1967, I, 63-98; Norman, 1971]. This problem is often very acute on small farms dependent mainly or entirely on family labour [Mabro 1971]. If farmers are attracted to grow certain food crops, it can only be at the expense of those food crops they have hitherto grown, or at the expense of export crops. It is not just a question of raising yields in West Africa, but of productivity per man, and hitherto the most obvious alternative of mechanization has proved too costly, partly because of the failure, except in a few cases, to produce completely mechanized systems of production. Many schemes, for example, have tried to marry mechanized clearance and tillage with hand weeding. More effective use of existing labour resources could produce additional food or export crops if the farming year could be extended by water control, if certain bottlenecks such as weeding could be removed by the introduction of labour saving techniques, if more effective rotations for labour utilization could be introduced, or if labour could be made more mobile. Beals and Menezes [1971] argue that in Ghana temporary migration is more effective than permanent migration in contributing to the growth of agricultural output, whilst in Nigeria Norman [1971] suggests that the improved technology at present being introduced has little potential for increasing incomes, when both land and labour restrictions are involved. Already we have a mass movement in West Africa of at least half a million agricultural workers. Many farmers would hire more labour if they had a little more working capital to enable them to pay wages before crops are sold. Could more short term agricultural credit provide cheaply some of the increase in both food production and export crops for which so many West African governments are looking?

References

Beals, R.E. and Menezes, C.F. (1970) Migrant labour and agricultural output in Ghana, *Oxf. Econ. Papers, N.S.* 22 (1) pp. 109-127.

Chevalier, A. (1951) Le riz, a-t-il un grand avenir en Afrique occidentale?, *Rev. Internat. de Bot, Appt. et d'Agric. Trop.*, 31, pp. 321-322.

Clark, C., and Haswell, M. (1964) *The Economics of Subsistence Agriculture*, London.

De Wilde, J.C. (1967) *Experiences with Agricultural Development in Tropical Africa* 2 vols., Baltimore.

F.A.O. (1941-42, 1945-46) *International Yearbook of Agricultural Statistics.*

F.A.O. (1948-70) *Yearbook of Food and Agriculture Statistics, Trade*, Rome.

F.A.O. (1954) *Food Composition Tables—Minerals and Vitamins*, Rome.

F.A.O. (1970) *Yearbook of Food and Agriculture Statistics, Production*, Rome.

Jack, D.T. (1958) *Economic Survey of Sierra Leone*, Govt. Printer, Freetown.

Johnston, B.F. (1958) *The Staple Food Economies of Western Tropical Africa*, Stanford.

Johnston, B.F. (1959a) *The Outlook for Wheat and Flour Imports in Tropical Africa*, Food and Agriculture Service, U.S. Dept. of Agric., M-48, Wash. D.C.

Johnston, B.F. (1959b) Tropical Africa: growing market for wheat and flour, *Foreign Agric.*, 3-5, 32 and 24.

Kilby, P. (1965) Patterns of bread consumption in Nigeria, *Food Res. Inst. Studies, Stanford*, 5, pp. 3-12.

Mabro, R. (1971) Employment and wages in dual agriculture, *Oxf. Econ. Pap., N.S. 23* (3) pp. 401-417.

Miracle, M.P. (1961) Seasonal hunger: a vague concept and an unexplored problem, *Bull. de l'Inst. Franc. d'Afr. Noire*, 23, pp. 273-283.

Morgan, W.B. (1963) Food imports of West Africa, *Econ. Geogr.*, 39 (4), pp. 351-362.

Morgan, W.B., and Pugh, J.C. (1969) *West Africa*, London, pp. 568-571.

Myrdal, G. (1970) *The Challenge of World Poverty: a World Anti-Poverty Programme in Outline, 1971.*

Norman, D.W. (1971) Initiating change in traditional agriculture, *Agric. Econ. Bull. for Africa*, 13, pp. 31-52 (UN Econ. Comm. for Africa, FAO).

Oluwasanmi, H.A. (1960) Agriculture in a developing economy, *J. Agric. Econ.* 14 (2) pp. 234-241.

Papy, L. (1951) La valleé du Sénégal, Cah. d'Outre-Mer, 4, pp. 277-324.

Paulme, D. (1957) Des riziculteurs Africains: les Baga, *Cah. d'Outre-Mer*, 10, pp. 257-278.

Poleman, T.T. (1961) *The Food Economies of Urban Middle Africa: The Case of Ghana*, Stanford.

Seers, D., and Ross, C.R. (1952) *Report on Financial and Physical Problems of Development in the Gold Coast*, Accra.

Stamp, L.D. (1958) The measurement of land resources, *Geogr. Rev.* 48, pp. 1-15.

Thompson, V., and Adloff, R. (1958) *French West Africa*, London.

U.N.O. (1969) *Yearbook of International Trade Statistics*, Rome.

Land Assessment for agricultural development

M. G. Bawden, M. A. Brunt and G. Murdoch

Introduction

In this paper the sequence of investigations which should precede agricultural development is described, and illustrated by reference to work by the Land Resources Division in Africa. Each stage of investigation is not necessarily required, but the need for each stage must be considered as, otherwise, critical factors may be omitted from the assessment and the wrong conclusions drawn. For example, in Tanganyika a quarter of a century ago the major error with the groundnut scheme was not in pronouncing the land suitable for development *per se,* but in deciding, without adequate evidence, that it was suitable for the development of large scale mechanised groundnut production. There are many other places in Africa where land suitable for development has been correctly selected, but where the subsequent development has been inappropriate; while there are others where the selection of land was itself inept.

The Land Resources Division (LRD) is one of the scientific units of the British Government's Overseas Development Administration, Foreign and Commonwealth Office. At present the Division employs 67 permanent scientific staff; this number is doubled if staff on contract to ODA and counterpart staff provided by local governments are included. Since it was established in its present form seven years ago, the Division has been involved in more than 40 projects throughout the developing world, most of them in the tropics and more than half in Africa. The purpose of the Division is to assist Governments with land appraisal and planning for agricultural development in its widest sense, including livestock—husbandry and forestry. To achieve this, the Division may be associated with some or all of a sequence of progressively more intensive investigations. These start with initial appraisal and reconnaissance to select areas with probable high development potential. This, in turn, may lead to more intensive investigation and assessment of selected areas and, finally, to development plans and pilot schemes. Four stages can be recognised in this sequence:

i)   project identification and appraisal;
ii)   reconnaissance;
iii) detailed development studies;
iv) pilot projects.

These stages are generally sequential. However, the methods of investigation used during the first three stages are usually the same; although in detail each investigation is designed to cater for the particular requirements of that project. It is therefore appropriate to describe the common methodology before illustrating the nature of each stage.

Methodology

Each LRD project is undertaken by an integrated team of scientists drawn from appropriate disciplines. Whatever the project, these teams aim to:-

(a)   investigate the area being studied and determine the boundaries and physical characteristics of *units of the environment* in terms of land form, soil, vegetation, climate and hydrology;
(b)   determine the size of the present *human and livestock populations* and the extent, pattern and type of *present land use*;
(c)   determine the *socio-economic basis* of present production;
(d)   assess development possibilities in the light of environmental and socio-economic *constraints* identified during a-c;
(e)   test the development possibilities so established against *market prospects* for the crops and production being considered.

To establish the basic environmental units, the area is usually divided first into physiographic regions, such as mountains, plateaux, plains or flood plains. Within this framework detailed investigations will then be made of the geomorphology, soil, vegetation, climate and hydrology. At the reconnaissance level, the mapping unit is called the land system, after Christian and Stewart [1953], who defined it as an area or group of areas throughout which there is a recurring pattern of topography, soils and vegetation. Land systems are mapped on the promise that this pattern of land will have a particular pattern of agricultural potential.

At a more intensive level of investigation the same methods are still applied but, instead of a broad framework of land systems, the subdivisions or component parts, called land facets, are studied.

The procedure of mapping land systems or their component facets is based on the concept that different types of country are expressed on aerial photographs by distinctive patterns, and that, by recognising these patterns on the photographs, different landscapes can be mapped. Aerial photographs are employed by the Division in all survey work. But it is at the reconnaissance stage that the greatest benefits are to be gained from air photographs as they provide a comprehensive picture of the landscape, and of the distribution of vegetation and land use upon it, and enable the investigator to study the landscape from the general to the particular with a minimum of time spent in the field, checking the internal consistency of observed units. Ground observations which are made from the particular to the general take far longer to acquire and are employed mainly at close density fieldwork stages subsequent to exploration and reconnaissance.

In some projects land system data have been combined with a survey of the existing land use, for which aerial photographs are also used. The vegetation or land use is identified at a series of random sample points on the photographs and the position of each point is recorded on published (or specially compiled) topographic maps. The land facet and land system within which each sample point falls is also recorded. A computer programme provides the area of each system and the proportion of each land use or vegetation category occurring on each land facet [Tuley 1971, Brunt 1967].

Project identification and appraisal

When an overseas government asks for a land resource investigation, it is first necessary to determine that the request makes good economic and ecological sense, and that socio-political factors are adequately considered. We must also establish what is already known about the area. Is the assessment to be at the exploratory, reconnaissance or detailed level (or at all three in sequence over all or part of the area)? Is the land under-used or already over-crowded; have there been previous studies of land that is analogous to this area; are specific development projects contemplated or is the future use of the land an open question? The project appraisal stage seeks to answer these initial questions by research into the antecedents of the proposed probject, reference to bibliographies and archival records, field investigation and discussion with the client government.

All the Division's projects have been preceded by an appraisal, but it is only recently, with the growth of requests for more intensive development studies, that comprehensive appraisal has become a necessary and distinct initial stage in the sequence of investigation. An investigation in the Bamenda Plateau region of West Cameroon is an early example of project appraisal by LRD. In this area there was land use conflict between the nomadic cattle owners and the settled farmers. A preliminary appraisal [Brunt 1959] led first to an air photo reconnaissance of present and potential land use [Bawden and Langdale-Brown 1961], and subsequently to more detailed ground investigations of the soils and ecology by FAO [Hawkins and Brunt 1965].

More recently, the Division has investigated the problems associated with the agricultural development of The Gambia. The Gambian Government has for many years appreciated the value of land resource studies for development planning and, following a soil survey by LRD in connection with oil palm development [Hill 1968 and 1969], the government asked for a land resource study of the whole country. During the project appraisal, the concept of this request was extended to include all the Gambia river basin [Brunt and Hill 1970], to be investigated as a co-operative Sene/Gambian– Anglo/French project. Subsequent negotiations showed this concept to be politically too advanced, and revised development proposals were prepared for The Gambia alone [Brunt and Robertson 1971]. These proposals were accepted and the project, which started in October 1971, consists of:-

i)   an integrated land resources study of The Gambia;
ii) enterprise studies to investigate and prescribe techniques and systems of production with particular reference to cotton, groundnuts, forage crops and arable crop by-products, and to the greater integration of livestock and crop production.
iii) selection and planning of areas for the intensive cultivation of rice and possibly of cotton.

In the Gambia, as in most other countries, sound agricultural planning and development based on ecological survey will only be productive if it can be demonstrated that the systems of production are technically feasible, economically worthwhile and socially acceptable. The Division's investigations will cover each of these conditions before making any final recommendations.

A final example is the LRD/ODA appraisal mission [Mutter 1972] of the Niger Valley below the Kainji Dam. The major problems in this area, following the construction of the dam, have been the loss of fishing in the swamps and pools of the flood plain, which are no longer flooded, and the changes in the amount of land suitable for flood irrigation. The purpose of the appraisal was to assess the area's potential and the action required to promote development. The team spent 3 months in the Niger Valley in late 1971 and the final report was issued in March 1972. As a result several possible irrigation sites were selected for more intensive study. First priority areas include 30 square miles of contemplated paddy rice farmland on alluvial flats previously inundated during the growing season. Aerial photography and detailed ground surveying of these areas began almost immediately, and soil survey and land classification will follow next dry season.

Without project appraisal, the dangers that wrong terms of reference will be drawn up for major surveys and development operations are great. Project appraisal in particular identifies the most pressing development problems and incorporates economic and social aspects at the first possible moment. This marks a significant movement away from surveys concerned primarily with natural resource inventory, towards surveys closely related to immediate development problems and attainable goals. The integrated team approach, with physical and social scientists working together, provides no guarantee of success, but it should at least ensure that all the relevant factors are considered.

Reconnaissance

Most of the Division's reconnaissance investigations in Africa have been based on the land system concept: Eastern Botswana [Bawden and Stobbs 1963], Lesotho [Bawden and Carroll 1968], Malawi [Stobbs in preparation], Zambia [Mansfield *et al* in preparation] and Nigeria [Bawden and Tuley 1966, and Aitchison *et al* 1972].

The land system reconnaissance in North East Nigeria was concerned primarily with possibilities for the eradication of tsetse fly and the consequences for development which eradication would create. The main contribution from LRD was to collate existing survey data [Higgins *et al* 1960, and Klinkenberg *et al* 1963], survey other areas in similar detail [Carroll 1970, Carroll and Hope 1970], and to infer land systems for the whole area. One hundred and twenty seven land systems, grouped into 25 regions and 5 provinces were defined and mapped [Aitchison *et al* 1972]. The possibilities for eradicating tsetse fly [Glover and Aitchison 1970] and the possibilities for agricultural development which might follow [Lesslie 1968] were investigated by specialist staff supplied to Nigeria under a technical assistance scheme. Their findings were combined with the land system data and with the results of an air-photo based land use survey, to give a comprehensive land resource study which contains both an inventory of existing resources and an appraisal of their development potential [Tuley 1972]. Some development possibilities have already been taken further. Tsetse fly have been cleared from large areas and both grazing and cultivation have extended into the cleared areas. Near Lake Chad more areas suitable for growing wheat under irrigation have been recognised, and a new irrigation scheme has been implemented.

Not all reconnaissance projects are based on land systems. Much depends on the nature of the land and its probable use. For example, in the Kalahari of Botswana, vegetation is by far the most important factor to be considered in assessing grazing potential. Although other factors, particularly the availability of water, were considered, investigation of the vegetation communities formed the major part of the Division's investigations in that region [Blair Rains and McKay, 1968, Blair Rains and Yalala, 1972].

The ecological survey of the Kenya Highlands, with which LRD is associated, provides another example. The vegetation communities are being mapped from aerial photographs and ground investigation, to provide reliable indicators of agricultural potential in a region of very variable climate.

In some places a sequence of progressively more intensive surveys may have to be undertaken before the development stage is reached. For instance, in the savanna zone of the Western State of Nigeria, a land use reconnaissance by Taylor *et al* [1962], which mapped the vegetation pattern and gross landform at 1:250 000 scale, was followed by an LRD soil survey [Murdoch *et al* in preparation], in which the soils of sample blocks, which covered 1% of the survey area, were mapped at 1:20 000 scale. This led, not only to the classification of new soil series in the savanna [Ojo-Atere, Murdoch and Varley 1971], but also—and more important from the standpoint of future development—to the identification of new associations between the soils, landforms and types of vegetation. Murdoch *et al* then bypassed the land system by recognising land facets, and subsequently mapping their distribution over the whole area by extrapolation from the sample blocks using aerial photographs.

Detailed development studies

Until recently the Division spent only a small proportion of its effort on detailed development studies, and it is too soon to report the results of work now in progress for the Gambia and Botswana.

In detailed studies the practical end-points of land resource investigations are tested, verified, and firm recommendations on future land use are made. Usually they cover a relatively small area or a single commodity. At the individual farm level in Swaziland, Murdoch [1968] found that 'soil series mapping provides an adequate basis for assessing land capability as their differentiae are directly or indirectly major influences on the farming activities of an area'.

In order to monitor surveys in Swaziland, particular sites were investigated in detail to assess maize productivity at middle altitudes, and growth increment in planted pine forests at higher altitudes. Both programmes relate output to site factors. The LRD contribution to the work on maize yield [Armitage, in preparation] relates crop performance to mapped soil series. In the timber study, supported by ODA, Evans [1972] found that elevation, slope angle, position on the slope and the type of soil together explained two-thirds of the variation in crown height of *Pinus patula*.

The Division is also involved with development studies in Malawi, where government is now concerned to develop rice production. Land systems have been mapped for the whole country [Young and Brown 1964, Stobbs in preparation] and, from these, certain sites were identified as potentially suitable for intensive rice cultivation.

An appraisal mission [Laurence 1968] concluded that the Dwangwa Delta, 100 miles north of Lilongwe, offered the best prospects for an economically viable project, but said that further detailed investigations were necessary to confirm their recommendations and to select the site for a pilot project. These investigations comprised:

i) topographic mapping of 90 square miles, followed by photogrammetric mapping of approximately 44 square miles at a scale of 1:10 000 with a contour interval of 1 metre.

ii) Collection of hydrological data from an automatic river gauging station to be established on the Dwangwa River.

iii) A soil survey of the total area, and a more detailed survey of 2 square miles to identify the pilot farm site.

Field work was completed in October 1969; the reports and associated maps followed in January 1970. The site proposed for the pilot farm was approved, and staff, equipment and buildings were provided, financed by British technical assistance. Successful completion of this pilot phase should lead to the development of between 20 and 35 square miles of the Dwangwa Delta for irrigated and alternative systems of cropping.

Pilot projects

Although the Division has only recently become involved with pilot projects, it is being increasingly realised that investigation of land resources must include pilot projects if development schemes are to be successfully implemented. In most of the areas in Africa where investigations by LRD have progressed to this stage, the local government or private companies and other agencies have been responsible for the pilot projects, although LRD staff have been closely related with the work. Progress to the pilot stage in the Dwangwa area of Malawi has already been described. A R Stobbs of the Division's staff has been involved in all stages of the project from the land systems reconnaissance.

In North East Nigeria the land systems mapped in the Gongola Valley showed areas which might be suitable for the development of estates to grow sugar cane under irrigation. Further investigation of the soils, the available water and the market potential led to selection of a pilot project which is being run for the North East State Government jointly by the Commonwealth Development Corporation and Bookers. Further north, near Lake Chad, land system mapping showed that there was extensive areas of land similar to that which was already being successfully used for growing wheat under irrigation. Detailed comparison of the soils confirmed the similarity, and a second irrigation scheme has been established. The first scheme served as a pilot project for the second.

Conclusion

The land resource studies made by the Land Resources Division encompass a wide range of investigational activities and are increasingly concerned with projects related to specific developments. All these investigations bear directly on both social and economic development. Studies of land resources are undertaken to make these resources more productive. The need to increase productivity needs no emphasis in the face of the dramatic increase in population throughout the continent. While land assessment is only one part of the problem to be tackled, it is nevertheless an essential foundation upon which successful rural development must be based.

Acknowledgements

The authors are grateful to the Acting Director of the Land Resources Division for permission to present this paper. They are also indebted to D J Pratt and C A Robertson for contributing advice about the format and content of the paper.

References

The abbreviation LRD refers to Land Resources Division.
Aitchison, P.J., Bawden, M.G., Carroll, D.M., Glover, P.E., Klinkenberg, K., Leeuw, P.N. de, and Tuley, P. (1972) The land resources of North East Nigeria. Volume 1, The environment. *Land Resour. Stud.* no. 9.
Bawden, M.G., and Carroll, D.M. (1968) The Land resources of Lesotho. *Land Resour. Stud.* no. 3.
Bawden, M.G., and Langdale-Brown, I. (1961) An aerial photographic reconnaisance of the present and possible land use in the Bamenda Area, Southern Cameroons. Tolworth, Surrey: Forestry and Land Use Section, Directorate of Overseas Surveys.
Bawden, M.G., and Stobbs, A.R. (1963) The land resources of Eastern Bechuanaland. Tolworth, Surrey: Forestry and Land Section, Use Directorate of Overseas Surveys.
Bawden, M.G., and Tuley, P. (1966) The land resources of Southern Sardauna and Southern Adamawa Provinces, Northern Nigeria. *Land Resources Stud.* no. 2.

Blair Rains, A., and McKay, A.D. (1968) The Northern Stateland, Botswana. *Land Resour. Stud.* no. 5.

Blair Rains, A., and Yalala, A.M. (1972) The Central and Southern State Lands, Botswana. *Land Resour. Stud.* no. 11.

Brunt, M.A. (1959) Tour notes. Matters indirectly related to the farmer-grazier problem and its solution, based on the land use survey (Bamenda, Cameroons) *Unpubd misc. Rep. Land Resour. Div. Overseas Dev. Adm.* no. 4.

Brunt, M.A. (1967) The methods employed by the DOS in the assessment of land resources. *Act 2 e Symp. int. Photo-Interpret. Paris 1966*, VI 3-VI 10.

Brunt, M.A., and Hill, I.D. (1970) Outline proposals for assistance to the Governments of The Gambia and Senegal for an integrated land resource study of the Gambia river basin. *Internal Rep. Minist. overseas Dev.*

Brunt, M.A., and Robertson, C.A. (1971) Proposals for a land resource development project in The Gambia. *Internal Proj. Prop. Land Resour. Div. overseas Dev. Adm.* PROP/5/71.

Carroll, D.M. (1970) The soils of the Maiduguri–Bama area. *Samaru Soil Surv. Bull.* no. 40.

Carroll, D.M., and Hope, W.A. (1970) Soil survey of the Biu-Mubi area. *Samaru Soil Serv. Bull.* no. 43.

Christian, C.S., and Stewart, G.A. (1953) General report on survey of Katherine Darwin region, 1946. *Land Res. Ser. CSIRO Aust.* no. 1.

Evans, J. (1972) An evaluation of the productivity of fast-grown conifer crops during the second rotation in Swaziland. Bangor: University of Wales. (thesis).

Glover, P.E., and Aitchison, P.J. (1970) The land resources of North East Nigeria. Volume 2. Tsetse and trypanosomiasis. *Land Resour. Stud.* no. 9.

Hawkins, P.A., and Brunt, M.A. (1965) Report on the government of Cameroon on the soils and ecology of West Cameroon. *FAO Rep.* no. 2083.

Higgins, G.M., Ramsay, D.M., Pullan, R.A., and Leeuw, P.N. de (1960) Report on the reconnaissance and semi-detailed soil surveys undertaken in northeast Bornu. *Samaru Soil. Surv. Bull.* no. 14.

Hill, I.D. (1968) An assessment of the possibilities of oil palm cultivation in Western Division, The Gambia. *Oil Palm News* no. 6, 4-7.

Hill, I.D. (1969) An assessment of the possibilities of oil palm cultivation in Western Division. The Gambia. *Land Resour. Stud.* no. 6.

Klinkenberg, K., Tomlinson, P.R., Higgins, G.M., and Leeuw, P.N. de (1963) The soils of the middle Gongola region. *Samaru Soil Surv. Bull.* no. 21.

Laurence, J.F. (1968) A reconnaissance survey of irrigation potential in Malawi. LRD *Unpubd. misc. Rep. Land Resour. Div. overseas Dev. Adm.* no. 59.

Lesslie, A. (1968) The present land use and development possibilities in N.E. Nigeria. *Unpubd Rep. Minist. overseas Dev.* no. A984.

Murdoch, G. (1968) Soils and land capability in Swaziland. *Bull. Minist. Agric. Swaziland* no. 23-25.

Mutter, N.E.S. (ed.) (1972) Niger valley survey appraisal mission, September–December 1971. Final report. *Internal Proj. Prop. Land Resour. Div. overseas Dev. Adm* PROP/6/72.

Ojo-Atere, J., Murdoch, G., and Varley, J. (1971) The first full descriptions of twelve soil series, found under savanna vegetation in the Western State of Nigeria, *Unpubd misc. Rep. Land Resour. Div. overseas Dev. Adm* no. 141.

Taylor, E.W., Baker, R.M., Leefers, C., and Rosayro, R.A. de (1962) Report on the land use survey of the Oyo-Shaki area in Western Nigeria. Internal Rep. Fd Agric. Org.

Tuley, P. (1971) An air photographic sample census survey of land use and vegetation in North East Nigeria. Tables of percentage areas, point counts

calculation of the sampling errors. An annex to Land Resource Study no.
9. *Suppl. Rep. Land Resour. Div. overseas Dev. Adm* no. 2.
Tuley, P. (1972) See under Aitchison P.J.
Young, A., and Brown, P. (1964) The physical environment of Central Malawi.
Zomba, Malawi: Government Printer.

Index